D1267199

The Labors of
SISYPHUS

The Labors of SISYPHUS

The Economic Development of Communist China

Maria Hsia Chang

TRANSACTION PUBLISHERS
New Brunswick (U.S.A.) and London (U.K.)

Copyright © 1998 by Transaction Publishers, New Brunswick, New Jersey 08903.

Library of Congress Catalog Number: 97–19298
ISBN: 1–56000–330–8
Printed in the United States of America

Library of Congress Cataloging-in-Publication Data

Chang, Maria Hsia.
   The labors of Sisyphus : the economic development of Communist
China / Maria Hsia Chang.
     p. cm.
   Includes bibliographical references and index.
   ISBN 1–56000–330–8 (cloth : alk. paper)
   1. China—Economic policy—1976– 2. China—Economic
conditions—1976–   .   I. Title.
HC427.92.C3388   1997
338.951—dc21
                                       97–19298
                                         CIP

To *A. James Gregor* and *Charles Elmo*
the love and light of my life

Contents

Acknowledgments

This book would not be possible were it not for the support and contributions of many individuals and institutions, to whom I owe my gratitude and profound appreciation.

Like most books, its contents are the distillation of many years of learning, research, and thought. In this case, the years began with the instruction I received in the political science department of the University of California at Berkeley, where I first learnt of China from Professor Chalmers Johnson, and of economic development from Professors Robert Price and Andrew Janos. What followed were some seventeen years of my own teaching at Washington State University, the University of Puget Sound, and the University of Nevada, Reno, where I benefited immeasurably from the students in my courses on China and on political economy.

The actual writing of this book began two years ago, the completion of which was entirely due to a Faculty Development Leave that the University of Nevada, Reno, graced me in Fall semester, 1996. For that leave, I am indebted to Professors Eric Herzik, Richard Ganzel, Bill Eubank, John F. Copper, and Yuan-li Wu for their letters of support. The book's completion was also assisted by a grant from the Pacific Cultural Foundation of the Republic of China on Taiwan.

A scholarly book is only as good as the source materials it employs. For those materials, I am grateful to the thoughtfulness of colleagues as well as students who funneled various books, articles, and newsclips to me. Among them are Xiaoyu Chen, Dr. John Scire, Steve Rogers, Professors Leonard Weinberg and John Dobra, and Robert Rigney. I am also appreciative of the Chinese language materials I obtained from the libraries of Taiwan's Institute of International Relations, as well as U.C. Berkeley's Center for Chinese Studies Library and the East Asian Library.

But the writing of a book needs more than source materials—it also depends desperately on the kindness of friends and colleagues. For that I am grateful to my brother, Dr. Peter H. Chang; my colleague, Professor Leah Wilds; my dear friend, Stephanie Helen Free; and our department secretary, Beverly Adams for their support, encouragement, and interest.

Most important of all, my undying gratitude goes to the two males in my life who make me laugh: my husband, Professor A. James Gregor, for the many years of peerless instruction, tireless support, wise counsel, and unfailing love; and to my boy, Charles Elmo, for his constancy, solace, occasional silliness, and devotion.

Maria Hsia Chang
Reno, Nevada

1

Introduction

It is almost half a century since the inception of the People's Republic of China (PRC). In that time, a charismatic leader ruled and died, leaving a wake of destruction in his quest to transform China. His utopian vision was repudiated, in actions if not in words, by his successor who would reform the country almost beyond recognition. In that time, too, the Soviet Union, mentor to the People's Republic, would dissolve after admitting that communism had failed. Half a century is more than enough time for a reassessment of the meaning and purpose of the Chinese Communist Revolution.

The attempt to study any country is a difficult undertaking. In the case of China, it is particularly problematic because of information shortfall. Although data gathering in the People's Republic has greatly improved since the initiation of economic reforms in 1979, as recent as August 1994, the Chinese government still decried the problem of officials and cadres falsifying statistics.[1]

Information shortfall could account for narratives by Sinologists in the 1960s and 1970s that entirely misrepresented Maoist China. As examples, one scholar thought China's science and technology to be "innovative." Another argued that Mao had discovered answers to a problem that plagued the United States—"the unbridled expansion of unresponsive bureaucracy." Yet another saw virtues in the PRC's penological system and recommended it to Americans for emulation.[2]

After his death, it was Chinese commentators who identified much in the China of Mao Zedong to be barbarous, irrational, brutal, destructive, wasteful, and oppressive. Few identified scientific innovation, the solution to bureaucratic indifference, and progressive penology as accomplishments of the system.

1

For their part, by the early-1980s, American academics similarly began to inquire why "a movement of class and human liberation" on the Chinese mainland devolved "into one of the most oppressive systems in Chinese history." By that time, Maoist China was recognized as a "totalitarian feudal fascism" from which even decadent America had little to learn. Little evidence of merit was found in Maoist science, bureaucracy, or penology.[3] What had passed for an understanding of China just a few years before was almost entirely abandoned or so significantly qualified as to reduce it to antiquarian interest.

Current efforts at understanding China have access to a richer repository of more credible evidence. International agencies now have contact with China through a variety of channels. So do journalists, social scientists, economists, artists, and intellectuals of a range of political persuasions. What emerges are far more nuanced impressions of a vast and variegated canopy.

There is no pretense that any single work has captured the evolving present in all its complexity and variety. Most analysts approach contemporary China with a recognition of their limitations. They understand that no account is pure, providing an "exact description" of some reality.[4] Nevertheless, every representation of complex events must be accorded structure because "Just to do history at all is to employ some overarching conception which . . . goes beyond what is given."[5]

That overarching conception usually ascribes "meanings" and purposes to historical and political events. Political figures have motives and intentions, conscious or unconscious, that provide a scaffolding for an illuminating narrative. Those goals and intentions are historical "projects" that concatenate events. Given the inherent epistemological and methodological limitations of history and the social sciences, describing those meanings and presumed projects in any one narrative has more the character of art than science. Nevertheless, the scholar is obliged to make the near-quixotic effort. To do otherwise would be to surrender the self to a universe of mysticism and infinitely regressing subjectivity.

The Meaning of the Chinese Communist Revolution

Historical events, such as the Chinese Communist Revolution, can be thought of as having meaning with reference to some larger temporal structure in which they are components.[6] In the case of the Chinese Communist Revolution, the larger temporal structure that gives meaning to the revolution is modern Chinese history that began in the mid-nineteenth century, a history framed by the mortal challenge that foreign imperialism posed to China.

Throughout the millennial history of China, its political rhythms had displayed a cyclical quality: dynasties were born, flourished, decayed, and gave way to a successor in a convulsion of populist insurrection. The *denouement* of a dynasty was marked by a series of increasingly intractable crises and disasters typically comprised of a precipitous decline in the availability of revenue, disintegration in the hydraulic water system, and a corresponding failure in agricultural production. All of this would be attended by an increase in banditry that took on more and more organized forms until active resistance threatened the very continuity of the dynasty. The mass migration of peasants, who were no longer able to sustain themselves through their traditional pursuits, swelled the ranks of populist armies. Communication from the provinces to the center could no longer be sustained; more and more local revenue failed to reach the capital. Corruption by officialdom became pandemic, further undermining the effectiveness of government. Increasingly, the regime was unable to deal with even relatively minor natural dislocations and disasters. It was said that heaven had withdrawn the mandate to rule.

By the beginning of the nineteenth century, the Qing (or Manchu) dynasty began to display all the characteristic features of a sunset regime. The burgeoning traffic with the Western seafaring nations was producing increasingly deleterious effects on the national economy. Opium became the imported commodity of choice; and the domestic currency was debased to meet the shortfall in foreign exchange. By the first quarter of the century, drug use had become prevalent among China's economic, political, and military elites. The attempt in 1840 to control the flow of opium into China precipitated the first war between China and Great Britain, the preeminent Western power in the Far East. China was soundly defeated two years later and was subjected to the indignities of what would be the first in a series of "unequal treaties" with foreign powers.

Thereafter, the political integrity of China began to unravel. China lost a second war against an Anglo-French expedition in 1856. With each defeat, the European powers exacted more concessions from an increasingly inert nation. More and more, China was pried open to foreign trade and missionary activities. At the same time, the inexorable dynamics of the dynastic cycle produced the characteristic traditional peasant uprising—the Taiping Rebellion (1851–1864) that endured for fifteen years, engulfing half of Imperial China.

Defeats in war, economic decline, and popular insurrection successively undermined the viability of the institutions of traditional China. Like similar crises in the past, it appeared that the mandate to rule was being withdrawn from the Qing dynasty. What was different in the nineteenth century was the presence, in the midst of regime crisis, of "barbarians" who could neither be suborned, bribed, nor deflected from their purpose. Unlike the Mongols and Manchus who had conquered China in the past, the new barbarians from Europe were not as easily absorbed or deflected. Not only were the Europeans equipped with superior armaments produced by modern industry and science, they were convinced of their moral and cultural superiority. Unlike past barbarians, the Europeans did not come as tributaries or supplicants. Their arrival at the shores of China marked the crest of Western Europe's outward expansion and colonization. Awed neither by the magnificence nor the size of Imperial China, the Europeans came as conquerors to bring progress to a retrograde civilization.

By the end of the century, China had degenerated into a hypo-colony: a society that was nominally independent but suffered from all the ills and disabilities of colonialism. Stopping short of formal colonization, the imperialist powers used war (and the threat thereof) to wrest concessions from the Chinese court. By the dawn of the twentieth century, the imperialist powers had established "spheres of influence" within China which were protocolonies in intention and effect.

The Chinese response to Western imperialism traversed the spectrum of possibilities from populist xenophobia to reasoned reformist movements. The Taiping Rebellion was a populist response to the first incursions of the Europeans. Championing a primitive communism and a naive Christianity, the Taipings were recruited from the ranks of Chinese laborers increasingly displaced by Western trade. The Taipings were followed by the Boxer Rebellion of 1900, a populist insurrection of xenophobic violence against the foreign presence in China.

The more enlightened of China's political and intellectual elites knew that unless radical reforms were undertaken, China's very survival would be imperiled. The first reformers, those of the failed

Tongzhi Restoration (1864–90), sought to reform China with minimal change by grafting Western science and technology onto the Chinese body politic and society. The Tongzhi reformers were succeeded by a new generation who realized that the modernization of China could not be achieved simply through the importation of Western science and technology. Instead, modernization would have to be total, affecting every sector of Chinese society from the economic and educational systems to include government itself.

Led by Kang Youwei and Liang Qichao, the new generation of Chinese reformers patterned their efforts after the Meiji Restoration of 1860 that transformed Japan into an industrial nation in the space of a few decades. Like the Meiji reformers, the Chinese also advocated the modernization of the imperial system by transforming it into a constitutional monarchy. Like the Meiji reformers, Kang and Liang had the support of a young Chinese emperor, Guangxu. Unlike the successful Meiji reform, however, the Chinese reformers were thwarted by obdurate conservatives in the Qing court, led by the aged dowager Empress Ci Xi. What became known as the Hundred Days' Reform ended ignominiously with Guangxu's house arrest, the fleeing of Kang and Liang to Japan, and the arrest and execution of their colleagues.

The failure of reform made it evident to another group of Chinese intellectuals that the dynastic system was moribund. Led by Sun Yat-sen (1867–1925), they believed that revolution was the only recourse and hope for China.

Sun was the penultimate marginal man, born and raised in China but educated, since the age of thirteen, in the West (Honolulu). He had witnessed China's spiralling disarray under the pressure of the Western powers. At the same time, he marvelled at their science, appreciated the efficacy of their laws, and sought his nation's salvation in the promise of economic growth and industrial development that had given the West its power. To regenerate China, Sun articulated a formula for economic and political modernization which would begin with the revolutionary overthrow of the dynasty. This would be followed by the tutelary rule of a single party whose purpose was industrialization and political development. In this manner, the conditions would be created for the ultimate instauration of a representative and constitutional democracy.

In 1911, Sun's efforts culminated in a revolution that ended the rule of China's last dynasty. A new government of the Republic of China was proclaimed, and fledgling efforts were made to introduce representative government. Beyond that, Sun enjoyed very little more in the way of success. He discovered that neither he nor the new republic commanded the authority and power to rule. Without the support of a national consensus, the new government could not wield effective authority. Lacking its own army, the revolutionaries did not have the coercive means that could enforce government decisions. Instead, the country degenerated into warlordism—an anarchic assortment of local and regional units, each dominated by a strongman—which lasted an entire generation.

Sun's death in 1925 precipitated the fracturing of his revolutionary Nationalist Party (the Kuomingtang or KMT) into contending factions. As commander of the Nationalists' newly created army, Chiang Kai-shek assigned himself the task begun by Sun of unifying China through a "second revolution." By 1928, as the consequence of military defeat or political compromise, Chiang managed to gather the various warlords under the nominal leadership of the KMT government at Nanjing.

For a decade after 1928, the Nationalist government attempted to reconstruct the Chinese economy. Efforts were made to stabilize and standardize the national currency; a modern banking system was introduced. In 1931, work began on the rehabilitation of the agricultural system, which succeeded in producing 182 million metric tons of principal food crops by 1937—a quantity not attained again until well after the Second World War. There were improvements in the varieties of rice, wheat, corn, and potatoes. Insecticides were made available to peasant farmers for the first time in Chinese history. In a number of provinces, experimental stations, demonstration farms, and educational extension systems were introduced. Agricultural machinery and parts were imported and the total amount devoted to those acquisitions grew from about half a million Chinese dollars between 1932–34 to over a million dollars in 1936. In the judgment of many experts, Nationalist China was on the threshold of self-sustained takeoff in agriculture by the end of the 1930s.[7]

At the same time, progress was made in the industrial sector. Between 1928 and 1936, the availability of roads and track doubled. For the decade of 1926–36, China sustained a compounded industrial growth rate of 8.3 percent per annum. This accomplishment was all the more remarkable because it was attained during a period when the major economies of the world languished in the Great Depression, with the general indices of production in the United States, France and Germany falling by about 50 percent.

It was Japanese aggression that played a pivotal role in ultimately thwarting the Nationalist effort at economic development. That aggression began in 1931 when the Japanese Guandong Army occupied China's northeastern provinces (Manchuria). By 1937, the vital regions of China—the industrialized northeast and the coastal cities—had fallen to the invading armies of Imperial Japan. The KMT government retreated from Nanjing into the Chinese heartland to wage a sustained defensive war. In its wartime capital of remote Chongqing, Nationalist China lapsed into a vicious cycle of defeat and devastation, corruption and incompetence, treachery and disorder, from which it was not to emerge.

Nationalist China never regained its equilibrium after the Second World War. What was to emerge from the cataclysm of war was a new China, the product of the transformative vision of Mao Zedong and the Chinese Communist Party (CCP).

The Historical Project of the Chinese Communist Revolution

In effect, modern Chinese history can be understood as a series of ineffectual responses to the challenge of foreign imperialism. That series began with populist movements and reformist efforts that failed to modernize and industrialize China, leaving only revolution as a last recourse. The Revolution of 1911 was the first, but it was only partially successful. Although the revolution succeeded in overthrowing the *ancien régime*, it failed at instituting a viable modern polity. Because of the unfinished Revolution of 1911, social turmoil and political chaos worsened, requiring successive revolutions in the continuing effort to accomplish China's historic mission of economic regeneration.

Viewed in the larger context of modern Chinese history, the Communist Revolution was not simply the event that took place in 1949. Instead, it was the continuation and culmination of the series of responses to foreign imperialism. Because of the failure of the traditional Chinese state to respond to the challenge of modernization, the process of industrialization was retarded for so long that "nothing short of . . . an explosive force could have broken the shackles of the old order. . . ."[8]

What had enabled the Westerners and, later, the Japanese to subjugate China were their superior military capabilities delivered by modern science, industry, and technology. If the Chinese were to effectively meet the imperialists' challenge, they must become economically modernized. In effect, from the very first reformist effort, through the 1911 Revolution, Chiang Kai-shek's "second revolution," and the Chinese Communist Revolution of 1949, the historical project of the Chinese had always been the economic development of China.

The Necessary Conditions of Economic Development

Economic development may be defined as the increase in the productive capacity of the economic system as a result of its structural transformation. In the history of humankind, the change from the hunting-and-gathering mode of production to that of agriculture was a revolution in economic development. The Industrial Revolution that began in mid-eighteenth-century England was another revolution in economic development in which production became mechanized, resulting in a quantum increase in economic capacity and the employment of most of the labor force in manufacturing. Today, the advanced industrialized countries of the world are undergoing yet another revolution in economic development, which some have called post-industrialization, post-modernization, or the knowledge revolution. Increasingly, knowledge supplants capital as the primary means of production, and the majority of workers are found in the service or tertiary sector of the economy.

There are many paths to industrial economic development. As W. W. Rostow put it, "Historical cases of take-off . . . have assumed many different forms. There is no single pattern."[9] In some cases, the effort was led and dominated by private initiative; in others, the state played a major role. In some societies, industrialization emphasized the production of consumer goods; in others, the emphasis was on producer goods. Western industrialization took the course of centuries; later industrializers took mere decades.

Whatever the route to industrial development, for the project to be successful, a number of necessary conditions must be fulfilled. The fulfillment of those prerequisites can be accomplished through varying methods and strategies, but the prerequisites themselves must be attained or else the success of modernization itself would be compromised. Simply put, there are five prerequisites. They are: capital formation and accumulation; intersectoral capital investment; innovation; social cooperation; and social order and stability.

Capital Formation and Accumulation

Industrial production requires large sums of capital for the purchase of plant, equipment, and labor. The source of capital can be domestic, foreign, or both, although modernization cannot be achieved by a reliance on only imported capital. The preconditions for industrial "take-off" must include "an initial ability to mobilize domestic savings productively, as well as a structure which subsequently permits a high marginal rate of savings."[10]

Given the necessary role that domestic capital plays in industrialization, attention needs to be given to any internal factor that affects a society's indigenous generation and accumulation of surplus capital. The latter refers to whatever that remains after consumption by the masses to meet basic needs of food, shelter, and clothing.

Among the many factors inherent in a society that may impact its ability to generate and accumulate surplus capital are cultural attributes. Whatever the particular culture, the observations first made by Max Weber on the importance of hard work and frugality for capital formation and accumulation are probably relevant to all societies that aspire to industrialization.[11] What may vary from culture to culture is that which promotes or discourages the work ethic. Weber emphasized the role that the Protestant religion, particularly Calvinism, played in promoting work and frugality. But that role can also be performed by secular mechanisms. As an example, it has been suggested that the Confucian culture is the Asian counterpart of the Protestant ethic. It is argued that in emphasizing hard work and frugality, the Confucian ethic played a significant role in the successful industrialization of Taiwan, South Korea, Singapore, and Hong Kong—the group of four variously called the Asian Tigers or NICs (Newly Industrialized Countries).[12]

Aside from culture, political ideologies could also affect a society's ability to accumulate capital. To illustrate, an ideology of radical economic egalitarianism may discourage individuals from working hard by removing the financial incentives that make work rewarding. A society's class stratification system could also affect capital accumulation. Scholars have noted that a rigid class system discourages work because class membership is determined by birth rather than achievement. In both cases, by discouraging work, the ideology and the class system ultimately act against the interests of economic development.[13]

Intersectoral Capital Investment

It is not enough that the society intent on industrializing generate and accumulate surplus capital, that capital must be transferred to and invested in the modernizing sector. Capital must be invested to develop the physical and human infrastructure of energy, transportation, communication, education, and public health which enables and supports industrial production. Most importantly, surplus capital must not flow into the hands of those who, instead of investing that capital, "sterilize it by hoarding, luxury consumption, or low-productivity investment outlays." Individuals who could be detrimental to the national effort of capital investment include corrupt officials and members of the upper class who engage in the conspicuous consumption of wealth. One estimate is that "a necessary though not sufficient condition" for industrial take-off is that the rate of productive investment be over 10 percent of national income or the net national product.[14]

Innovation

The intersectoral transfer of capital, in turn, requires a society that has a positive attitude toward change and innovation because human creative genius is at the root of economic growth. Entrepreneurs, in particular, are needed because they function as the "critical catalyst" for development.[15] These are individuals in the private or public sector who accept borrowers' risk[16] and who act "with confidence beyond the range of familiar beacons" to reform or revolutionize the pattern of production.[17]

There are other innovators. Aside from business and industrial entrepreneurs, economic development also depends on the vital inputs of intellectuals—individuals with the disposition and training to be critical thinkers, who challenge established patterns with unconventional methods and perspectives. Among them, those trained in science and technology and in management are especially needed for successful industrialization. The developing society must therefore value, promote, and invest in all levels of education, from kindergarten to university. Not only does education transform an agrarian population into a literate industrial labor force, education also produces a corps of skilled personnel who could operate and maintain the sophisticated machinery and technology that are imported from the advanced industrial societies. Eventually, that skilled personnel must be capable of creating their own technology if their society aspires to sustained development.

Social Cooperation

Effective economic development also requires the cooperation and coordination of individuals who are strangers unrelated to each other. In the agrarian society, the population is widely dispersed among geographically isolated villages; family members make up the basic work unit; and interactions between strangers are rare occurrences. In the industrial society, in contrast, the population is concentrated in large cities; the factory is the work unit; and strangers must work and live in close proximity to each other.

The industrial economy therefore requires the social cooperation of the masses so that they can work together to produce goods, solve common problems, and maintain stability. Social cooperation, in turn, is contingent on people being able to compromise as well as having basic trust in others. Interpersonal trust, in turn, is dependent on the existence of a system of laws and ethics that govern relations among strangers. Where there are widespread interpersonal distrust and suspicion, a weak tradition of compromise, and an expectation of injustice in interpersonal relations, the stability of expectations that is crucial to the successful operation of a modern economy is severely impaired. Instead, corruption and nepotism are the norm; and "the self-discipline necessary to keep a society working well"—as in the payment of taxes and resistance to the temptation to steal—will be correspondingly weakened.[18]

Order and Stability

The preceding four preconditions for economic development—capital accumulation, capital investment, innovation, and social cooperation—require the antecedent prerequisite of social order and stability. Order and stability provide the context for hard work and innovation for, in their absence, individuals cannot count on being able to enjoy the fruits of their labor and ingenuity. Similarly, for capital investment to take place, social order and stability are needed because investors must be assured that profits are forthcoming. Finally, without the stability and continuity that are "crucial to development,"[19] instead of social cooperation, there would be constant confrontation with deleterious consequences on industrial production.

The Role of the State in Economic Development

In all this, government can exercise an important role because, among its many responsibilities, the state is charged with maximizing a society's capacity to realize collective goals.[20] The state may be defined as a set of organizations invested with the authority to make and implement binding decisions for people juridically located in a particular territory. Since economic development takes place within the broad framework of an entire society, the way society and government function necessarily affects the productive process. At a minimum, good government can assure stability and continuity, without which investment and production will falter.[21]

The role of government becomes even more critical in the case of societies that are late in their quest to modernize. Alexander Gerschenkron and Barrington Moore, Jr. were among the first to suggest that the later the effort at economic modernization, the greater and more important the state's role becomes.[22] Alexander Eckstein was even more direct, asserting that "The more backward the economy in relative terms . . . the greater will be the need for . . . [massive state] intervention if a breakthrough . . . is to be attained."[23]

State intervention in the economic development of retarded societies is needed because "Certain major obstacles to industrialization *must* be removed and certain things propitious to it *must* be created before industrialization can begin."[24] One reason for state intervention has to do with considerations of national security. Industry is the foundation of modern military power—the capacity to wage war depends on the ability to produce weaponry and to provide a reservoir of skills for its maintenance and operation.[25] As the guardian of the universal interests of society,[26] the government of an underdeveloped society surrounded by advanced powers is compelled to assume the role as the primary agent propelling economic development.[27]

Furthermore, since the underdeveloped society has a paucity of entrepreneurs or "risk-taking profit maximizers," the state becomes an additional, if not the primary, agent of capital accumulation.[28] Typically, government in a backward society also becomes the major capital investor in vital sectors of the economy, namely, the production of producer goods and the development of an industrial and social infrastructure. Having a long period of gestation, the prospective current return of such large overhead capital items is insufficient to attract private investment.[29]

A strong state's role is also needed in order to remove whatever societal, cultural, religious, or ideological barriers that impede modernization. Those barriers might include a traditional elite who is threatened by change and jealously guards its privileges. Traditional attitudes that discourage achievement, hard work, and innovation also impede modernization. Finally, a general condition of interpersonal suspicion and distrust thwarts social cooperation toward common objectives, economic development included.[30]

If the state were to be effective as a modernizing agent, it will have to satisfy a number of conditions. J. J. Spengler listed four sets of "minimal requirements."[31]

A first set consists of "minimal public services" that must be provided by the government. Those public services include: (1) the maintenance of law, order, and security; (2) the support of education and public health; (3) the issuance and regulation of paper money and bank credit; (4) the creation of banks to assemble savings and supply credit; (5) the provision of a legal and administrative structure for the functioning of business organizations, the maintenance of private and public property, and the prevention of excessive monopolies; and (6) the attraction of as much foreign personnel and capital as are warranted and desired for economic development.[32]

A second set of "minimal requirements" is comprised of "growth-supporting and growth-stimulating arrangements" that the state must provide. Those arrangements include: (1) the raising of tax revenue in a manner that "diminishes very little" the incentive to economic activity and the propensity to form capital; (2) governmental expenditure that is conducive to economic growth; (3) economic decision making and a climate of opinion that encourage innovation and entrepreneurship; (4) state support of basic research and applied technology; (5) a five-year plan and a developmental corporation to help administer the plan; (6) the control of inflation; and (7) independent agencies with access to the information requisite for periodical assessments of governmental economic policies and performance.[33]

A third set of "minimal requirements" that must be satisfied by the government of a late-developer, in the interest of economic development, pertains to "governmental personnel." The paucity of qualified personnel in an underdeveloped society demands that government must increase the stock of qualified personnel through investment in appropriate education and other measures. At the same time, there must also be judicious use of whatever personnel that is available. Most importantly, qualified governmental personnel "should not be engaged in the performance of tasks which nongovernmental personnel can do quite (if not more) effectively."[34]

A fourth, and final, set of "minimal requirements" consists of "political instruments." It is suggested that a single-party system is preferable to non- or multiparty systems because a well-entrenched party is better able to keep the ideology of development effectively alive. A single party is better at imposing the necessary costs of development on the population, and at remaining in office long enough to get economic growth effectively under way. Another necessary political instrument is a minimal welfare state, if at all, so that state capital is not diverted to welfare assistance, and economic growth is not consumed by real wage increases.[35]

In addition to Spengler's list of minimal requirements for effective state intervention in economic development, Dietrich Rueschemeyer and Peter B. Evans identified four other "prerequisite" features of the successful developmental state. They are: (1) relative autonomy of the state from the dominant class so that collective goals can be formulated and implemented; (2) an extensive, internally coherent bureaucratic machinery; (3) decentralization, so as to avoid the loss of information, distortion of commands, and general lack of initiative endemic to highly centralized bureaucracies; and (4) a limited state enterprise sector (if at all) and the preservation of the market in order to establish some limits on inefficiency and corruption, as well as provide "a metric" of prices, production, and profits that allows the central bureaucracy to keep rough track of performance.[36]

The Role of Ideology in Economic Development

If government is a primary actor in the economic development of latecomers, how its ideology conceives of that enterprise is crucial to the success or failure of the project. An ideology is a logically related collection of empirical and normative beliefs about the world, a function of which is to inform and mobilize mass action towards some common purpose. Given the dominant profile of the state in developing countries, the purposive policy role of ideology is magnified. Mary Matossian referred to such ideologies as "ideologies of delayed industrialization" because of their similarity of historical context as well as their common objective of economic development.[37]

As the underlying value system of society, to be effective, an ideology of delayed industrialization must display certain characteristics. For Matossian, such an ideology should, above all, be pragmatic in its approach to the "three main problems" of industrially backward countries. Those problems are: (1) what is to be borrowed from the West? (2) what is to be retained from the nation's past? and (3) what characteristics, habits, and products of the masses are to be encouraged? In resolving these problems, the ideology should use as its criterion the pragmatic standard of whatever that "will tend to strengthen the nation."[38]

That pragmatism also informs S. N. Eisenstadt's notion that, for economic development to succeed, the society's dominant value system (be it religion, culture, or political ideology) must have "transformative capacity." By that, Eisenstadt means "the capacity to legitimize," in the value system's own terms, the development of new motivations, activities, and institutions that were not part of the "original impulses and views" of that value system.[39] In other words, to be an effective developmental ideology, its ideational contents must be open to interpretation. Along with ideational porosity is a weak authority structure that offers "less resisting power" against change and innovation.[40] In effect, a developmental ideology that insists on adherence to dogma and relies on a rigid hierarchical power structure is not conducive to modernization. An ideology with such characteristics stifles rather than encourages creativity and initiative.

Finally, W. W. Rostow also identified a number of features or "propensities" of the efficacious developmental ideology. Such an ideology must possess the propensities to develop fundamental physical and social science; to apply science to economic ends; to accept innovations; and to seek material advance.[41]

Conclusion

Given the importance of the state and its guiding ideology in the economic development of backward societies, an examination of the performance, policies, and ideologies of the government of the People's Republic of China is recommended. The fact that after almost a half-century of Communist Party rule, China still labors under the yoke of poverty and underdevelopment is suggestive of major deficiencies in the government and its ideology.

Those flaws are all the more magnified because the single party that governs China, from its inception, chose to pursue Marxist nostrums in its approach to problems as well as install a totalitarian system where the state controls every aspect and intrudes into every niche and crevice of society and the economy. That decision has had a major impact on the history and economic performance of the People's Republic.

The Marxist-Leninist ideology is a system of beliefs and values that is rigid in its convictions. It embraces central planning by bureaucrats and cadres who are selected more for their ideological zeal and political skills than their economic acumen. The ideology abjures the market and its guiding signals. It promotes social division and confrontation, identifying select classes as targets for extirpation. All of which are pernicious for economic development.

In China, the inherently flawed ideology of Marxism-Leninism was exacerbated by the contributions from Mao Zedong thought. Mao redefined "class" to mean the content of an individual's beliefs, a radical departure from classical Marxism's definition of class by the objective criteria of an individual's occupation and property ownership. The new meaning that Mao gave to "class" assured that the Communist Revolution in 1949 did not bring class struggle to a decisive conclusion. Instead, members of "black" classes would continue to be born anew as individuals deviated from Mao's prescribed thinking. Under Mao, the Chinese Revolution would have to be "continuing," leading to continuous and unceasing class warfare and social turmoil.

Mao's antipathy to intellectuals, who became the targets of countless campaigns, could not but stifle creativity and innovation. The

Communist Party's promotion of the personality cult elevated Mao, an individual untutored in economics, to be the unchallenged policymaker for an entire nation. None of this could be remotely conducive to economic development.

It is no wonder that after Mao's death in 1976, the Communist Party found a country demoralized by his Cultural Revolution and in economic disrepair. Mao's "continuous revolution" had exacted some 35 million lives. China's average annual per capita gross national product (GNP) was only $253 in 1978, making it one of the poorest nations in the world. A third of the peasantry lived below subsistence level.[42] After thirty years of socialism, China's annual per capita food grains output in 1978 managed to be less than that in 1936 under Nationalist rule.[43]

The disastrous legacy of Mao convinced the Communist Party that reform was needed. Under the leadership of Deng Xiaoping and guided by his ideas, beginning in 1979, the CCP undertook a series of economic reforms that significantly improved the material and social circumstances of the Chinese people. Economic growth, however, has been uneven. The coastal provinces have become prosperous, while the inland regions in western China remain mired in poverty. Seemingly entrenched inflation, as well as overpopulation, threaten to erode economic advancements. Pandemic political corruption is an acid that corrodes not only the economy, but may eventually bring down the government.

Like the labors of Sisyphus, China seems consigned to a never-ending struggle out of underdevelopment. Whether Deng's reforms are sufficient to propel China into the ranks of the industrialized nations remains to be seen.

Notes

1. "Firmly Oppose False and Deceptive Reports," *Renmin ribao* (*People's Daily*), 17 August 1994, as reported in *Shijie ribao* (*World Journal*, hereafter *WJ*), 18 August 1994, p. 12A.
2. Michel Oksenberg, ed. 1973. *China's Developmental Experience* (New York: Praeger, 1973), 2, 3.
3. Tang Tsou, "Back from the Brink of Revolutionary-`Feudal' Totalitarianism," in *State and Society in Contemporary China*, eds. Victor Nee and David Mozingo (Ithaca, NY: Cornell University, 1983), 56. See Edward Friedman, "The Societal Obstacle to China's Socialist Transition: State Capitalism or Feudal Fascism," ibid., 148–171; and Benedict Stavis, "The Dilemma of State Power: The Solution Becomes the Problem," ibid., 175–193.

4. See W. H. Walsh, *An Introduction to Philosophy of History* (London: Hutchinsons' University Library, 1951), 31; and L. O. Mink, "The Anatomy of Historical Understanding," in *Philosophical Analysis and History,* ed. William Drey (New York: Harper & Row, 1966), 184–191.
5. Arthur C. Danto, *Analytical Philosophy of History* (London: Cambridge University, 1965), 115.
6. Ibid., 8.
7. See Arthur N. Young, *China's Nation-Building Effort, 1927–1937: The Financial and Economic Record* (Taipei: Rainbow-Bridge Book Co., 1976).
8. Alexander Eckstein, "Individualism and the Role of the State in Economic Growth," in *Political Development and Social Change*, eds. Jason L. Finkle and Richard W. Gable (New York: John Wiley and Sons, 1971), 182.
9. W. W. Rostow, "The Take-Off into Self-Sustained Growth," in Finkle and Gable, *Political Development*, 153.
10. Ibid., 148.
11. See Max Weber, *The Protestant Ethic and the Spirit of Capitalism* (New York: Charles Scribner's Sons, 1956).
12. See Robert N. Bellah, ed., *Religion and Progress in Modern Asia* (New York: Free Press, 1965); Tu Wei-ming, ed., *Confucian Traditions in East Asian Modernity: Moral Education and Economic Culture in Japan and the Four Mini-Dragons* (Cambridge, MA: Harvard University, 1996); and ch. 3 of Lawrence Harrison, *Who Prospers?: How Cultural Values Shape Economic and Political Success* (New York: Basic Books, 1992).
13. Arthur W. Lewis, *The Theory of Economic Growth* (Homewood, IL: Richard D. Irwin, 1955).
14. Rostow, "Take-Off," 155, 145.
15. Lawrence E. Harrison, *Underdevelopment is a State of Mind* (Boston, MA: Madison Books, 1985), 24.
16. Joseph A. Schumpeter, *Capitalism, Socialism, and Democracy* (New York: Harper Brothers, 1950), 155.
17. Ibid., 132.
18. Harrison, *Underdevelopment is a State of Mind*, 8.
19. Ibid.
20. J. J. Spengler, "Economic Development: Political Preconditions and Political Consequences," in Finkle and Gable, *Political Development*, 166.
21. Harrison, *Underdevelopment is a State of Mind*, 2.
22. See Alexander Gerschenkron, *Economic Backwardness in Historical Perspective* (Cambridge, MA: Harvard University, 1962), and Barrington Moore, Jr., *Social Origins of Dictatorship and Democracy* (Boston: Beacon, 1966).
23. Alexander Eckstein, "Individualism," 179.
24. Ibid., 31.
25. Harry G. Johnson, "The Ideology of Economic Policy in the New States," in Finkle and Gable, *Political Development*, 104.
26. Dietrich Rueschemeyer and Peter B. Evans, "The State and Economic Transformation: Toward an Analysis of the Conditions Underlying Effective Intervention," pp. 46–47 in *Bringing the State Back In*, eds. Peter Evans, Dietrich Rueschemeyer, and Theda Skocpol (London: Cambridge University, 1985).
27. Alexander Gerschenkron, *Economic Backwardness*, 17.
28. Rueschemeyer and Evans, "The State and Economic Transformation," 45.
29. J. J. Spengler, "Economic Development," 172.
30. See Lawrence Harrison, *Undevelopment is a State of Mind*, chs. 1–2.

31. Spengler, "Economic Development," 171.
32. Ibid., 171.
33. Ibid., 171–172.
34. Ibid., 172–173.
35. Ibid., 174–175.
36. Rueschemeyer and Evans, "The State and Economic Transformation," 49, 50, 55, 58.
37. See Mary Matossian, "Ideologies of Delayed Industrialization," in Finkle and Gable, *Political Development*, 113.
38. Ibid., 122, 120.
39. S. N. Eisenstadt, "The Protestant Ethic Thesis in an Analytical and Comparative Framework," in *The Protestant Ethic and Modernization*, ed. S. N. Eisenstadt (New York: Basic Books, 1968), 10.
40. E. Troeltsch, *Protestantism and Progress* (Boston: Beacon, 1958), 90–91.
41. W. W. Rostow, *The Process of Economic Growth* (New York: W. W. Norton, 1962), chs. 1–3.
42. Jan S. Prybyla, "China's New Economic Strategy: Defining the U.S. Role," *Backgrounder* (Washington, DC: The Heritage Foundation, 1985), 3.
43. Cheng Chu-yuan, "Economic Reform in Mainland China: Consequences and Prospects," paper presented at the Fifteenth Sino-American Conference on Mainland China, Taipei, Taiwan, 8–14 June 1986, 4.

2

Mao Zedong Thought

There is general consensus in the literature that ideology can play a critical role in economic development. Whether originally conceived to serve the purpose of development, ideologies have been adapted to that end, particularly in backward societies attempting delayed industrialization.

Of all the ideologies pressed into the service of development, classical Marxism may be among the most ill-suited. It was originally conceived as a solution to the problems that Karl Marx anticipated would afflict post-industrial societies. Instead, Marxism or some variant was employed by eponymous revolutionaries of a surprising number of less-developed nations as a policy guide for rapid industrialization.[1]

If Marxism itself was an inappropriate ideological vehicle for economic development, Maoism, among all the variants, may well be one of the most counterproductive. If an ideology of delayed industrialization is required to display reasoned judgment concerning socioeconomic programs, then Maoism was manifestly unsuitable. If an ideology of late development is expected to provide incentives for innovation, achievement, and the judicious application of science and technology, then Maoism was a poor candidate. If an ideology of development requires the fostering of interpersonal trust, and of social order and stability, then Maoism must be considered an abject failure.

The Role of Ideology in China

When the Chinese Communist Party acceded to power in 1949, it proceeded to transform China into an "ideocracy": a political system in which government is legitimated by an ideology that claims to be absolute and comprehensive, presuming to know as well as explain all aspects of reality.[2] The ideology's claim to exclusive knowledge of the truth extends beyond empirical matters to the normative domain.

Ideocracies are not totally inimical to the task of economic development. Their moral certitude potentially can provide the normative basis that, like religion, could promote social order and stability.[3] More than that, ideocracies are by their nature authoritarian—and some authoritarian systems have shown themselves to be compatible with, and even conducive to rapid industrialization.

From its inception, the legitimating ideology of the People's Republic of China was Marxism-Leninism-Mao Zedong Thought, a monistic ideology that assumes there is an abstract model of society, the truth of which has been demonstrated "once and for all."[4] Believing that the final stage of human evolution is communism—a society of material abundance, classless equality, and direct self-government—the PRC's ideology is also utopian. Being utopian, the ideology carries incentives that could inspire individual and collective effort for rapid industrial development.

The utopian character of Marxism-Leninism-Mao Zedong Thought implies that the ideology has an "unconstrained vision" of human nature and human potential. Men and women are believed to be perfectible, particularly in regards to their moral perfectibility. In contrast, for example, to classical liberalism's conviction that human beings are inherently *both* good and bad, the Chinese Communists believe instead that "moral improvement has no fixed limit."[5]

But the remolding of women and men into perfect moral beings requires the direction and guidance of an elite—the Communist Party—who alone comprehends the ideal in its entirety. Armed with the Truth, as embodied in the absolutist ideology, the elite assigns to itself the role of society's vanguard. With the acquisition of total power, this self-appointed vanguard undertakes a program of comprehensive social engineering in order to remold human nature and transform society.

In that quest, the vanguard party relies on its ideology for inspiration, legitimation, as well as guidance. In the case of the Chinese Communists, those separate functions are performed by two analytically discrete ideological components. The CCP's ideology of Marxism-Leninism-Mao Zedong Thought is divided into "theory" (*lilun*) and "thought" (*sixiang*). "Theory" provides the Party with its philosophy, its *Weltanschauung*, and its objectives, and is believed to contain "universal truths" for all humankind. The purpose of "theory" is to explain, inspire, and legitimate.

The problem is that, by their very nature, "universal truths" are too broad and general to serve as an effective guide to specific action. "Theory" therefore requires interpretation for it to be translated into concrete policies. The interpretation, translation, and application of "theory" to the concrete circumstances of China would be the purview of "thought." As Franz Schurmann put it, the CCP's "theory" is its "pure ideology," and "thought" its "practical ideology." Schurmann explained that,

> Pure ideology is a set of ideas designed to give the individual a unified and conscious world view; practical ideology is a set of ideas designed to give the individual rational instruments for action. . . . Without pure ideology, the ideas of practical ideology have no legitimation. But without practical ideology, an organization cannot transform its *Weltanschauung* into consistent action.[6]

The Communist Party identifies the ideas of Marx and Lenin to comprise its "theory" and those of Mao to be its "thought." It is claimed that in his lifetime, Mao selected from among the elements of Marxism-Leninism those he considered relevant for China at any particular time.[7] As expressed by the 1945 CCP Constitution, "Mao Zedong Thought is the thought that unifies the theory of Marxism-Leninism with the realities of the Chinese revolution."[8] Put in Marxist terminology, Mao's thought is understood to be the "dialectical synthesis" of the "thesis" of Marxism-Leninism with the "antithesis" of China's concrete conditions. This is why even during the convulsion of the Cultural Revolution, Maoist enthusiasts refrained from insisting that Mao Zedong Thought was the "universal truth for the whole world."[9]

Long before Mao rose to political dominance, his followers already identified him not only as China's "savior" but as a "brilliant" leader who was to convey great truths to his people.[10] By the time he reached the pinnacle of power during the Great Proletarian Cultural Revolution (GPCR), it was unselfconsciously affirmed that "Every sentence of Chairman Mao's is truth, and carries more weight than 10,000 other sentences."[11] Mao's thought was more than simple truth. It was a talisman that drove lorries when engines failed; restored sight to the blind; enabled the lame to walk; assured bumper crops; cured the constipation of pigs; and protected all from harm. Everything of any consequence that had transpired in China for most of the twentieth century was attributed to the influence of Mao Zedong Thought.

Even after Mao's death in 1976 and his party's admission that he had made many mistakes, the CCP still insisted that Mao's thought remained its guide to action. Only recently have references begun to be made to an alternative "thought" of Deng Xiaoping.

Given its importance in China's political life, Mao Zedong Thought necessarily exerted a critical impact on the course of the country's economic development. It was Mao who, from the very founding of the People's Republic, "shaped much of China's economic developmental efforts."[12] Whether Mao's thought can be considered an appropriate ideology of delayed industrialization is another matter. To determine all that, it is necessary to undertake a review of the origins, cognitive character, and the employments of Mao Zedong Thought.

The Origins and Nature of Maoism

Quite independent of its role in shaping the economic trajectory of the People's Republic, Mao Zedong Thought was the inspiration, the guide, and the legitimating rationale for the system that dominated the lives of a fifth of humankind for half a century. For all that, we are not even certain to what the expression "Mao Zedong Thought" refers.

Mao's thought, more often than not, was treated by Chinese authorities as the unique product of his personal reflections. Whenever theoreticians on the Chinese mainland spoke of the specific content of Mao's thought, they referred exclusively to his writings. Similarly, Liu Shaoqi, in his report to the Seventh CCP National Congress in 1945, defined Mao Zedong Thought as "Those theories that are expressed in comrade Mao Zedong's various writings. . . ."[13]

The picture, however, is more complicated than that. In 1981, when the Communist Party undertook a critical review of its history and of Mao's role, it concluded that his thought was a "theoretical synthesis of the collective wisdom of the Chinese Communist Party" with "comrade Mao Zedong as its greatest representative." According to the CCP,

[Even] Mao Zedong himself never thought Mao Zedong Thought was the product of his individual wisdom. As early as the 1940s . . . he recognized that Mao Zedong Thought was the product of the Party's collective wisdom, with himself as merely one representative. . . . In March 1964, commenting on *The Selected Works of Mao*

Zedong, Mao wondered "How could this be my work alone? The material contained in *The Selected Works* are taught to us by the masses. . . ."[14]

In 1979, at the fourth plenum of the Eleventh CCP Central Committee, Marshal Ye Jianying declared that "Mao Zedong Thought is . . . the product of Mao's comrades-in-arms, the Party, and the wisdom of the revolutionary masses."[15] In 1981, then CCP General Secretary Hu Yaobang stated that Mao Zedong Thought was the product of a collective enterprise to which even "revisionists" and "capitalist roaders" such as Li Lisan and Liu Shaoqi contributed.[16]

More important than its origins is the question of how suitable a source of truth Mao Zedong Thought might be. If Mao's thought was to unerringly guide the nation, one would expect evidence of its veridicality.

In fact, there is considerable ambiguity concerning how much truth is to be found in Maoism. There were times when the Party insisted that Mao's thought was a "correct theory" sustained by a "body of correct principles. . . ."[17] On other occasions, the Party leadership seemed prepared to allow that Mao Zedong Thought was not a repository of impeccable truths, but contained both truth and error. Despite being the Party's guiding ideology, Mao's thought harbored "mistakes," contained both "rights and wrongs," and allowed itself to be influenced by "subjective factors" and extrinsic "social causes."[18] All of which did not bode well for the programs it inspired.

In their attempt to explain the thought's fallibility, Party stalwarts argued that because Mao Zedong Thought was the *application* of the "universal truths" of Marxism-Leninism to the concrete conditions of China, the application sometimes resulted in mistakes. The problem was that no one, including Mao himself, was capable of identifying error on the occasion of its occurrence. As Mao admitted, "Flowers that wear the cap of Marxism sometimes are not necessarily Marxist." Although his thought was supposed to be the sole guide to policy and conduct for an entire nation, there were no clear criteria for the unambiguous identification of the content and meaning of his "Thought" or for separating truth from falsity. Instead, errors of judgment and mistakes in behavior could be unproblematically identified only after the fact.

The result of this ambiguity was mistakes that were often tragic and monumental in scope. As an example, in 1957, responding to his own question of whether there had been any people "unjustly killed," Mao admitted that at the time of the "great" campaign "to eliminate counter-revolutionaries" in 1950, 1951, and 1952, "there were" people who had been "unjustly killed."[19]

When Mao embarked upon the creation of vast People's Communes in the late-1950s, we were told at the time that the effort constituted a major "creative development" of Marxism-Leninism and an instance of the genius of Mao Zedong Thought.[20] Through the creation of communes, "courageously and with extraordinary brilliance," Mao solved the problems posed by Lenin and Stalin concerning the advent to communism. China would make "a great leap forward" into communism through the collectivization of agriculture, "walking on two legs,"[21] and an equality of status between physical and mental labor, and between peasants and cityfolk.[22]

After Mao's death, however, his Party judged the creation of the people's communes to be a monumental mistake that stemmed from "smugness" and an "impatience for quick results." "The role of man's subjective will and efforts" in the productive process had been "overestimated."[23] And it was none other than Mao himself who had committed those errors.[24]

Mao further erred in not accepting the criticisms of the communes proffered by his colleagues, most notably Peng Dehuai, during the Lushan Party plenum in 1959. To make matters worse, Mao misidentified those criticisms as instances of "class struggle" and extended the 1957 Anti-Rightist Campaign into the Communist Party itself. Beginning in the early-1960s, he "widened and absolutized the class struggle" and committed a series of "Left" errors. "Theoretical and practical mistakes . . . became increasingly serious," so that persons, institutions, and enterprises were subjected to "unwarranted, inordinate political criticism." The central committee of the Party "failed to rectify [those] mistakes in good time." Those failures, in turn, provided the occasion for the subsequent enormities inflicted upon the Chinese people in the Cultural Revolution. All of which constituted one of the "most serious mistakes" made since the founding of the People's Republic.[25]

At the time of those enormities, however, neither Mao nor the Party, armed with his thought, could identify errors or mitigate their effects until they achieved biblical dimensions. Mao's thought, presumably employing all the "universal truths" of Marxism-Leninism, nonetheless led China into catastrophe.

How Marxist is Mao Zedong Thought?

While it might have been misapplied, the thought of Mao was presumably a concrete expression of the ideological fountainhead of Marxism-Leninism, upon which Mao's claim to truth is contingent. The verisimilitude of Mao's thought, therefore, depends on the extent to which it was Marxist in any meaningful sense.

Although there are those who characterized Mao's thought as "truly Marxist"[26] and others who spoke of his writings as having a "Marxist ring,"[27] still others have argued that Mao never possessed "a correct idea of Marxism." The latter maintained that Mao was but little familiar with classical Marxism, the writings of Karl Marx and Friedrich Engels[28]—"the theoretical basis of Marxism . . . remained unknown territory for Mao."[29] Instead of the primary works of Marx and Engels, Mao's "main source for the study of Marxism were popular writings, mainly textbooks by Soviet philosophers. . . ."[30]

More importantly, Mao seemed never to have fathomed the theoretical coherence of classical Marxism. As a result, his thought was innocent of the sophistication and complexity, and much of the content, of classical Marxism. That cognitive failure was to have tragic consequences for the Chinese economy.

For Marx and Engels, a socialist revolution could only be undertaken by the proletarian majority of an advanced industrial society. Urban wage workers, schooled in the responsibilities of machine production by industrial capitalism, would accede to political control during one of the predictable economic crises that Marx and Engels fully expected to attend modern society. The anticipated socialist revolution would inherit the vast productive capabilities of monopoly capitalism, free workers from the control of a propertied minority, and the oppression of poverty. It would be a "leap from the world of necessity to that of freedom."

In the anticipated socialist society, Marx expected a sophisticated working class to practice self-governance through the instrumentalities of universal suffrage, referendum and recall. They would abjure "hierarchical investiture" as alien to a liberating revolution that would, at one and the same time, envelope all the advanced industrial countries of the world. Under these benign circumstances, the state would wither away along with the antagonism of classes, and humankind would bask in the peace, abundance, and freedom of communism.

It was V. I. Lenin who confounded the coherence of classical Marxism by introducing revisions into the Marxist corpus. Those changes were necessitated by severe disjunctures between Marxist theory and reality. One such disjuncture was the failure of the proletariat of the advanced capitalist economies in Western Europe to embark on the revolution predicted by Marx. Another disjuncture was the same proletariat's commitment to their respective nations during the First World War, which contradicted Marx's dictum that "the working man has no fatherland."

To account for these disjunctures, Lenin explained that capitalism, in its highest and most advanced stage, had evolved into imperialism. Instead of exploiting the workers of Europe, Western capitalists found new and cheaper workers among the less developed peoples of the world. The latter's exploitation was made all the easier because of Western governments' collusion with the capitalists. Through the colonization of the world's less developed communities, the transformation of monopoly capitalism into imperialism was complete. The new imperialists now could reap super profits from the colonies which were used to purchase peace at home by suborning the proletariat of Europe with increased wages, improved work conditions, and the right to organize unions. In this manner was the European proletariat shorn of its revolutionary impulse and deflected from its historic mission, becoming instead a new "labor aristocracy."[31]

It was this mutation of advanced capitalism into international imperialism that accounted for the failure of socialist revolution to erupt in capitalist Europe. But the proletarian revolution had been merely delayed. For that to occur, Lenin argued, the lifeline between the colonies and the capitalist "metropolis" must be severed. The colonial peoples must be mobilized to revolution through an appeal to nationalism and independence. These nationalist "bourgeois" revolutions would be followed by a second, socialist revolution led by a communist party that, upon victory, would install itself in power in the name of the "dictatorship of the proletariat." All of which would be the preamble to socialist revolutions in the West. In this manner, some semblance of integrity would be restored to classical Marxism.

By the end of his life, Lenin became aware that international socialist revolution might well be delayed for an entire epoch. In the interim, Lenin asked, "Shall we be able to hold on with our small proletariat and very small peasant production . . . until the West-European capitalist countries consummate their development towards socialism?" However economically retrograde and unsuited for socialism, the Soviet Union would have to defend itself from external enemies. Revolutions in colonial India or ravaged China would insulate the Soviet Union from external threat while the world waited for the advent of socialism in the industrial democracies.[32]

This was the logic that led Josef Stalin, in 1926, to enjoin the Chinese to embark on revolution. Although Stalin recognized that Marxism's final victory could be won only by the proletariat of all the advanced countries of the world, like Lenin, he insisted that the protection of the Soviet Union required uprisings among the peasants of the oppressed colonial nations, including China.[33] Marx himself had never conceived peasant revolutions as socialist and thought that the peasantry was irremediably "counterrevolutionary."[34] For his part, Engels, in his *Peasant War in Germany*, warned that any revolution that inherited a primitive economic base would inevitably decay into a repressive and rapacious dictatorship.

It was this kind of revised and uncertain Marxism to which Mao gave his allegiance, a "Marxism" that was more Leninist-Stalinist than Marxist. Gone was the recognition that socialist revolution required the provision of an antecedent economic base capable of producing the abundance that would assure a satisfied, educated and self-directed proletariat. If there are "universal truths" to be found at the base of Mao Zedong Thought, they are not Marxist. Whatever truths there are have been modified by Lenin and Stalin who transformed some of the central theses of classical Marxism in order to defend and secure the Soviet Union.[35]

More than that, Mao did not even seem to remain true to the convictions of his Soviet mentors. It is difficult, if not impossible, to identify the specific Leninist truths to which Mao Zedong Thought is unequivocally committed. Not only was Mao's class analysis of the peasantry entirely non-Marxist, the alternatives he posed for the CCP leadership were non-Leninist as well. To Mao, the Chinese peasants possessed a natural revolutionary impulse. "Several hundred million" strong, they would rise like a "mighty storm" that "no power" could contain. In the face of that elemental force, the Communist Party had few choices. It could "march" at their head, "trail behind them," or "oppose them."[36] None of this was Leninist in character or inspiration.

Mao seemed convinced that revolution was the spontaneous result of poverty—a Marxist and Leninist heresy. So convinced was Mao that poverty was sufficient to precipitate revolution that he celebrated the fact that China was poor, for "If China becomes prosperous . . . then [people] will not want revolution."[37] Being poor was good, according to Mao, because "the poor want revolution."[38] All the sophistication of Marxism and Leninism had dissolved into a platitude.

Mao, the Philosopher

If a developmental ideology were to guide an entire nation in economic construction, it must give evidence of a commitment to rational analysis and calculation. In that regard, an examination of the philosophical content of Mao Zedong Thought recommends itself.

During his lifetime, Mao's supporters and adherents proclaimed that he had "creatively" developed Marxism to a "higher level" of truth. Their claim was constructed on Mao's presumed authorship of a few essays on epistemological and ontological matters, the two most important are *On Practice* and *On Contradiction*. These two seem to have been part of an intended larger work entitled *On Dialectical Materialism* and were probably written in the winter of 1939–40.[39]

Enthusiasts and defenders of Mao notwithstanding,[40] it is difficult to find logical analysis, even less, philosophical profundity, in the thought of Mao. Some critics have simply dismissed him as a thinker entirely because "We shall not find in his writings anything approaching a serious attempt to elaborate on or give a popular exposition of problems of philosophy, natural science, the theory of cognition, logic and so on."[41]

Very few of Mao's pronouncements are *argued*. Neither the vast generalizations concerning human psychology, the role of will power and enthusiasm in history, nor the supposed dynamics of class and revolution are ever supported by evidence or logic. His understanding of logic and of scientific laws, so critical to rational programming, was rudimentary, at best, as evidenced in the following exegesis by Mao on the subject of logic:

> Formal logic is very like elementary mathematics; dialectical logic is like advanced mathematics. . . . Formal logic contains quite a few incorrect major premises. Therefore, it cannot arrive at a correct judgment; but from the perspective of formal logic [that judgment] is not at all incorrect.[42]

If this was Mao's understanding of logic, it was an understanding suffused with confusion and incoherence. Such confusion could only frustrate any attempt to deal with formal systems or employ logic in the resolution of problems.

Mao's comprehension of science and its laws, so critical to any program of economic development, was no better than his grasp of formal logic. To him, science meant that "people have to eat, that's scientific, and shouldn't be abolished."[43] Despite his manifest ignorance of science and logic, he never permitted that ignorance to restrain his programmatic enthusiasm. As a case in point, at the time of the Great Leap Forward, in an effort to hasten the industrial development of China, Mao commanded peasants to commit all their resources to the fashioning of iron in backyard furnaces. Convinced that China could surpass the output of Great Britain in a matter of years, his enthusiasm was unconstrained by natural law, the properties of metals, or the necessity of collateral inputs. With little understanding, if any, of physical laws and their intrinsic constraints on human enterprise, Mao invariably chose to interpret the laws of nature voluntaristically. This would explain his inability to comprehend why technologically backward Chinese peasants required ten tons of coal to produce a ton of iron, when foreigners with technologically advanced facilities could produce the same ton of iron with only two tons of coal.[44]

Mao's writings are replete with other impenetrable curiosities. In his major philosophical work, *On Contradiction*, Mao dealt with complex matters with abandon. He spoke of the "universality of contradictions," of contradictions "inside things," and of contradictions as the "cause of things, without which nothing would exist." We are told that contradictions are both absolute *and* relative; that they "permeate all things" but still remain "particular." Despite the ambiguous nature of contradictions, Mao insisted that they constitute the "essences" of things, for to "deny contradictions is to deny everything."[45]

All of which tells us very little. The term "contradiction" is used so loosely that it refers to any dissimilarity between things, literal opposites, any tension or opposition between things or aspects of things, any tension in general, any conflict or inconsistency, as well as any difference or antagonism. Just how cognitively empty this is becomes evident when one considers how any of it might be applied with any positive consequence.

By way of illustration, in expounding on the "unity of opposites,"

Mao said: "Quantitative change and qualitative change form the unity of opposites. Everything has its relative regularity. . . . Cut the circumference [of a circle] into tens of thousands of pieces and it'll become square. Circles and squares are the unity of opposites."[46] Not only do opposites unite, they also "interpenetrate" each other, thereby confirming the "universality of contradiction." Expounding further on the "interpenetration of opposites," Mao provided the following illustrations:

> International affairs influence each other, permeate each other. . . . Thus I am part of you, [and] you are part of me. Now the world, too, is like this, the world is two mud bodhisattvas. There is something of us inside the capitalist mud bodhisattva, and something of them inside the socialist bodhisattva. Thus inside you is me, [and] inside me is you. . . .[47]

How any of that could have assisted China's leadership in the formulation of policy remains a mystery. Equally mysterious is the function of Mao's conception of Marxist dialectics, and how that might be put to cognitive or programmatic use.

For Mao, dialectics meant that "things will develop in the opposite direction when they become extreme; the more that bad things are done, [ultimately] the good will emerge. . . . [I]n every bad thing one should see good; in the good, one should see bad. In misfortune there is fortune, in fortune there is misfortune."[48] More than its banality, Mao's understanding of Marxist dialectics is steeped in opacity, as is almost all of his thought. In one talk, for instance, he sought to justify his directive on the formation of People's Communes with the following incomprehensible lecture on dialectics:

> It's always been the majority obeying the minority, because the minority [has always] reflected the opinion of the majority. . . . The world's first, marsh gas, is H_4C; farts are H_2S; gypsum is calcium sulphate. From this perspective, the opinion of the minority reflects the opinion of the majority.[49]

It was not enough that he had "creatively developed" Marxism-Leninism in such fashion—Mao was convinced that his thought was superior to that of his ideological mentors! Commenting on the writings of Marx, Engels, Lenin, and Stalin, Mao opined that "They had little experience, so naturally their views are vague and inexplicit. Don't think the ancestors all fart fragrantly and fart no foul farts."[50] In particular, Mao thought Lenin and Stalin to be deficient in their understanding of contradictions and of dialectics. According to Mao:

[I]n Lenin's time, he would not fully investigate this question; [and still] lacking experience, he died. For a long time Stalin did not admit that socialist society had contradictions. . . . Therefore . . . we say that Stalin was somewhat deficient in dialectics. . . . I say his dialectics are bashful dialectics, are coy dialectics, or could be called hesitant dialectics.[51]

Not only was Mao's thought obtuse, it entertained diametrically opposite positions on any number of issues. As an example, in his talk of 27 February 1957, Mao regarded China's large population to be a grave problem: "Our nation. . . has so many people, a population of 600 million. Here [we] need birth control; it would be great [if we] could lower the birth [rate] a bit."[52] By August 1958, however, he had changed his mind completely and now insisted that "[Our] views on population should change. In the past I said that [we] could manage with 800 million. Now I think that one billion plus would be no cause for alarm."[53]

Similarly, Mao was of two minds with regards to the functional value of material incentives. In 1942, in a report on the Shaanxi-Gansu-Ningxia Border Region that was controlled by the CCP, Mao forebade the cadres from adopting "a policy of egalitarian distribution" and compensation, proposing instead a "progressive piecework wages system." An egalitarian system of wages, Mao maintained, "destroys the distinction between skilled labour and unskilled labour and the distinction between industriousness and laziness, thus lowering work enthusiasm." By paying workers in accordance with how much actual labor they had performed, not only would their "work enthusiasm" increase, it would also "raise production."[54]

But by the second half of the 1950s, at the time of the Great Leap, Mao had completely reversed his position. He now questioned the value of a differential wage system that he had once advocated. "Why do [we] have to use a wage system?", Mao queried. "Too great a reliance on material rewards . . . won't do" because it would be "a concession" to the "bourgeoisie." Instead of material incentives, "We should put into practice some of the ideals of utopian socialism." For, afterall, "If human beings only live to eat, isn't that like dogs eating shit?"[55]

These kinds of judgments were offered as mutually exclusive truths which were more than a little confusing for those who had to render them into actual policy. Far from being a creative development of Marxism, Mao Zedong Thought was a bowdlerized, simplistic rendering of entire passages drawn from Soviet material, paraphrased and edited for inclusion in Mao's writings,[56] having very little relevance to anything in the Chinese environment and having largely pernicious consequences on the growth and development of the Chinese economy. If Mao Zedong Thought was to serve as an ideology of delayed industrialization, much of it was dysfunctional.

Mao Zedong Thought as Political Expediency

Given the opacity and inconsistencies in Mao Zedong Thought, it is very hard to imagine how it could serve convincingly as a prescriptive guide to economic conduct. Far from being the guiding ideology of a developmental regime, Mao Zedong Thought was apparently designed to serve the political needs of the Communist Party elite. Where the thought proved to be most useful was in the arena of political expediency. Mao's "theoretical" concepts were "twisted and reduced to a tool of policy, and a very convenient tool indeed. . . ."[57] The real purpose of Maoist methodology was to serve as "the ideological and propaganda defense of Maoist policies."[58]

Mao Zedong Thought allowed Mao, and those around him, to embark upon arbitrary and capricious changes in assessment and behavior by pretending they were the result of dialectical insights. It allowed and allows every unprincipled alteration in public policy to masquerade as "dialectics." The use of the dialectic allowed "unities" to "transform" themselves into "opposites," and "nonantagonistic contradictions" to quickly become "antagonistic." In so doing, Mao Zedong Thought was and is almost exclusively politically expedient, serving political ends known only to a self-selected CCP "vanguard."

Thus, at one time the "big bourgeoisie" was part of the revolution;[59] at another, it was not. At one time the government under the Communist Party included the industrial workers, the peasants, the partisans, the urban petty bourgeoisie, the national bourgeoisie, and the "enlightened gentry." Whatever the "contradictions" among them were judged to be "nonantagonistic." All these classes "would together accomplish the political, economic and cultural tasks of the new-democratic state."[60]

Before long, however, Mao would argue that the class struggle in China had grown "acute."[61] Campaigns against the gentry, the national bourgeoisie, and the petty bourgeoisie were instigated, only to be followed by more campaigns against intellectuals, "capitalist roaders," and an ill-defined class of felons identified only as members of the "new bourgeoisie." By the time of the Cultural Revolution, Chinese theoreticians, using Mao's dialectical method, spoke of a "long and tortuous and at times . . . very acute" class struggle among the leaders of the "proletarian party" itself, close comrades of Mao's who had been dialectically transformed into a "new bourgeoisie."[62]

There have been many such "dialectical transformations" in Mao Zedong Thought. At one time Mao's revolution sought to enhance capitalist industrial enterprise in China.[63] But then, "things often turn into their opposites,"[64] so it should not come as a surprise that by the late-1950s, Mao had decided that private enterprise in China was to be abolished.[65]

At one time Mao identified the Soviet Union as the necessary guide for the liberation of humanity. The Chinese were compelled by "objective reality" to "lean to the side of the Soviet Union."[66] For all that, it was not long before the Soviet Union dialectically transformed itself into "social imperialism" to betray "the people of the socialist countries" and "attack Marxism-Leninism itself."[67]

The dialectical quality of Mao Zedong Thought made changes of policy in the People's Republic very difficult to anticipate or comprehend. For more than three decades China lurched from one developmental strategy to another. At one time, between 1953 and 1957, that strategy was a replication of the Stalinist program that oversaw the industrial development of the Soviet Union. By 1958, however, China's strategy had become its dialectical opposite. Emphasis was no longer simply on capital accumulation and capital intensive growth, but on moral incentive and labor intensive investments. That was itself subsequently transformed into a program of unorthodox economic retrenchment of the early-1960s, to give way, once again, to the moral enjoinment, and the ethic of sacrifice and commitment of the Cultural Revolution.

Each and every peremptory policy reversal was presumably illuminated by the "scientific theses" that comprise "the thinking of comrade Mao Zedong."[68] All of which suggests that there was no specific substance to Mao Zedong Thought, and that his thought was often employed to justify the requirements of the moment.

In fact, discovering truth in Mao's China was so difficult that the most senior members of the Communist Party regularly fell into error. During the time of the Cultural Revolution, for example, it was found that eleven of the fifteen members and alternate members of the Party's secretariat had fallen so deeply into error that they constituted a "black gang," an "anti-Party clique." PRC Chairman Liu Shaoqi was identified as an "anti-Marxist-Leninist."[69] Deng Xiaoping, Liu's second-in-command, was identified as a "black bandit" and would follow Liu into infamy, only to be followed himself by Lin Biao. Lin, who had previously been annointed as Mao's successor, was discovered to be the leader of an anti-Marxist "anti-Party clique."

Possessing the "truths" of Mao Zedong Thought seemed to provide few advantages to China's ruling elite. Mao expected continual schisms among the Party leadership. In 1971, he observed that there had already been ten "splits" in China's vanguard party and fully expected that "this may happen another 10, 20, or 30 times."[70] After Mao's death, Hua Guofeng and Ye Jianying fell from the political pantheon of China's ruling elite. They had apparently "fragmented" Mao Zedong Thought, "distorting" and "debasing it."[71] Subsequently, Hu Yaobang and Zhao Ziyang, both protégés of Deng Xiaoping, similarly lapsed into error. In fact, there has hardly been a single leader in the highest reaches of the Communist Party who has not fallen into serious error at one time or another, irrespective of the abundance of truths and the policy guidance made available by the thought of Mao.

It is not difficult to understand why almost every prominent CCP leader lapsed into error because, within the confines of the vagueness, opacity, and vagaries of Mao Zedong Thought, there was no clear way to distinguish truth from error. Curiously enough, Mao was convinced that the masses, in particular the peasants, had the ability to understand his thought when the best educated and most informed of the Communist Party elite repeatedly failed. He consistently prided himself as having some special intuitive rapport with the masses. Whenever his colleagues and subordinates failed to unite behind his standard, Mao would force his program through over their resistance by an appeal to the masses.[72]

From all this, it would seem that Mao conceived the masses to be an inexhaustible source of creativity, intelligence, and ingenuity. Inexplicably, that was not the case, for Mao characterized the masses as passive "blank" receptors of his policy injunctions. According to him, the Chinese people's "cultural and scientific level is not high. . . ." In the last analysis, the masses "are like a blank sheet of paper which is good for writing on."[73] Being "blank sheets of paper," the masses were told to simply follow whatever Mao instructed. "Everything in line with Mao Zedong's thought should be supported and followed; everything not in line with Mao Zedong's thought should be opposed and resisted."[74] At the height of the Cultural Revolution, the Chinese people were enjoined simply to "fulfill the instructions of Comrade Mao Zedong regardless of whether we have or have not yet understood them."[75]

All of which means that in the ideocratic system of the People's Republic where political rectitude was all-important and the consequences of error were profound, there were no clear criteria for identifying truths and for distinguishing truth from falsehood. Obedience to Mao Zedong was the sole imperative of the system. Mao instructed the masses in much the same fashion that Rousseau advised teachers to educate their charges. Mao was the final arbiter of what his thought implied; no other political leader could divine the truth. In practice, Mao Zedong Thought could only be applied by Mao himself.

However much Mao Zedong Thought might have been conducive to economic development—by instilling in the masses an ethic of work, sacrifice, and obedience—its arbitrary, confusing, and capricious nature bred anxiety, social strife, and alienation that were counterproductive to development. The tactical policies of investment, the recoupment of capital innovation and infrastructural articulation all suffered from the erratic and constantly changing directives that were a hallmark of Mao's tenure in power.

The Core of Mao Zedong Thought

If Mao's thought failed as an ideology of delayed industrialization, it was not due to a lack of recognition of China's need to industrialize. Mao saw his country's economic retardation as having "caused the Chinese people to remain poverty-stricken and illiterate, and to be looked down upon by other peoples of the world."[76] This was why, he went on, "we must build our country into a great industrial power"[77] through "down-to-earth and effective economic development."[78]

Some of Mao's ideas for economic development were appropriate and eminently sensible, if commonplace. Time and again, he exhorted his countrymen to "wipe out bureaucratic airs" and "be on the same plane as the common people." The Chinese must be "industrious and thrifty," "individual consumption should be kept down." He proposed that "Every province should put up a proclamation banning gambling," and that weddings and funerals "should all be kept simple."[79]

The value Mao placed on manual labor and work in general; his emphasis on frugality; his objections to waste, status display, and bureaucratic impediments—these were all conducive to modernization. Beneath all of that, however, were a set of convictions that, more emphatically than any other, were to militate against all of his more sensible ideas.

For all of the vagueness and ambiguity that made it unsuitable as a tactical guide to comprehensive and sustainable development, Mao Zedong Thought contains a set of strategic imperatives, inherited from classical Marxism, the implications of which were clear and unambiguous. Both Marx and Engels had enjoined their followers to renounce private property and the market economy that sustained it. Those notions would exercise their influence on the thought of Mao until his disappearance into history. However ignorant Mao might have been about economic matters, he was nonetheless committed to a set of fundamental beliefs about how an economy ought to work, and how it could be transformed into communism. Those beliefs would exact a tragic price from the people of China.

Implicit in the abandonment of a free market was the necessity of an alternative guide for the allocation of resources; the investment of capital; the establishment of prices; the assignment of wages; and the distribution of goods. To replace the free market and the private economy, Mao looked to the command economy of Lenin and Stalin. Like the Soviet Union, the entire Chinese economy would be governed exclusively from the administrative center by government planners.

But the command model, if it worked at all, is dependent on the economic training and expertise of the planners who, in turn, are dependent on their access to accurate and reliable data, economic and otherwise. Given China's primitive information infrastructure, the economic model of central planning could not be more ill-suited. Mao was not unaware of that problem, as evidenced in a conversation between him and an associate during the ill-fated Great Leap Forward.

In that conversation, Mao inveighed against an epidemic of "fake reports" and falsified statistics which provoked him to inquire, "In the last analysis, are there really 8.5 million tons of good steel this year? Do they really exist or have they [just] been reported?" Despite the information shortfall that led him to conclude that "I think, in fact, there is not that much [good steel],"[80] Mao nevertheless insisted on setting production targets that were entirely unrealistic. He fully expected that "after only three years of arduous struggle," agrarian China could surpass Japan in the overall number of machine tools produced. On steel production, his expectations were even more grandiose. Noting that the United States produced "100 million tons" of steel and exported "a bit over 10 million tons," Mao remarked, "On an impulse, [I] thought of a figure and came out with it. Can we make 30 million tons of steel next year?"[81]

Not only was Mao seemingly unaware of the inherent flaws of the command model that he borrowed from his Soviet mentors, he did not seem to realize that the model was unsuited even for the Soviet Union. Mao's ignorance is amply revealed in the following exchange with a subordinate. The conversation would be farcical if the consequences were not so tragic. In response to Mao's assurance that "The U.S.S.R. is on relatively firm ground, honest and frank, producing every year 50 million tons of steel," his associate remarked: "Not necessarily, the U.S.S.R. also falsifies."[82]

There was one potential benefit to the suppression of private property, the abandonment of the market, and the imposition of a command economy—the elimination of class differences as a source of social conflict. But Mao succeeded in precluding even this potential benefit by introducing his own "innovative" notions about the nature of "class" and class conflict.

It may be that Mao was uninformed as to the classical Marxist notion of class; it may also be that he was simply indifferent to a concept which is critical to the integrity of Marxism. Whatever the reason, Mao redefined social "class" to mean not an individual's relationship to the means of production but the content of her thoughts and beliefs. The result of Mao's reconception of "class" and class membership was that, although the property-owning classes in China had been thoroughly extirpated in the campaigns of the early-1950s, Mao insisted that "feudal" remnants and incipient capitalists still exerted their influence on the thinking of people.[83] All of which led him to the expectation that "there will still be ideological and political struggle (or call it revolution)"[84] under socialism. Mao provided the following explanation:

> There are two kinds of abolition of classes: One concerns classes that engage in economic exploitation; they are easily abolished, and we now can say they are already abolished. The second concerns classes in terms of political thinking (landlords, rich peasants, the bourgeosie, including their intellectuals); these are not easily abolished, and they have not yet been abolished. . . .[85]

More than that, Mao apparently was convinced that class thinking was so insidious that children could inherit it from parents—"The bourgeoisie has a bourgeois ideology; the sons of the bourgeoisie also have a bourgeois ideology."[86] This was why, in his judgment, "The struggle between proletarian ideology and bourgeois ideology will last decades,"[87] necessitating an "uninterrupted" and continuous revolution. "Enemies of the people" were apparently ineradicable: "Once smashed, they regenerate; once they regenerate they have to be smashed again."[88]

Like almost everything in the thought of Mao, it was difficult to precisely define and identify the "black" classes who were the "counter-revolutionary" "enemies of the people." The definitions provided by Mao were not illuminating. According to him, "rightists" must be censured because they were "oppositionists." On the other extreme were the "left opportunists" who also required "re-education" because they were overly enthusiastic in carrying out his injunctions. Between the two extremes were the "middle-of-the-roaders" whom Mao also found objectionable because they were "doubters."[89] It did not help that even Mao had difficulty. He once confessed that he himself had trouble sorting out China's social classes with anything like precision.[90]

Given the deceptive and shifting character of class membership, the only way to ferret out members of the "black" classes who were the people's "enemies" was through "practice." According to Mao, "All genuine knowledge originates in direct experience. . . . There can be no knowledge apart from practice." Thus, "only through personal participation in the practical struggle to change reality can you uncover the essence of that thing or class of things and comprehend them."[91]

What that meant is very difficult to fathom, for Mao admitted that practice or experience itself can be deceptive and misleading. According to him, "sometimes, in fact, a few experiences that are backward experiences, are labeled as advanced experiences, [though] in reality they are backward experiences."[92] Despite that uncertainty, Mao nevertheless was adamant that only through the experience and practice of "struggle" could "the people" be distinguished from its "enemy," and the "non-antagonistic contradictions" that occur among the "people" be distinguished from the "antagonistic contradictions" that take place between the "people" and its "enemy." As he put it, "Contradictions will sooner or later become apparent, so it's good to create a disturbance."[93] To add to the problem, since both the "people" and their "enemy" were defined by their thoughts and behaviors, it was entirely possible that, in the course of a given struggle, "people" could suddenly turn into the "enemy" and what started out as "non-antagonistic" could abruptly become "antagonistic."[94]

None of this would be of much consequence if Mao had not prescribed entirely different methods to deal with the two kinds of contradictions. According to him, contradictions that were "non-antagonistic" would be resolved through "peaceful" means of education, persuasion, and criticism. "Antagonistic contradictions," in contrast, must be dealt with with "dictatorial" methods that could include compulsion, labor reform, and death.[95]

All of which meant that under the guidance of Mao Zedong Thought, China became a society where rule of law was disdained and dismissed as "bourgeois." In its place were social chaos and mob justice, over which ruled Mao's supreme will. As the Great Helmsman once said, "[We] can't rule the majority of the people by relying on law. . . . Who could remember so many clauses of a civil code or a criminal law?. . . . The more bourgeois freedom is destroyed, the more proletarian freedom there is."[96]

Instead of the order and stability so crucial to economic development, China under Mao degenerated into a society where political turmoil and social chaos were celebrated as virtues in the belief that "The more the struggle, the more enriched [life will become]. . . ."[97] As Mao put it in his inimitable fashion, "it's good to have a bit of disturbance." In a population of 600 million, he observed, "to have one million cause trouble in a year is normal."[98] After all, "if there is no struggle with the germs, then there can't be immunity from the disease. . . . [G]etting sick regularly is a good thing. . . ."[99]

On top of all the disabilities of a command economy, and the stresses attending the effort to comprehend and follow political dictates that were vague and shifting, Mao had added the extra burden of a continuous "class" struggle. All of which were ruinous of economic development, to say nothing of the society's overall well-being. In the years immediately following his death, his own party would arrive at the same judgment.

Notes

1. John H. Kautsky, *Communism and the Politics of Development* (New York: John Wiley & Sons, 1968).
2. Jaroslaw Piekalkiewicz and Alfred Wayne Penn, *Politics of Ideocracy* (Albany, NY: State University of New York, 1995), 27.
3. Waldemar Gurian, "Totalitarianism as Political Religion," in *Totalitarianism*, ed. Carl J. Friedrich (New York: Grosset and Dunlap, 1964), 122.
4. Jean-Francois Revel, *The Totalitarian Temptation* (New York: Penguin, 1977), 44.
5. Thomas Sowell, *A Conflict of Visions: Ideological Origins of Political Struggles* (New York: William Morrow, 1987), 25–26.
6. Franz Schurmann, *Ideology and Organization in Communist China* (Berkeley: University of California, 1966), 22, 23.
7. Ibid., 24.
8. *Guanyu jianguo yilai dangde rougan lishi wenti de jueyi* (*Resolution on Certain Historical Problems of Our Party since the Founding of the People's Republic of China*) (Beijing: People's Publisher, 1983), 486.
9. *Liberation Army Daily*, 3 November 1967, as cited in *The "Miracles" of Chairman Mao*, ed. George Urban (Los Angeles: Nash, 1971), 153.
10. Jerome Ch'en, ed., *Mao: Great Lives Observed* (Englewood Cliffs, N.J.: Prentice-Hall, 1969), 20.
11. "Fighting Cancer with Revolutionary Optimism," Beijing radio, 13 September 1968, cited in Urban, *The "Miracles"*, 9.
12. John G. Gurley, "The Formation of Mao's Economic Strategy, 1927–1949," *Monthly Review* 27 (July-August 1975): 58.
13. Liu Shaoqi, "On the Party," *Selected Works* I(Beijing: Foreign Languages, 1984), 331; see pp. 330–335.
14. *Guanyu jianguo yilai*, 487.
15. Ibid., 488.
16. *Resolution on CPC History (1949–81)* (Beijing: Foreign Languages, 1981), 94–98.
17. Ibid., 57.
18. "Communiqué of the Sixth Plenary Session of the Eleventh Central Committee of the Communist Party of China," in Cohen, *The Communism of Mao Tse-Tung*, 124.
19. Ibid., 142.
20. See the entire discussion of Arthur A. Cohen, *The Communism of Mao Tse-tung* (Chicago: University of Chicago, 1964), ch. 6.
21. Mao meant by this the coequal development of agriculture and industry.
22. Chen Boda, "Under the Banner of Comrade Mao Zedong," *Red Flag* 4 (16 July 1958), as cited in Cohen, *The Communism of Mao Tse-Tung*, 176.
23. *Resolution on CPC History*, 28.
24. See the discussion in James Peck's introduction to Mao Zedong, *A Critique of Soviet Economics* (New York: Monthly Review, 1977), 7–29.
25. *Guanyou jianguo yilai*, 324–335 (*Resolution on CPC History*, 27, 30–32).
26. Philipped Devillers, *Mao* (New York: Schocken, 1969), 35.
27. Stuart R. Schram, *The Political Thought of Mao Tse-tung* (New York: Praeger, 1969), 30, 35.
28. There are many competent treatments of classical Marxism, independent of subse-

quent Leninist re-interpretation. See A. G. Meyer, *Marxism: The Unity of Theory and Practice* (Ann Arbor: University of Michigan, 1963); Karl Federn, *The Materialist Conception of History: A Critical Analysis* (London: Macmillan, 1939); M. Bober, *Karl Marx's Interpretation of History* (Cambridge: Cambridge University, 1948); and A. James Gregor, *A Survey of Marxism* (New York: Random House, 1965), ch. 5.

29. O. E. Vladimirov, ed., *Maoism As It Really Is* (Moscow: Progress Publishers, 1981), 41.

30. F. V. Konstantinov, M. I. Sladkovsky, and V. G. Georgiyev, eds., *A Critique of Mao Tse-tung's Theoretical Conceptions* (Moscow: Progress, 1972), 27.

31. See Vladimir I. Lenin, *Imperialism: The Highest Stage of Capitalism* (New York: International, 1939).

32. V. I. Lenin, "Better Fewer, But Better," in *Collected Works* 33 (Moscow: Progress, 1966): 499–500.

33. J. V. Stalin, "The Prospects of the Revolution in China," *Works* 8 (Moscow: Foreign Languages, 1954): 375.

34. Karl Marx anticipated a revolution in China, but it would not be a socialist uprising. It would serve to precipitate the trade and business crises in Western Europe which Marx identified as necessary for revolution among the advanced industrial economies. See Karl Marx, "Revolution in China and in Europe," *New York Daily Tribune*, 14 June 1853, in *Marx on China* (London: Lawrence and Wishart, 1968), 4, 9.

34. See Theodore H. Von Laue, *Why Lenin? Why Stalin?* (New York: Lippincott, 1964), ch. 8.

35. Mao, "Report on an Investigation of the Peasant Movement in Hunan (March 1927)," *Selected Works* I (Beijing: Foreign Languages, 1977), 24.

36. Mao, "On the Correct Handling of Contradictions," in Roderick MacFarquhar, Timoth Cheek, and Eugene Wu, *The Secret Speeches of Chairman Mao: From the Hundred Flowers to the Great Leap Forward* (Cambridge, MA: Council on East Asian Studies, Harvard University, 1989), 180.

37. Mao, "On the Ten Major Relationships," *Selected Works* 5: 306; Vladimirov, *Maoism*, 122–123.

38. Karl A. Wittfogel, "Some Remarks on Mao's Handling of Concepts and Problems of Dialectics," *Studies in Soviet Thought* 3, no. 4 (December 1963): 255.

39. See, for example, Bob Avakian, *Mao Tse-tung's Immortal Contributions* (Chicago: RCP Publications, n.d.), 132. Some effort was made to add depth to Mao's thought by Frederic Wakeman, Jr., *History and Will: Philosophical Perspectives of Mao Tse-tung's Thought* (Los Angeles: University of California, 1973) with arguable success.

40. Fedor Burlatsky, *Mao Tse-tung: An Ideological and Psychological Portrait* (Moscow: Progress, 1976), 222.

41. Mao, "Talks at the Hangzhou Conference (Draft Transcript) (3–4 January 1958)," in MacFarquhar et al., *The Secret Speeches*, 382.

42. Mao, "Talks at the Wuchang Conference (21–23 November 1958)," in ibid., 513.

43. Mao, "Talks at the First Zhengzhou Conference (6–10 November 1958)," ibid., 471–472.

44. Mao, "On the Correct Handling of Contradictions Among the People," *Selected Works* 5: 384–399.

45. Mao, "Talks at the Hangzhou Conference," 382.

46. Mao, "On the Correct Handling of Contradictions," in MacFarquhar et al., *The Secret Speeches*, 182.

47. Ibid., 179–180.
48. Mao, "Talks at the Beidaihe Conference (Draft Transcript) (17–30 August 1958)," in ibid., 427.
49. Ibid., 441.
50. Mao, "On the Correct Handling of Contradictions," in ibid., 162–164.
51. Ibid., 159.
52. Mao, "Talks at the Beidaihe Conference," 403.
53. Mao, "Economic and Financial Problems (December 1942)," in *Mao Zedong and the Political Economy of the Border Region* by Andrew Watson (Cambridge: Cambridge University, 1980), 95, 162.
54. Mao, "Talks at the Beidaihe Conference," 417, 410, 414.
55. See Mao, "On Dialectical Materialism," *Studies in Soviet Thought* 3 (December 1963), 270–277; V. I. Krivtsov, ed., *Maoism Through the Eyes of Communists* (Moscow: Progress, 1970), 37; and Konstantinov, Sladkovsky, and Georgiyev, *A Critique of Mao*, 32.
56. Cohen, *The Communism of Mao*, 162, 163.
57. Vladimirov, *Maoism*, 14, 17.
58. From the early version of Mao, "The Chinese Revolution and the Chinese Communist Party," as cited in Schram, *The Political Thought*, 230.
59. Mao, "On Coalition Government," *Selected Works* 3: 280.
60. Mao, *A Critique of Soviet Economics*, 63.
61. Zhang Chunqiao, *On Exercising All-Round Dictatorship Over the Bourgeoisie* (Beijing: Foreign Languages, 1975), 4, 13.
62. See the discussion in Mao, "Report to the Second Plenary Session of the Seventh Central Committee of the Communist Party of China (5 March 1949)," in *Selected Works* 4: 361–375.
63. Mao, "On the Ten Major Relationships," 297.
64. Mao, *A Critique of Soviet Economics*, 64; Cohen, *The Communism of Mao*, 115–116.
65. Mao, "Stalin: Friend of the Chinese People," *Selected Works* 2: 335 and "On the People's Democratic Dictatorship," 2: 415, 417.
66. *Communiqué of the Eleventh Plenary Session of the Eighth Central Committee of the Communist Party of China* (Beijing: Foreign Languages, 1966), 6.
67. See the discussion in Chu-yuan Cheng, *China's Economic Development: Growth and Structural Change* (Boulder, CO: Westview, 1982), ch. 9; *Circular of the Central Committee of the Chinese Communist Party (16 May 1966)* (Beijing: Foreign Languages, 1967), 17; Chou Yang, *The Fighting Task Confronting Workers in Philosophy and the Social Science* (Beijing: Foreign Languages, 1963), 52.
68. Mao, "Talks at Three Meetings with Comrades Zhang Chunqiao and Yao Wenyuan," in *Chairman Mao Talks to the People: Talks and Letters, 1956–1971*, ed. Stuart Schram (New York: Pantheon, 1974), 279.
69. Yao Wenyuan, *On the Social Basis of the Lin Biao Anti-Party Clique* (Beijing: Foreign Languages, 1975), 17.
70. See Deng Xiaoping, "Mao Zedong Thought Must be Correctly Understood as an Integral Whole," *Selected Works of Deng Xiaoping (1975–1982)* I (Beijing: Foreign Languages, 1984), 55.
71. Mao, "On Some Important Problems of the Party's Present Policy," in *Selected Works* 4: 186. See the discussion in Lowell Dittmer, "The Legacy of Mao Zedong," *Asian Survey* 20 (May 1980): 552–553.
72. Mao, "On the Ten Major Relationships," 306; see Boris Leibson, *Petty Bourgeois Revolutionism* (Moscow: Progress, 1970), 144.

73. *People's Daily*, 26 June 1967, as cited in Urban, *The "Miracles,"* 154.

74. *People's Daily*, 16 June 1967, as cited in Konstantinov, Sladkovsky, and Georgiyev, *A Critique of Mao*, 149.

75. Mao, "On Ideological Work (Talk at a Conference Attended by Party Cadres from People's Liberation Army Units under the Nanjing Command and from Jiangsu and Anhui Provinces) (19 March 1957)," in MacFarquhar et al., *The Secret Speeches*, 325.

76. Mao, "Talks at the Beidaihe Conference," 409.

77. Mao, "Economic and Financial Problems," 59.

78. Mao, "Talks at the Hangzhou Conference," 384, 381, 380.

79. Mao, "Talks at the Wuchang Conference," 506.

80. Ibid., 512, 485.

81. Ibid., 510.

82. Mao, "Talk at the Forum of Heads of Propaganda, Culture, and Education Departments from Nine Provinces and Municipalities," in MacFarquhar et al., *The Secret Speeches*, 198.

83. Mao, "Talks at the Hangzhou Conference," 389.

84. Mao, "Talks at the Wuchang Conference," 490–491.

85. Mao, "Talk at the Forum," 205.

86. Ibid., 198.

87. Mao, "Talks at the First Zhengzhou Conference," 457.

88. Mao, "Talks at the Hangzhou Conference," 377; and "On Practice," in *Four Essays on Philosophy* (Beijing: Foreign Languages, 1968), 18.

89. Mao, "A Talk with Literary and Art Circles (8 March 1957)," in MacFarquhar, et al., *The Secret Speeches*, 228.

90. Mao, "On Practice," 8, 9.

91. Mao, "On the Correct Handling of Contradictions Among the People (Speaking Notes) (27 February 1957)," in MacFarquhar, et al., *The Secret Speeches*, 173, 189.

92. Mao, "Talk at Yinian Tang (16 February 1957)," in MacFarquhar, *The Secret Speeches*, 119.

93. See Mao, "On the Correct Handling of Contradictions Among the People," in *Four Essays on Philosophy*, 79–96.

94. Mao, any version of "On the Correct Handling of Contradictions."

95. Mao, "Talks at the Beidaihe Conference," 424.

96. Mao, "Talk at Yinian Tang," 126.

97. Ibid., 122.

98. Mao, "On the Correct Handling of Contradictions," in MacFarquhar, *The Secret Speeches*, 174.

3

The Need to Reform

Being an ideocracy, governing in the People's Republic of China requires an appeal to its legitimating ideology. All of the aspiring leaders of mainland China had sought just such legitimation. When Liu Shaoqi was second only to Mao in the ranks of the Communist Party, he certified his right to rule by identifying himself with the "theory of Marxism-Leninism and the methods of Mao Zedong."[1] Similarly, when Lin Biao aspired to rule, he insisted that rule would be by virtue of "Marxism-Leninism and the thought of Mao Zedong."[2] When Jiang Qing and her Gang of Four undertook to seize control of China, they likewise insisted that their policies would be "charted by Marxism-Leninism-Mao Zedong Thought."[3]

Although continuing rule by the Chinese Communist Party (CCP) requires an appeal to the thought of Mao, there is something in that thought that his successors found manifestly objectionable. Thus, after Mao's death, while Deng Xiaoping insisted that the regime on the mainland of China remained inspired by Mao Zedong Thought, Deng found it necessary to denounce and reject some of its content. In retrospect, it does not seem difficult to identify the offending elements.

The Socialist Command Economy

However little Mao read of classical Marxism, in a life filled with revolutionary activity, he could hardly have misunderstood the enjoinments, prescriptions, and proscriptions about economic planning so prominent in the writings of Marx and Engels. Whatever else classical Marxism taught Mao Zedong, it taught him that the market exchange of commodities would necessarily cease with the advent of socialism.

In one of the more popular writings of Engels, an exposition we know that Mao read, the co-founder of Marxism stated that with the victory of socialism, the production and market exchange of commodities would be "done away with." The anarchy of capitalist production and distribution through market exchanges would "capitulate" to production upon "a definite plan." "Anarchy in social production [would be] replaced by plan-conforming, conscious organization."[4]

The logic of this position is clear.[5] Commodities, for the founders of Marxism, were goods produced for sale. Sale took place in commodity markets in which capitalists sought profit. The search for profit drove capitalists to decrease workers' wages to subsistence levels in order to reduce costs and secure the highest possible profit margins for their products. That entailed substituting machinery for human labor, since machines not only do not demand wage increases but make workers redundant, thereby increasing the available "reserve army of labor." The pool of unemployed, in turn, would further depress wages.

The capitalist search for profits amidst intense competition would ultimately drive the system into monopolies and monopsonies, enabling the "ruling bourgeoisie" to dictate prices, only to ultimately reduce effective demand in their own economies. As low wage rates reduced the capacity of workers to purchase goods at a price that could return a profit, domestic producers were driven to seek market supplements in the world community. That, in turn, initiated a cycle that would ultimately assume a global dimension—a cycle of product marketing, overproduction, underconsumption, and renewed crisis. The "inevitable" consequence would be socialist revolution, in which the working class would seize the means of production and produce goods to serve human needs instead of profit. Socialism would be triumphant, capitalist market arrangements would disappear, and production would be planned on "a rational basis."

In effect, classical Marxism taught that socialism and its planned economy were possible (and necessary) only when "the actual conditions" for their realization were present. Those conditions involved the antecedent "complete development of modern productive forces," which would generate an "excess of supply over demand, over-production, glutting of the markets, [and] crises every ten years. . . ." A planned economy thus required, as a necessary condition for effective implementation, a fully matured industrial system as a foundation. Only then could a "single vast" and "definite plan" be conceivable, which would set about to harmonize "the modes of production, appropriation, and exchange with the socialized character of the means of production."[6]

All of this was understood by every knowledgeable Marxist for almost an entire generation after the death of Engels in 1896. The founders of Marxism advocated the planned economy for advanced industrial economies; they had very little to say to underdeveloped productive systems. The historical irony was that "socialist" revolutions exploded in the economically backward periphery of the industrialized world.

To render classical Marxism applicable to the economically backward communities of the world, recourse was made to V. I. Lenin's "creative development" of the inherited belief system, which transformed an ideology for liberation of the industrialized West into a doctrine for revolution on the periphery of capitalism. Lenin's revision of Marxism, however, did not license a command economy for industrially underdeveloped Russia. It was not Lenin who attempted the planning of a backward economy. That was left to Josef Stalin.

Stalin, heir to the transformed revolutionary doctrine, made Marxism-Leninism a revolutionary developmental creed for retrograde economies. Stalinism imposed a bureaucratic, centrally controlled, developmental plan on partially industrialized, premodern Russia. Not surprisingly, that imposition would generate deleterious side effects.

Economic growth and development under Stalin were achieved at the expense of the living standard of the Soviet people. Heavy rates of investment (about 30 percent of GNP), accumulated through compulsory savings, were sustained at the expense of consumption. Investment was showered on heavy industry to the neglect of the consumer goods industries. In a "workers' paradise," urban and rural workers were exploited to underwrite the expansion of the power, metallurgical, machine fabrication, and defense industries.

More than the exploitation of workers and consumers was at stake. The question was whether the state plan could assure that investment was efficiently employed and that the sacrifice of workers was not in vain. By the time of Stalin's death, there was increasing evidence that the entire economic system of the Soviet Union was characterized by static and dynamic imbalances.

Shortages and surpluses made efficiency extremely difficult; duplication and underutilization of resources were commonplace. Since the price structure was artificial, governed by decisions at the center of the system, the correction of malfunctions was difficult and time consuming. Guaranteed full employment, combined with universally low wages made labor immobile and its use unreflective of system needs. Waste was pandemic.[7]

The typical leadership response to these endemic problems was to tinker with the system. Output targets were redefined. Production was no longer measured in weight, volume, and number of units, instead "value-added" was introduced, calculated in terms of bureaucratically fixed prices. Enterprise managers were allowed some discretion in the use of state grants of capital. Bonuses were offered as incentives; profits were permitted and sometimes employed as measures of enterprise success. All of which, by the mid-1960s, had done little to change the Soviet economic system or remedy its disabilities.[8]

Most quantitative analyses indicate that after 1960, there was a slowdown in the growth of productivity in the Soviet Union in terms of both resource extraction and total factor productivity.[9] In fact, there had been a gradual deceleration in the efficiency and productivity of the Soviet economy since the late-1950s. After 1975, in particular, there was a steady decline in output per capita in the Soviet Union, when compared to productivity in the United States.[10]

In 1988, very few intellectuals in the international community were surprised when Soviet leader Mikhail Gorbachev admitted that, except for sales of vodka and oil, the Soviet economy had not grown in real terms for about two decades.[11] By that time, Soviet economists themselves reported that between 1981 and 1985 there was essentially no economic growth in the Soviet Union. In fact, between 1979 and 1982, the production of industrial goods, together with agricultural productivity, actually declined.[12]

By the mid-1980s, it was an open secret that centrally administered, planned economies had everywhere given evidence of serious systemic shortcomings. By that time, socialist Yugoslavia, Hungary, and Poland had all experimented with market supplements to the planned economy. The Hungarians claimed some successes from reform, mainly due to the expansion of profit-driven enterprises in the small private, as well as the increasingly large cooperative, sectors.

The Maoist Economy

Despite all the irrationalities inherent in the imposition of central planning on a retrograde economy, it was the Stalinist plan that Mao Zedong thrust upon agrarian China in 1949. In the early-1950s, a familiar slogan among Chinese revolutionaries was: "The Soviet Union today is our tomorrow."[13]

It was Stalinism, not Marxism or Leninism, that provided the economic core of Mao Zedong's thought.[14] Mao once acknowledged that "in the first five-year plan we [did] no more than copy the Soviet Union's methods."[15] However inappropriate planning was for an economy that lacked the requisite material conditions, Mao adopted and adapted the Stalinist model to backward China, insisting that production and distribution in industry and agriculture be conducted according to a "predetermined" and "unified plan."[16]

While he deplored "bureaucratism" and touted provincial "independence" in problem-solving, Mao made it clear that the provinces would have to submit their resolutions to the scrutiny of the "central planning authority with administrative headquarters in Beijing," who would exercise "firm control over the general lines of development of the Chinese economy." In this manner, enterprise management was put directly under the "guidance of the party."[17]

But Mao did more than simply adopt Stalinism. The structural center of Mao's economic program for China, while shaped by Stalinist planning, had unique traits of its own. For some, Mao's developmental strategy constituted a "clear rejection of essential components" of Stalinist planning, and a "clear departure from the Soviet path."[18]

To begin with, Mao was remarkably ignorant of elementary economics, as he himself admitted. In 1959, he told his followers that "I have only just begun recently to study economic work." In another conversation in 1962, he acknowledged that "In our work of socialist construction, we are still to a very large extent acting blindly....I haven't got much understanding of industry and commerce. I understand a bit about agriculture, but this is only relatively speaking—I still don't understand much."[19]

Mao's ignorance of economics could account for his unique conceptualization of economic problems that left almost everyone adrift. A case in point is the Marxian notion of the "law of value." Mao never seemed sure about what to do with the concept. At one time, he maintained that "the law of value serves as an instrument of planning," but "should not be made the main basis of planning." At another time, he insisted that "the law of value does not have a regulative function" in planning.[20] For Mao, the law of value was a "bourgeois category" that somehow unhappily survived into the socialist epoch.[21]

The law of value is one of those theoretical concepts in classical Marxism that leaves traditional economists confused and unconvinced of its serviceability in planning and analysis.[22] The concept is an entailment of Marx's labor theory of value: the conviction that the labor embodied in products determines their value. According to Marx, while the market value of commodities might vary because of extraneous factors such as scarcity or demand, it was concretized labor time embodied in a product that constituted its "real" value.

Thus Engels concluded that in order to "arrange a plan of production," society needed only "calculate how many hours of labor" would be required to satisfy collective needs, given the available "means of production." Planning for a socialist society would initially employ the law of value as a guide. Ultimately, when society had outgrown its "bourgeois origins" and become communist, when production was undertaken to fulfill needs rather than to gain profit, the law of value would no longer serve any purpose. Until that time however, the law of value was an essential tool in socialist planning, delivering rationality into the capitalist anarchy of production.[23]

However Mao understood the law of value,[24] it did not enter into any of his economic calculations. As Mao put it, "commodity exchange laws governing value play no regulating role in our production. This role is played by planning."[25] But that planning was essentially arbitrary, governed not by technical assessments of factor endowments, opportunity costs, or allocative rationality, but by ideological conviction.

In the economy he dominated for more than a quarter century, Mao insisted on price stability with no regard for prevailing conditions. Costs, wages, and prices would be fixed by political fiat. In order to increase production, one must simply put "politics in command." It was not technical planning that increased production but "political consciousness"—the "spiritual inspiration from political ideology."[26]

This emphasis on political rectitude ("red") over technical know-how ("expert") would lead Mao to foment continuous class struggle, including the Cultural Revolution, the most destructive class struggle of all. Mao's faith in the miraculous power of sheer masses of people energized by political enthusiasm would lead him to the colossal blunders of the Great Leap Forward. Without capital and productive resources Mao imagined that output in China could be "greatly expanded...through the release of powerful latent energies and abilities of the masses of peasants and workers. . . ." Peasants and production line workers were expected to increase output by engaging in political campaigns that would liberate their "proletarian genius."[27] Scarce capital was invested in monumental construction that never matured into anything of consequence. Millions of people were periodically mobilized to undertake some vast project, such as reforesting areas as large as France or excavating irrigation trenches covering enormous territories, only to allow the effort to be wasted through poor planning, lack of maintenance, or simple indifference.[28]

There was a great deal of vagueness, ambiguity, and simple confusion in what passed as planning in the economy of Maoist China. Mao had imposed an erratic, fitful, ill-governed, ill-informed, and uncertain economic system on the People's Republic. Throughout most of his tenure, the Communist Party engaged in the economic planning of one of the largest nations of the world without reliable data, a meaningful pricing structure, or any efficient means for transmitting, processing, or coordinating information. The absence of any rational price structure made resource allocation, assessment of opportunity costs, enterprise activity, wage payments, and the merit of output assortments almost entirely arbitrary. The People's Republic entered into a recurring cycle of centralization leading to rigidity, rigidity leading to complaints, complaints leading to decentralization, decentralization leading to disorder, and disorder leading to recentralization.[29]

This was exacerbated by the unceasing upheaval and turmoil from Mao's political campaigns. By the end of the 1960s, in his effort at a "continuous revolution," Mao almost succeeded in dismantling the planning bureaucracy and, with it, the economy of the People's Republic itself.[30]

The Effort at Reform

From the beginning, Mao had opposed the economic revisionism that surfaced in Eastern Europe, the Balkans, and Khrushchev's Soviet

Union. He saw such reform efforts as not only a "sabotage" of the socialist planned economy, but an attempt at a "full restoration of capitalism."[31] The Soviet leaders, Khrushchev, Brezhnev, and Kosygin, "imitated" the methods of capitalist management by introducing the "principle of profit seeking."[32] In so doing, they were undermining the "highly centralized guidance" that distinguished socialism from the "anarchy" of industrial capitalism.[33]

Whatever the fulminations in China's official press against Moscow's revisionism, the inherent disabilities of the command economy were recognized by many thinkers on the Chinese mainland. It had become clear by the early-1960s that something was fundamentally wrong with the command economy. There was incredible waste in the system; initiative and enterprise were lacking. More than that, China was in the throes of one of the most devastating famines in modern Chinese history, the aftermath of Mao's ill-conceived Great Leap Forward. Massive failures in the agricultural sector led to perhaps as many as 30 million deaths between 1959 and 1962, as well as one to two hundred million cases of malnutrition.[34]

It was during those tragic years that some in the highest echelons of the Chinese Communist Party began to recognize that the command collectivist economy had failed.[35] "The inefficiencies of the economy had to be corrected or else the Communist Party's legitimacy in the eyes of the Chinese people would be compromised."[36] Liu Shaoqi, for one, urged Mao to move slowly in socializing the primitive Chinese economy. Deng Xiaoping and Chen Yun advocated allowing peasants to farm their own plots and operate small secondary industries, such as basketry and weaving, and sell their produce in essentially unregulated markets.[37] At the same time, the economist Sun Yefang recommended market adjuncts to reduce the allocative irrationalities and general wastefulness of the command economy.[38]

Mao's response to these recommendations was to embark on a vendetta against those who offered them. He sought to silence the "capitalist roaders" in the leadership ranks of the Party. Ultimately, he was to invoke the anarchic violence of the Red Guards to destroy the opposition and to preclude any revisionism of communist China.

To the natural question of why Mao insisted on maintaining the flawed system, part of the response must be that he sincerely believed that Marxism-Leninism, as he understood it, was the salvation of China and ultimately the world. Equally probable was the fact that the institutional arrangements the CCP had contrived after its accession to power ensured the Party's and Mao's own tenure. Any major changes in the system might very well threaten both.

Even before the death of Mao, elements in his Party attempted to restore some semblance of rationality to the system. In 1975, several documents attributed to Deng Xiaoping made their appearance.[39] They were immediately attacked by Maoist enthusiasts as "poisonous weeds" comparable to the revisionist efforts of Khrushchev and Liu Shaoqi.

In those documents, Deng sought the improvement of conditions in the agrarian sector, even if it meant the restoration of family farming. He proposed emphasizing quality production, discipline in the workplace, and a return to formal technical training. Beijing was no longer to tolerate "fake statistics." Responsible data would have to be generated; its storage, retrieval, and effective employment were recommended. Resources were to be conserved and available factors of production efficiently utilized.

More significant still was Deng's proposal that the primitive industrial base of China be modernized through the transfer and acquisition of foreign technology and skills. After 1949, the Soviet Union had provided the technology for China. Hundreds of turnkey plants, technical manuals, and the selective skills necessary to modern industry were imported from the Soviet Union in the early-1950s. But the Sino-Soviet rift that led to the abrupt withdrawal of all Soviet economic aid and assistance in 1960 left China with aging plant and obsolescent technology.

Since that time, episodic efforts at upgrading were attempted through foreign purchase and transfer, but Mao's general disposition was to achieve and sustain self-sufficiency. According to Mao, the Sino-Soviet rupture left China surrounded by enemies. On one side was capitalist "world imperialism," on the other was Soviet "social imperialism."[40] In a hostile world, China must create an autarkic economy that would provide the Chinese with survival advantage by prevailing on their own domestic resources.

In contrast to Mao, Deng's proposals anticipated an entirely different strategy. Deng advocated that China attract foreign capital, skills, and investment into its closed economy. Doing so would require major reforms in the foreign policy and economic strategies that had brought the People's Republic to the brink of ruin.

However subversive of Maoism, all of Deng's revolutionary proposals were couched in Maoist language. In an established ideocracy, such behavior was expected. Deng made constant appeal to the "directives of Chairman Mao" and spoke of the absolute necessity of studying "Marxism-Leninism-Mao Zedong Thought" and "dialectic materialism." Mao had provided the "guidelines, policies and methods...for the entire historical period of socialism." His thought was the "soul" and the "standard" of all efforts by members of the Communist Party. To depart from that thought was to betray the revolution. Deng even urged his Party to "consolidate" the "successes" won in the very Cultural Revolution that had purged him.[41]

What is nonetheless clear is that beneath the ideological trappings, Deng was suggesting massive revisions of the Maoist dispensation. That was clear to the ardent Maoists and their leaders, the Gang of Four. They accused Deng of neglecting class struggle and the socialist revolution. Deng had failed to keep "politics in command," and was intent on restoring capitalism itself.[42]

With the death of Mao in 1976, swiftly followed by the arrest of the Gang of Four, forces in China quickly mobilized under Deng's leadership to reform the economic system. That the Party embarked on major reforms of an economic system identified by its own economists as "irrational"[43] is a testament to the gravity of the situation. In the judgment of the economists, the "chaos of [Mao's] Cultural Revolution" had, in fact, "pushed the economy to the brink of collapse."[44]

Two years after Mao's demise, the Party's Eleventh Central Committee convened its third plenary session. Its communiqué noted: "We are now, in the light of the new historical conditions and practical experience, adopting a number of major new economic measures, conscientiously transforming the system and methods of economic management."[45] What was being rejected was the general economic and political strategy embodied in Mao Zedong Thought. Whatever else Mao believed was largely a matter of indifference. All the obscure notions of dialectics, the "interpenetration of opposites," and the "blank" but powerful peasants were abstractions that bore little consequence for a China that found itself facing external threat and endemic poverty.

In 1981, five years after the death of Mao, the Chinese Communist Party, by that time securely under the leadership of Deng Xiaoping, undertook a "basic appraisal of the history of the People's Republic" under Mao's rule. The Party concluded that it had made "mistakes" of "enlarging the scope of class struggle and of impetuosity and rashness in economic construction." Those mistakes were the consequence of failures on the part of Mao himself who was held "chiefly," though not exclusively, responsible for "all those errors." Mao had been "smug," and "overestimated the role of man's subjective will and efforts." He failed to adequately understand Marxist theory so that "Many things denounced as revisionist or capitalist during the `cultural revolution' were actually Marxist and socialist principles." The "capitalist roaders" vilified and abused during the Cultural Revolution in fact "formed the core force of the socialist cause." Mao had apparently misunderstood everything.[46]

Such Chinese economists as Xu Dixin, Liu Suinian, Liang Wensen, Dong Fureng, and Liao Jianxiang provided a catalog of Mao's economic policy failures. "Leftism" had derailed the economy of socialist China. Agriculture was all but totally neglected. Low yields in the rural economy reduced the general standard of living of all Chinese, and failed to provide a domestic market for national industries. The policies of import substitution and economic autarky had hopelessly impaired China's growth and modernization. China's comparative advantage for labor-intensive exports was totally neglected. The protection of domestic industries resulted in high costs, low efficiency, and poor product quality. There was a chronic overinvestment in heavy industry and a critical neglect of investment in agriculture, the infrastructure, and small enterprise. State-run industries produced goods of poor quality for which there was no market. Inventories were overstocked; the cycle for the turnover of capital was excessively long. Competence was systematically neglected in the pursuit of political correctness.

Because of all that, China's entire economic system had become increasingly sclerotic, handicapped by obsolete technology and antiquated notions of management. There was little incentive to modernize. The failure to import the advanced technology of the industrialized countries to offset domestic shortcomings made it extremely difficult for China to begin to compete with the productivity of capitalist economies.[47]

Reform of the Maoist system was initiated in 1979. By the mid-1980s, the Chinese economy had been transformed. "Rationality" began to be introduced into economic arrangements: pricing policy began to reflect "objective values" and increasingly, markets were established. Both results meant that productive and consumer goods could be exchanged at a price close to their real costs without the arbitrary interference of the central authorities. Despite the continual reference to "national plans," markets were expected to perform more and more functions.

By the time of its Thirteenth Congress, the CCP was referring to the reformed Chinese economy as a "socialist planned commodity economy" where production would be "regulated" by both planning and the market. Planning would no longer be "mandatory," while mandatory planning would be "drastically" reduced.[48] "Competitive and open" "socialist markets" would be introduced to provide incentive for "increased efficiency and a rational division of labor." They would include not only commodity markets and capital goods, but markets for all the principal factors of production including capital, labor, technology, information, and real estate. In effect, the Maoist economy was being transformed into a "socialist" market economy that displayed all the features of profit-driven enterprise, albeit in an environment of imperfect competition.[49]

All of this was to be undertaken under the guidance of "the scientific system of Mao Zedong thought comprehensively and precisely" understood.[50] Mao Zedong Thought was to remain the light of the system, but it was to be "precisely" understood. In reality, this meant that Mao Zedong Thought would have to be reformed by Deng Xiaoping, China's new paramount leader, into a belief system divested of its economic substance as well as its propensity for political turbulence.

In a system devoid of any meaningful popular participation, political legitimacy must derive from some other source. Despite Mao's mistakes, his historical stature was such that his thought would have to remain as the source of the Party's right to rule. As long as Deng ruled under the mantle of Mao Zedong Thought, he could pretend to legitimation through a secular form of apostolic succession.

Deng was fully prepared to make Mao Zedong Thought a pillar of the governance of post-Maoist China. But that thought would have to be defanged of its most destructive features. These included Mao's "erroneous economic policies,"[51] as well as his notion of an "uninterrupted revolution." The rest of Mao's thought—the empty formulations about "dialectics" and its "antagonistic" and "non-antagonistic" "contradictions"—was tolerable and sometimes useful in the Byzantine politics of Communist China. But Maoist crash programs involving the dissipation of vast human and capital resources would never again be permitted, nor would Maoist mass upheavals against class enemies.

Divested of its worst features, Mao Zedong Thought might well serve the Communist Party of China under the leadership of Deng, as a certification of authority. And that appears to be precisely how Deng employed the thought of Mao. He has reformed it sufficiently so that it no longer hobbles the nation's economy and the effort to industrialize.

All this had been anticipated by Jiang Qing, Mao's wife and the most ardently "leftist" of his followers. Years before Deng initiated his reforms, Jiang had characterized him as a "revisionist fascist dwarf" who would "deceive everyone." Once he acceded to power, she warned, he would "change everything."[52]

Notes

1. Liu Shaoqi, *How to Be a Good Communist* (Beijing: Foreign Languages, 1965), 22.
2. Lin Piao, *Long Live the Victory of People's War* (Beijing: Foreign Languages, 1968), 5.
3. Zhang Chunqiao, *On Exercising All-Round Dictatorship Over the Bourgeoisie* (Beijing: Foreign Languages, 1975), 25.
4. Friedrich Engels, *Anti-Duehring: Herr Eugen Duehring's Revolution in Science* (Moscow: Foreign Languages, 1962), 388, 380, 383.
5. See the discussion in "II Theoretical," in ibid., 365–391.
6. Ibid., 386, 406–407, 390, 380–382. That such an interpretation is substantially correct is attested to by all the central documents of the classical Marxist tradition. See the discussion in Karl Kautsky, *Die soziale Revolution: Am Tagen ach der sozialen Revolution* (Berlin: Vorwaerts, 1904).
7. Jan S. Prybyla, *Market and Plan under Socialism: The Bird in the Cage* (Stanford: Hoover Institution, 1987), 39–41.
8. See Philip Hanson, "Discussion of Economic Reform in the USSR: The Novosibirsk Paper," *Radio Liberty Research Bulletin* (September 1983) RL 356/83.
9. See Abram Bergson, "Technological Progress," in *The Soviet Economy: Toward the Year 2000*, eds. A. Bergson and H. Levine (London: Allen and Unwin, 1983).
10. Philip Hanson, "Brezhnev's Economic Legacy," in *The Soviet Economy After Brezhnev*, ed. Philip Joseph (Brussels: NATA, 1984), 41–55.
11. "Communiqué on the Plenary Session of the Central Committee of the Communist Party of the Soviet Union," reported in *Pravda* and *Izvestiva*, 18 February 1988, 1; see also, Abram Bergson, "Gorbachev on Soviet Growth Rate," *Radio Free Europe*, 25 March 1988.
12. Abel Aganbegyan, *The Economic Challenge of Perestroika* (Bloomington: Indiana University, 1988), 3.
13. As cited in James Peck's "Introduction" to Mao Zedong's *A Critique of Soviet Economics* (New York: Monthly Review, 1977), 10.

14. See the insightful discussion in Andrew Walder, "Cultural Revolution Radicalism: Variations on a Stalinist Theme," in *New Perspectives on the Cultural Revolution,* eds. William A. Joseph, Christine P. W. Wong, and David Zweig (Cambridge: Harvard University, 1991).
15. Mao, *A Critique of Soviet Economics*, 122.
16. Ibid., 54, 73.
17. Ibid., 73, 103. Paul M. Sweezy, "China: Contrasts with Capitalism," *Monthly Review* 27 (July-August 1975): 4–5.
18. Harry Magdoff, "China: Contrasts with the USSR," *Monthly Review* 27 (July-August 1975): 12–13, 42.
19. Mao, *Chairman Mao Talks to the People: Talks and Letters, 1956–1971* (New York: Pantheon, 1974), 175, 154.
20. Mao, *A Critique of Soviet Economics*, 87, 147.
21. Mao, *Chairman Mao Talks to the People*, 131.
22. See the discussions in Fred M. Gottheil, *Marx's Economic Predictions* (Evanston, IL: Northwestern University, 1966), ch. 2; H. W. B. Joseph, *The Labour Theory of Value* (London: Oxford University, 1923); R. L. Meek, *Studies in the Labour Theory of Value* (London: Lawrence and Wishart, 1956).
23. Engels, *Anti-Duehring*, 424–425.
24. Mao seemed genuinely confused about the "law of value." In one place he equated the "law of value" with the "exchange of equal values" and "remuneration according to work done." See Mao, *Chairman Mao Talks to the People*, 135.
25. Ibid., 83, 133.
26. Mao, *A Critique of Soviet Economics*, 87–88, 90, 130.
27. Mao Zedong, "Sixty Points on Working Methods," in *Mao Papers: Anthology and Bibliography*, ed. Jerome Ch'en (New York: Oxford University, 1970), 57, 61, 64; John G. Gurley, "The Formation of Mao's Economic Strategy, 1927–1949," *Monthly Review* 27 (July-August 1975): 61–63.
28. See the poignant account in Li Honglin, "'Right' and 'Left' in Communist China: A Self-Account by a Theoretician in the Chinese Communist Party," *The Journal of Contemporary China*, no. 6 (Summer 1994): 1–8.
29. Jiang Yiwei, "The Theory of an Enterprise-Based Economy," *Social Sciences in China* 1, no. 55 (March 1980).
30. Jan S. Prybyla, *Reform in China and Other Socialist Economies* (Washington, DC: American Enterprise Institute, 1990), 12.
31. *On Khrushchev's Phoney Communism and its Historical Lessons for the World* (Beijing: Foreign Languages, 1964), 26–28.
32. See "The Promotion of Capitalist Economy in all Fields," *How the Soviet Revisionists Carryout All-Round Restoration of Capitalism in the U.S.S.R.* (Beijing: Foreign Languages, 1968), particularly pp. 1–7.
33. *Leninism and Modern Revisionism* (Beijing: Foreign Languages, 1963), 4–5.
34. Pat Howard, *Breaking the Iron Rice Bowl: Prospects for Socialism in China's Countryside* (Armonk, NY: M.E. Sharpe, 1988), 37. After Mao's death, the Chinese Communist Party admitted to 15 million deaths in the famine that followed the Great Leap.
35. See Li Honglin, "'Right' and 'Left,'" 3–6.
36. Peter M. Lichtenstein, *China at the Brink: The Political Economy of Reform and Retrenchment in the Post-Mao Era* (New York: Praeger, 1991), 37.
37. See Uli Franz, *Deng Xiaoping* (New York: Harcourt, Brace, Jovanovich, 1988), chs. 9 and 10.
38. See Steve Reglar, "The Law of Value Debate: A Tribute to the Late Sun Yefang,"

in *Chinese Marxism in Flux 1978–84*, ed. Bill Brugger (Armonk, NY: M.E. Sharpe, 1985).

39. The Deng Xiaoping documents are found in their substantial entirety in Chi Hsin, *The Case of the Gang of Four—With First Translation of Teng Hsiao-ping's "Three Poisonous Weeds"* (Hong Kong: Cosmos Books, 1977), 203–272. The text of "On the General Program for All the Work of the Whole Party and the Whole Country" is found in its entirety in *Teng Hsiao-ping and the "General Program"* (San Francisco, CA: Red Sun, 1977). The Working Draft, "Some Problems in Accelerating Industrial Development" (2 September 1975) is in Chi Hsin, *The Case of the Gang of Four*; pp. 239–272 are particularly instructive.

40. See King C. Chen, ed., *China and the Three Worlds: A Foreign Policy Reader* (White Plains, NY: M. E. Sharpe, 1979).

41. Deng Xiaoping, "On the General Program," in Chi Hsin, *The Case of the Gang of Four*, 203, 204, 206, 233, *passim*. See also "Teng Hsiao-ping's Self-Criticism," in Chi Hsin, *Teng Hsiao-ping: A Political Biography* (Hong Kong: Cosmos Books, 1978), particularly pp. 62–63.

42. "Reversing Correct Verdicts Goes Against the Will of the People," *Beijing Review*, no. 11 (12 March 1976); "Counter-Revolutionary Political Incident at Tiananmen Square," ibid., no. 15 (9 April 1976); Hsiang Chun, "An Attempt to Restore Capitalism Under the Signboard of Opposing Restoration," ibid., no. 33–34 (1977).

43. Zhou Shulian, "Changing the Pattern of China's Economy," in *China's Economic Reforms*, eds. Lin Wei and Arnold Chao (Philadelphia: University of Pennsylvania, 1982), 57.

44. Wang Zhenshi and Wang Yongzhi, "Epilogue: Prices in China," in ibid., 225.

45. *Beijing Review*, no. 52 (1978): 11.

46. *Resolution on CPC History (1949–81)* (Beijing: Foreign Languages, 1981), 16–17, 27, 28, 30, 31–32, 33, 34.

47. See Xu Dixin, ed., *China's Search for Economic Growth: The Chinese Economy Since 1949* (Beijing: New World Press, 1982); George C. Wang, ed., *Economic Reform in the PRC in Which China's Economists Make Known What Went Wrong, Why, and What Should be Done about it* (Boulder, CO: Westview, 1982); Yu Guangyuan, *China's Socialist Modernization* (Beijing: Foreign Languages, 1984); Xue Muqiao, *China's Socialist Economy* (Beijing: Foreign Languages, 1981); Liu Suinian and Wu Qungan, eds., *China's Socialist Economy: An Outline History (1949–1984)* (Beijing: Beijing Review, 1986).

48. Between 1981 and 1985, the central government's mandatory plans were reduced from over 300 to just 60. The number of goods distributed according to "unified state planning" decreased from 256 to 26.

49. *The 13th Party Congress and China's Reforms* (Beijing: Beijing Review, 1987), 48, 51–52.

50. Liu Suinian and Wu Qungan, *China's Socialist Economy*, 434.

51. Ibid., 417.

52. Ross Terrill, *Madame Mao: The White-Boned Demon* (New York: Simon and Schuster, 1992), 383, 403.

4

The Developmental Nationalism
of Deng Xiaoping Thought

The Evaluation of Deng Xiaoping's Thought

The designation by the Chinese Communist Party of a political leader's ideas as "thought" (*sixiang*) is a momentous decision. Throughout the history of the People's Republic of China, only the ideas of Mao Zedong were accorded that status. Although Deng's reformist ideology has served as the guide and legitimation for China since 1978, his party had refrained from identifying it as "thought," calling it instead the "spirit" (*jingsheng*), "line" (*luxian*), or the "reformist thought" (*gaige sixiang*) of Deng Xiaoping.[1]

The Party's reservation began to change in 1992. The May issue of the CCP's internal document, *Neibu tongxin*, revealed that before his death, Marshal Nie Yongzhen had recommended that "Deng Xiaoping thought" be formally incorporated into the work report of the soon-to-be-convened Fourteenth Party Congress. In June, in a conversation with Holland's prime minister, PRC Premier Li Peng was the first Chinese official to publicly employ the expression, "Deng Xiaoping thought," calling it "China's precious treasure."[2] And when the Fourteenth Party Congress convened that October, Nie's dying wish was more than fulfilled. The expression "Deng Xiaoping thought" was inscribed into both the Congress' work report as well as the Party's revised Constitution. Deng's thought had achieved an equal plane with that of Mao.[3]

Thereafter, Party and government leaders began making lavish public accolades to Deng, contrary to his oft-stated admonition that the

Party must eschew "the cult of personality and placing individuals above the organization."[4] As an example, in his report to the Fourteenth Party Congress, CCP chief Jiang Zemin called Deng "the chief engineer of the reform and modernization of Chinese socialism." All across China, newspaper editorials trumpeted that "Deng Xiaoping thought is the spiritual foundation of the people."[5] It was announced that an annotated compilation of Deng's speeches, "The Thought of Deng," would soon be published. Billboards of Deng appeared throughout Beijing. There were also a documentary, a special portrait, books, and tapes on Deng, all employing the inflated language that was once used for Mao during the Cultural Revolution. Deng was a "giant," a "superman," "a history-making great man," and a "warm spring breeze blowing across the great land of China."[6]

The next year, in 1993, Deng's stature appeared to have been elevated to yet a higher level. That May, in a speech at the Thirteenth National Congress of the Chinese Communist Youth League, CCP Standing Committee member Hu Jintao characterized Deng's collection of ideas on "building socialism with Chinese characteristics" as "theory" (*lilun*). That "theory," Hu maintained, was the "newest fruit" produced by the union of Marxism with China's concrete conditions. It was the "Marxism of contemporary China," and the "tool for leading the party to realize its new historical mission."[7] In effect, Deng's ideas were no longer mere "thought," they have attained the rarefied status of "theory," previously accorded to only Marxism and Leninism.[8]

In June 1993, the Communist Party determined that Deng Xiaoping was "the outstanding representative and glorious exemplar of the defense, maintenance and development of Marxism-Leninism-Mao Zedong Thought." The next month, in an article in *People's Daily*, Shanghai Municipal Party Secretary Wu Bangguo wrote that Deng Xiaoping's "theory of building socialism with Chinese characteristics" was "the most precious spiritual wealth of the Party and the nation."[9]

In August 1993, on the eve of Deng's eighty-ninth birthday, the Communist Party called Deng Xiaoping theory the "fountainhead for realizing socialist modernization." Li Ruihuan, then chairman of the CCP's Political Advisory Commission, revealed that Deng was hard at work proofreading the third volume of his *Selected Works* in the hope that his thought would replace that of Mao Zedong. At the same time, Shanghai's Social Science Academy established an Institute for the Study of Deng Xiaoping Theory.[10]

In October 1993, during a visit to the National Defense University, Central Military Affairs Commission Vice Chairmen Liu Huaqing and Zhang Zhen called on the People's Liberation Army to use Deng's thought as a "theoretical weapon" to guide the military's modernization. Liu and Zhang stated that Deng's "theory on building socialism with Chinese characteristics" was the "successor and developer of Mao Zedong Thought."[11]

The publication of the third volume of the *Selected Works of Deng Xiaoping* in November 1993 was the occasion for a nationwide campaign to "conscientiously study" his thought.[12] According to the Hong Kong magazine, *Jingbao*, the campaign's scope and methods were reminiscent of past campaigns that exalted Mao.[13] Jiang Zemin called Deng Xiaping theory "the scientific compass that guides the continuous victorious progress of China." More than that, party elder Bo Yibo, in an interview with a CCP publication, *Dangxiao luntan*, said that Deng "found a way to build socialism with Chinese characteristics which Mao Zedong had sought for but was unable to find."[14]

In July 1994, at a Party symposium on theory and propaganda in Beijing, Deputy Director of the CCP's Propaganda Bureau Zheng Bijian called on the participants to "raise Deng Xiaoping theory to a higher level to become the spiritual pillar of the entire Party and nation." That August 8, an article in China's *Guangming ribao* insisted that Deng "had pioneered a new territory within Marxism" and, "in building socialism with Chinese characteristics, accomplished a major contribution of historic importance."[15]

Various commentators have interpreted the ascension of Deng's ideas to the level of "thought" and "theory" as an effort either by a dying old man to purchase immortality, or by his followers to fortify their position in the imminent struggle for succession.[16] It is also commonplace among Western Sinologists to deal with the thought of Deng Xiaoping as primarily "pragmatic," a collection of essentially ad hoc solutions for the grave economic problems left behind by Mao Zedong.[17]

Although the conditions in which China found itself at the time of Mao's death gave urgency to Deng's reforms, the political character of the regime compels the Party to seek doctrinal legitimation. In the ideocratic system of the People's Republic, major policy changes require putting together a new theoretical rationale. While it is true that Deng's reformist policies had been necessitated by the catastrophic state of the Chinese economy, that does not mean Deng did not make an independent ideological case for his reforms, or that the case made is void of theoretical interest.

A Return to Classical Marxism

Deng, in a very real sense, is a better Marxist theoretician than Mao Zedong. As had been argued, Mao Zedong Thought displays little grasp of the intellectual complexity of classical Marxism. Deng, on the other hand, seems to be familiar with the essentials of classical Marxism. In Moscow's Sun Yat-sen University, Deng was enrolled in a course devoted to historical materialism—the philosophy of history of Marx and Engels.[18] He also received instruction on Marxist economic theories from a standard textbook by Karl Kautsky, entitled *The Economic Theory of Karl Marx.*

Like Mao, Deng rarely cited references in developing his arguments. Unlike Mao, Deng often displayed a certain grasp of some of the central theses of Marxist social and economic theory, in particular the classical Marxist conception of the relationship between productive forces and productive relations. This was evident in the following quote from Deng's "On the General Program of Work for the Whole Party and the Whole Nation" in 1975:

> Marxism holds that, within the contradictions between the productive forces and the relations of production, between practice and theory, and between the economic base and the super-structure, the productive forces . . . and the economic base generally play the principal and decisive role. *Whoever denies this is not a materialist.*[19]

In effect, in 1975, Deng already assumed a position on a theoretical issue that challenged some of the central tenets of Mao Zedong Thought. He was criticizing nothing less than Mao's conception of the role of the "super-structure" in revolution, social change, and economic development.[20] For Deng, it was economics and not politics that should be in command. The Maoists at the time immediately identified Deng's proposal as the "revisionist theory of the productive forces."[21] A spate of articles appeared castigating him as an "unrepentant capitalist roader in the Party" who had devised a "revisionist program" to defeat Mao's Marxism and restore China to capitalism.[22]

Deng evidently anticipated that his "General Program" would make him the object of vicious political attack. In order to protect himself, he larded over his "General Program" with profuse denunciations of the "rightists," "capitalist roaders," and "revisionists" in the Party, who included Liu Shaoqi and anyone else who was ever the object of Maoist abuse.[23] Later, when Deng was safely in power, he would restore to the pantheon of true Marxists almost all whom he had denounced in the "General Program."

The issue of the primacy of productive forces is not an arcane Marxist preoccupation but involves, instead, some of the most basic problems that have collected around revolutionary Marxist regimes since the Bolshevik revolution. Until V. I. Lenin revised the conceptual schemata of classical Marxism, no informed Marxist believed that socialist revolution could come to economically immature communities.

Marx had been clear on the determinant role of the forces of production. In the *Poverty of Philosophy*, he maintained that "in acquiring new productive forces, men change their mode of production; and in changing their mode of production, in changing the way of earning their living, they change all their social relations."[24] As productive forces change, social relations change; as social relations change, all of life changes.

According to Marx, "the multitude of productive forces accessible to men determines the nature of society"[25] as well as the "forms of intercourse" between human beings. Even the "phantoms formed in the human brain"—religious convictions, ethics, and law—were "sublimates" of the more fundamental processes of production. "Life is not determined by consciousness, but consciousness by life."[26] History proceeds as a function of the development of the material forces of production. In the final analysis, the "productive forces . . . are the basis of all . . . history."[27]

The relations of production were conceived by classical Marxism to be clearly subordinate to and contingent upon the productive forces. According to Engels, "every change in the social order, every revolution in property relations" could only be "the necessary result of the creation of new productive forces. . . ."[28] In the 1859 Preface to his *Critique of Political Economy*, Marx wrote that "in the social production of their life, men enter into definite relations that are indispensable and independent of their will. . . ." Those relations "correspond to a definite state of development of their material productive forces."

The "sum total" of the relations of production, and the productive forces to which they correspond, constitutes the "real foundation" upon which a "superstructure" of social, political, and intellectual life is erected.[29]

It follows that socialism could only be a product of a fully developed economy in that a primitive economic base could hardly support the advanced productive and distributive relations of socialism. As early as the *German Ideology* of 1845, Marx had insisted that while peripheral, economically less developed areas might be drawn into revolution, socialist revolution could come only to advanced industrial systems, for only those systems would inherit the productive potential to fully satisfy human need without making recourse to invidious class distinctions and oppressive political rule. If an attempt were made to introduce socialism into an economically underdeveloped environment, Engels believed that the only result possible was a "slide back . . . to [the] narrow limits" of the old system. True socialist liberation was a function of "the level of development of the material means of existence." To build communism on a primitive economic base would be a "chiliastic dream fantasy."[30]

Thus, the issue of socialist revolution in economically backward countries divided orthodox Marxists from their Leninist confreres. The issue had made some of Europe's foremost Marxist theoreticians anti-Leninist.[31] For them, the effort to achieve a socialist revolution in an industrially retarded community was theoretically bankrupt.[32]

It was no surprise to the orthodox Marxists that Lenin and his followers were faced with the problems created by their premature revolutions in Russia and elsewhere. Those revolutions grafted advanced productive relations on top of economies of primitive productive forces. Impatient Leninists abolished private property, eliminated material incentives and pursued egalitarianism in the futile effort to create communism in primitive economies.

In what were to be the last years of his life, Lenin recognized that contradiction when he attempted to develop the Soviet Union's retarded economic base with his New Economic Policy. For all the talk of socialism, Lenin reintroduced capitalist modalities, including differential wages. Notwithstanding his theory of capitalism as international imperialism, Lenin courted foreign investors and leased out extractive rights to natural resources. All in an effort to create socialism in a backward economy.

The Chinese Communist Revolution was undertaken in an even more primitive economic system. Mao never seemed to fully grasp the problem of the disjuncture between China's primitive productive forces and the socialist productive relations imposed by his party. Mao conceived the superstructure, not the productive forces, to be primary in the process of socioeconomic change. He was determined that superstructural elements like revolutionary commitment, political intransigence, personal sacrifice, and selfless dedication would shape reality to his utopian vision.[33] In effect, Mao seized on the power of his convictions "to change the world arbitrarily,"[34] in his quest to create socialism out of thin air.

In contrast, Deng, like the first Marxists, argued that it was not productive relations but the development of the "forces of production" that constituted the engine of progressive history. Deng recognized that China's poverty was a consequence of its immature industrial and technological base. It follows then that the dream of socialism required the resources of a fully developed industrial system.

By 1978, two years after Mao's death, Deng was no longer coy in his anti-Maoist beliefs. He identified the fundamental task that faced the People's Republic to be that of economic development. Deng was prepared to draw the outlines of a strategy for economic development in which emphasizing the "forces of production" would become the primary theoretical justification for reforming the system inherited from Mao.

The Developmental Nationalism of Deng Xiaoping

Mary Matossian, in her seminal piece, "Ideologies of Delayed Industrialization," noted the prevalence of a certain type of ideology among the less developed nations. Seemingly disparate ideologies all share a common mission in an environment of delayed industrialization. Irrespective of its particular contents, Matossian believed that the most effective developmental ideologies use pragmatic standards "to determine exactly" what elements should be included and excluded.[35]

As an example, an appeal to nationalism can be useful for economic development in that it imparts to people a sense of collective identity, pride, and purpose. A developmental ideology may seek to inspire with a vision of a utopian future, spurring heroic efforts of sacrifice and economic construction. The ideology may also urge the importation of sophisticated technology and skills from advanced industrial societies, including the West.

What is essential, according to Matossian, is that none of the elements exists "as an axiomatic, self-justified good." Whatever is borrowed from the West, retained from the past, or envisioned for the future, should be employed only as a means towards the advancement of the greater national good. In the final analysis, the ideology's contents must meet the pragmatic test of that which "will tend to strengthen the nation."[36]

The reformist ideology fashioned by Deng is just such an ideology of developmental nationalism. For the most part, it employs a pragmatic standard for the selection of its idea contents. Whatever its Marxist inspiration, an argument can be made that Deng's ideology is more nationalist and developmental than it is Marxist.

Historic Mission

To begin with, Deng has returned to the historic mission of twentieth-century-Chinese revolutions. He stated that the fundamental purpose, "the first thing," of the Chinese Communist revolution was economic development, understood by Deng to be the elimination of poverty through "the emancipation of the productive forces."[37] In his judgment, from 1957 until the death of Mao, the Party was not able "to figure out what socialism is and how to build it" and thus "made a lot of mistakes."[38] The ideas and policies of the "Left" had "plagued" China, which hindered economic development and resulted in a "sluggish" economy. The standard of living of the people was "very low," with a per capita GNP in 1978 of less than $250.[39] Deng further explained,

> Many strange things happened in those days. . . . [P]eople were told that they should be content with poverty and backwardness and that it was better to be poor under socialism and communism than to be rich under capitalism. That was the sort of rubbish peddled by the Gang of Four. There is no such thing as socialism and communism with poverty. . . . According to Marxism, communist society is a society in which there is overwhelming material abundance. Socialism is the first stage of communism; it means expanding the productive forces. . . .[40]

The Primary Stage of Socialism

The disagreement between Deng and the Maoists on the development of the productive forces centered on a more basic issue of whether China, after 1949, had successfully and securely entered into the period of socialism. The answer to that question would determine the identity of the principal contradiction in post-revolution Chinese society.

After the collapse of the Great Leap and the growing Sino-Soviet dispute, Mao began to seriously doubt whether a socialist system really had come into existence in the People's Republic. By 1962, he decided that socialism was a sustained and arduous process in which the abolition of private property was merely a first necessary step. During that long process, socialism would be continuously imperiled by the constant reproduction of "new bourgeois elements." Despite the revolution of 1949 that abolished private ownership and socialized the means of production, there would still be "classes" in nominally socialist China, as well as "class struggles" between the "proletariat" and the "bourgeoisie," and between the "people" and its "enemies." That class struggle constituted the primary contradiction in socialist China, a struggle that Mao expected to be "a protracted, complex, sometimes even violent affair." These were the ideas that subtended Mao's theory of "continuing the revolution," which was adopted as official CCP ideology in 1969 and reaffirmed in 1973.[41]

Being a better Marxist than Mao, Deng had always thought otherwise. In contrast to Mao, Deng believed that "material conditions," not superstructural elements, were "the foundation" of socialism.[42] As early as 1956, in his "Report on the Revision of the Constitution of the Communist Party of China," Deng was convinced that socialism had taken secure roots in China. The abolition of private ownership and the socialization of the means of production had brought about "a fundamental change" in class relations. Classes no longer existed because the bourgeoisie as a class was "on its way to extinction" and the working class had become "the leading class."[43] As Deng explained:

Casual labourers and farm labourers have disappeared. Poor and middle peasants have all become members of agricultural producers' co-operatives, and before long the distinction between them will become merely a thing of historical interest. . . . The vast majority of our intellectuals have now come over politically to the side of the working class. . . . The conditions in which the urban poor and the professional people used to exist as independent social strata are virtually no longer present. . . . What is the point, then, of classifying these social strata into two different categories? And even if we were to try and devise a classification, how could we make it neat and clear-cut?[44]

All of which meant that class warfare was no longer a concern in socialist China. According to Deng, the cause for concern, as well as the principal contradiction in society, was the "very low" level of China's productive forces. Reforming the economy to raise the level of the productive forces would be the Party's "central task."[45]

Deng maintained that China was still in a "primary" or "underdeveloped" stage of socialism because the Chinese had been building socialism for only a few decades.[46] The concept of a "primary" stage of socialism, though expedient, was nevertheless an ingenious innovation, given the situation Deng had inherited. It allowed him to explain away mistakes of the past and present, as well as justify the economic reforms that would follow. On the one hand, Deng made it very clear that China had moved into the period of socialism. Being socialist meant that ownership of the means of production must be public, and that the Communist Party would rule as the "vanguard" of the "dictatorship of the proletariat." On the other hand, however, because the People's Republic had entered into merely the first stage of socialism, it was understandable for there to be superstructural detritus from the country's feudal past. Those feudal remains included the one-man rule of Mao and his "patriarchal" cult of personality, as well as the bureaucratism and political sinecure of the Party and government.[47] Being in the "primary" stage of socialism could also explain China's economic backwardness and the need for market reforms to develop its productive forces.

Deng further maintained that China's backwardness was made worse because of Mao's misguided policies. Because of those policies, China "wasted twenty years . . . while . . . the world developed rapidly."[48] With Mao dead and the Gang of Four under arrest, the country would make up for lost time. Through a program of the Four Modernizations (in agriculture, industry, national defense, and science and technology), China would be transformed into "a modern and powerful socialist state."[49] As Deng put it, "Pauperism is not socialism, still less communism." Nor does socialism mean a development that is "too slow." The Party must "find a way" to develop rapidly.[50]

World View

The urgency of modernization was informed by Deng's *Weltanschauung*, which saw the world as dominated by advanced industrial "hegemonist" and "imperialist" nations who used their power to "bully" the less developed nations, "interfering" in the latter's efforts at economic development and political independence.[51] Even more than in the past, the contemporary world was inhospitable for poor countries. Their environment had become more difficult, requiring that they "struggle even harder."[52]

In the case of China, quite aside from its poverty, other factors made its circumstances even more challenging. Deng warned that "There are many people in the world who . . . are out to get us." Not only had the fall of communism in Eastern Europe and the Soviet Union made China one of the last bastions of socialism in the world, the People's Republic was also surrounded by newly developed economies that could "move ahead" of China and capture its export markets. China must be particularly wary of capitalist industrialized countries because "Capitalists want to defeat socialists in the long run." In the past, those capitalists had employed weapons and atomic bombs in their effort to vanquish socialist states. Their ploy today was the "peaceful evolution" of China to lure it away from socialism. Given a hazardous and threatening global environment, if China were to remain underdeveloped, it "would have no future."[53]

Nationalism

In a difficult and hostile world, nations remain the basic units that could ensure the collective well-being of peoples. Deng insisted that China must "look after [its] own" and safeguard its own interests, sovereignty, and territorial integrity[54]—particularly in view of its past history of failures.

Stating that "I am a Chinese, and I am familiar with the history of foreign aggression against China,"[55] Deng recounted the litany of humiliations the Chinese endured for over a century since the Opium War at the hands of the imperialist powers. That was a time when Chinese were "looked down upon" by foreigners.[56] Deng maintained that it was the founding of the People's Republic that restored dignity to the Chinese. As he put it, "The modern image of China was not created by the government of the late Qing Dynasty, nor by the northern warlords, nor by Chiang Kai-shek and his son. It is the People's Republic of China that has changed China's image."[57] With the PRC's founding, the Chinese people finally "achieved status" and "stood up."[58]

Under the leadership of the Communist Party, China had become a proud and independent nation. Foreign countries could no longer expect China to be their "vassal." Nor could they expect China to submit to anything that was deleterious to its national interest.[59] After all, the Chinese were no less intelligent or talented than other peoples. Although they had felt inferior for more than a century, the Chinese now were confident in themselves and would no longer be intimidated.[60]

Notwithstanding their innate intelligence and talents, Deng believed that the Chinese could be effective only when they were united.[61] Just as the Communist revolution restored self-respect to the Chinese people, only through the continuation of the People's Republic could their international independence and dignity be assured. "Only socialism can save China, and only socialism can develop China." It was the People's Republic's unique brand of socialism that gave it autonomy. Without socialism, China would eventually become "a dependency" of other countries, subject to "the will of the Americans, or of people in other developed countries. . . ."[62]

Deng clearly saw the Chinese nation as being larger than the People's Republic, encompassing all of the world's ethnic Chinese. He believed that, "no matter what clothes they wear or what political stand they take," all Chinese had a sense of pride and identification with the Chinese nation and would want China to become strong and prosperous. Interestingly, Deng drew a distinction between the Chinese nation and the PRC state, insisting that "We don't demand that . . . [Chinese] be in favour of China's socialist system; we only ask them to love the motherland. . . ."[63] Appealing to what he believed to be their innate sense of nationalism, Deng called on the "tens of millions" of ethnic Chinese across the world to "love our country and help to develop it." For in the last analysis, "The image of China depends on the mainland, and the prospects for China's development also depend on the mainland."[64]

Economic Modernization

But simple nationalism was not enough. Deng believed that true national autonomy could come only from economic strength and prosperity.[65] Only economic development could deliver the advanced military capabilities that would enable China "to stand firm forever" among the nations of the world.[66] Deng explained that,

> If it were not for the atomic bomb, the hydrogen bomb and the satellites we have launched since the 1960s, China would not have its present international standing as a great, influential country. These achievements demonstrate a nation's abilities and are a sign of its level of prosperity and development.[67]

Because China lagged behind the industrial nations by two to three decades, Deng argued that the "overriding" nationwide task "for a considerable time to come" must be that of working "single-mindedly" for economic modernization. Nothing less than the country's "destiny for generations to come" hinged on the success or failure of that effort,[68] a process that was conceived by Deng to consist of three stages.

The goal of the first stage in China's economic development was the doubling of the country's per capita GNP from $250 in 1980 to $500 by 1990. That doubling of GNP would "ensure that the people have adequate food and clothing." By 1988, "ahead of time," Deng declared the first stage to have been accomplished.[69]

Stage two's goal was another doubling of the per capita GNP to $1,000 by the year 2000. By that time, Deng expected that China "will have shaken off poverty and achieved comparative prosperity." Its GNP of $1 trillion would make it "quite powerful," placing it "in the front ranks of countries." China would become a power to reckon with in the world. As Deng put it, even a modest defense allocation of one percent of the GNP would mean a sum of $10 billion, with which "a great deal" could be accomplished.[70]

A GNP of $1 trillion, in turn, would serve as "a new starting point" from which the last stage of China's economic modernization would be launched, a stage that would conclude by 2030 or 2050. By that time, according to Deng, China would have become fully industrialized, achieving parity with moderately developed countries.[71]

For all that to happen, for China to attain economically developed status, a number of instrumentalities was necessary. To begin with, the command economy of Stalin and Mao would have to be reformed.

The Reform of the Command Economy

Deng evidently regarded the command economy to be a major obstacle to the development of the productive forces. He stated that the Party made a mistake when it adopted the Soviet command model in the early-1950s. The management of the command economy was entrusted to a political bureaucracy that was overstaffed, burdened with overlapping organizations, and characterized by complicated procedures and "extremely low" efficiency. Such a bureaucracy was "utterly incompatible with large-scale production." The result was that quantity instead of the quality of goods was emphasized, so that the entire Chinese economy became "hampered."[72]

Another problem of the command model was an irrational pricing system. All prices were set by the state, "contrary to the law of value." Lacking a rational pricing policy, the state had to assume the "heavy burden" of providing subsidies in "tens of billions of yuan" a year to make up for the disparity between purchasing and selling prices. Those subsidies diverted precious resources away from investment in education, science, and culture—to the detriment of economic development.[73]

The dysfunctional command economy of irrational pricing and state subsidies would have to be reformed. Market mechanisms must be introduced to improve productivity and efficiency. The pricing system would have to be rationalized. State subsidies would have to be reduced, if not eliminated altogether. The economy would have to be freed from the mismanagement of the political bureaucracy by devolving power to local governments and to the managers of state-owned enterprises. Private businesses would have to be sanctioned.

All of this would be anathema to Mao Zedong. Accordingly, Deng justified his proposals by insisting that adopting some of the features of capitalism did not mean that China was abandoning socialism. According to Deng:

> [T]he difference between capitalism and socialism is not a market economy as opposed to a planned economy. Socialism has regulation by market forces, and capitalism has control through planning. Do you think capitalism has absolute freedom without any control?. . . . Both a planned economy and a market economy are necessary. If we did not have a market economy, we . . . would have to reconcile ourselves to lagging behind.[74]

Opening to the West

Another instrumentality that Deng advocated in the interest of economic development was the opening of China to trade, investment, and other contacts with the world, including and especially the capitalist advanced industrial democracies. In so advocating, Deng again assumed a position that was in direct contrast with that of Mao.

Under Mao, the People's Republic had pursued economic autarky as a necessary virtue. Deng's outlook was entirely different. He understood China's backwardness to be the result of centuries of isolation during the Ming and Qing dynasties, which was extended by Mao into the twentieth century. In so doing, "for a country to isolate itself," China closed itself to the world "only to its own disadvantage." For China to develop, it must instead "persist in opening to the outside world". There must not be "blind opposition" to anything that is foreign. China must sustain a long-term policy of learning from the advanced industrial nations so that it could "catch up with and surpass them." More than that, the policy of opening to the world must continue even after China had become developed because there would still be the need to learn from other countries "in areas where they are particularly strong."[75]

Under Deng's plan, China would trade with other countries and import their capital, skills, and technology. Special Economic Zones (SEZs) and open cities would be established, offering favorable terms and conditions to attract foreigners to invest in joint and solely-owned enterprises. International academic exchanges and scientific cooperation would be expanded.

In advocating contact with the outside world, Deng reasoned that not "everything developed in capitalist countries is of a capitalist nature." Science, technology, and advanced management techniques "have no class character" and are useful in any society. Deng argued that China would ultimately benefit from its open policy as long as Chinese national interests were served. Foreign imports must serve, not threaten, the integrity of "socialist production." And so long as China interacted with other countries "on the basis of equality and mutual benefit,"[76] national sovereignty and dignity would be preserved.

The Enhancement of Science and Technology

Deng's view on science and technology constituted another example of his departure from Maoism. Deng sought his justification in classical Marxism, maintaining that "Marx said that science and technology are part of the productive forces." More than that, Deng identified science and technology to be a "primary" productive force that governs, not simply the modernization of agriculture, industry, and defense, but the "rapid development" of the entire economy itself.[77]

Speaking very much like a technological determinist, Deng exulted that "Science is a great thing" and urged that "its importance" be recognized through the allocation of more "money and effort." Scientific research and training should be enhanced.[78] Education must be expanded, "even if it means slowing down in other fields." As Deng put it, "We have already wasted twenty years. . . . If we paid no attention to education, science, and technology, we would waste another twenty years, and the consequences would be dreadful to contemplate."[79]

The Treatment of Intellectuals

The promotion of science and technology would require attendant changes in the relations of production pertaining to intellectuals. Here, Deng's views once again depart significantly from those of Mao.

Mao was suspicious of, and antipathetic to, intellectuals. To him, intellectuals were members of the "black" capitalist class because they were more "expert" then "red." The very things that made them intellectuals—their professional knowledge, training, and expertise—made them politically suspect. As a consequence, under Mao's tenure, intellectuals were often singled out for special abuse.

Deng could not adopt a more different position on this matter. He derided the Maoists for their celebration of ignorance, a particularly vivid example of which was the Maoists' elevation of "an ignorant reactionary clown" who handed in a blank examination paper to be a model of "redness."[80] Deng refused to categorize intellectuals as bourgeois. Instead, he believed that "Everyone who works, whether with his hands or with his brain, is part of the working people in a socialist society." Unlike their counterparts in capitalist societies, intellectuals in socialist China were not "exploitative" because they had been trained by and were in service to "the working class." China's intellectuals differed from other workers "only insofar as they perform different roles in the social division of labour."[81]

Having identified intellectuals as members of the working class, Deng also dismissed the Maoist dichotomy of "red" versus "expert." "Red" was redefined by Deng to mean anyone who "loves our social-ist motherland and is serving socialism. . . ." In effect, an "expert" could also be "red," provided that the individual's work contributed to the motherland and, in his words and action, the individual refrained from taking "a reactionary political stand" against the Communist Party. As Deng explained, "So long as they keep to the socialist politi-cal stand . . . their devoted work is a concrete manifestation of their socialist consciousness."[82]

Under Deng, intellectuals would no longer be vilified simply be-cause they are intellectuals. On the contrary, Deng urged that they be raised "to first place," given more respect, and rewarded with higher salaries. The Party and the community-at-large must value knowledge; teachers must be better remunerated, no matter "how many difficulties we have." Everything must be done to encourage the return of the thousands of Chinese students studying abroad, "regardless of their previous political attitudes." To encourage their return, Deng proposed that a comprehensive scientific research center be created to increase employment opportunities. "Otherwise," he warned,"these people will not come back, and it will be a great loss to the country."[83]

Material Incentives

Intellectuals were not the only people who would be provided mate-rial incentives. Deng apparently believed that human beings in general would work harder and better if they could benefit directly from their labor. It would be "idealism" to ask that people work in selfless sacri-fice, because "revolution takes place on the basis of the need for material benefit." Ever the pragmatist, Deng cautioned that expecting people to be selfless was a strategy that simply "won't work in the long run."[84]

The Promotion of Achievement

While he believed that all people were motivated by material re-wards, Deng proposed that the high achievers and the talented should be particularly rewarded. They should be accorded special treatment, such as promotion "without hesitation," pay raises of "more than one step at a time," and "free rein" in their work.[85]

Let Some Get Rich

In advocating the principle of "more pay for more work," Deng was not unaware that it could lead to differential income and wealth, but thought it "only fair that people who work hard should prosper." He was convinced that egalitarianism would not work. Instead, Deng saw the rich as performing a potentially useful function by becoming "an impressive example" that would motivate others to excel. In this manner, Deng was convinced, the whole economy would "advance wave upon wave."[86]

To avoid a permanent "polarization" between the rich and poor, Deng imagined that when the time was "right," the government would enforce a redistribution of wealth, via taxes and voluntary contributions, from the rich to the poor, and from the prosperous coastal to the economically backward inland regions. But Deng was rather vague as to when that time would be, and cautioned against "overhastiness" because it would "only cause damage to economic development." Although Deng was evasive as to exactly when the right time would be for reducing the wealth gap spawned by his reforms, suggesting only that the Party "study when to raise this question and how to settle it," he did mention the year 2000 as possibly "the right time." By that time, he expected that the Chinese people would be living "a fairly comfortable life" with a per capita GNP of $1,000, and could afford to share their wealth.[87]

Order and Stability

Aside from the instrumentalities that would bring about a reform of the economy, Deng Xiaoping thought also addressed certain necessary conditions that must precede or accompany economic modernization. Of these necessary conditions, order and stability were paramount.

Deng believed that the successful development of China was entirely dependent on the maintenance of stability and order. More than that, he was convinced that order and stability in China were also in the world's interest. Deng maintained that if China were to descend into "turmoil," the situation would be far worse than during the Cultural Revolution because China no longer had "prestigious leaders" like Mao and Zhou Enlai who could hold the country together. Without that glue, China would deteriorate into civil war, with each region dominated by a faction and "blood flowing like water." The economic and transportation systems would be devastated, and "hundreds of millions" of refugees would flee into China's neighboring countries. The result would be a "disaster on a world scale."[88]

Party Dictatorship

China's "overriding interest" therefore must be stability. Given that, anything that could help maintain that stability was "good."[89] For Deng, the "democratic dictatorship" of the Chinese Communist Party was one of those "good" things. Although he recognized that the Communist Party had made many mistakes, Deng still insisted that it was "the centre" that ensured political stability and unity.[90]

To perform that critical function, the Party must first be internally cohesive. It must not degenerate into factional rivalries. Among the many factions that could divide the Party, Deng was particularly wary of the "Leftists" who opposed his reforms and "would like nothing better than nationwide confusion." Deng feared their resurgence and warned darkly: "Don't think that there can be no more chaos in China. . . ."[91] Much depended on the ability of CCP leaders to stay united on major policy goals and directives. As long as the leaders "remain stable and firm," Deng was convinced that "nobody will be able to do anything against China."[92]

Ideological Solidarity

Party unity, in turn, was contingent on the ideological solidarity of its members, a solidarity that was constructed on "Marxism-Leninism and Mao Zedong Thought."[93] For that reason, Deng refrained from the total denunciation of Mao, although he held Mao and his policies to be responsible for untold human suffering and economic devastation. Instead, Deng implored his party to refrain from being "too critical of the mistakes Mao made in his later years." Mao was the founding father and charismatic leader nonpareil of Chinese Communism. If the Communist Party were to reject Mao, there would be "ideological confusion and political instability" because its own legitimacy would be jeopardized. As Deng put it, "To negate the contributions of such a great historical figure would mean to deny all our achievements during an important period of the country's history."[94]

Bourgeois Liberalization

More than party unity, political and social stability also required a continuous effort to combat "bourgeois liberalization." By bourgeois liberalization Deng meant the rejection of socialism and Communist Party rule, and especially the "wholesale Westernization of China."[95] The exponents of bourgeois liberalization were those who "worship" Western notions of "democracy," "human rights," and "freedom." Deng evidently equated such notions with the anarchic "mass democracy" of the Cultural Revolution, and was convinced that the "evil trend" of unchecked bourgeois liberalization "would plunge the country into turmoil once more."[96]

Deng expected that the struggle to combat bourgeois liberalization would be protracted for fifty to seventy years until China had become economically developed. Although Deng urged that "bourgeois liberalization" must be resisted and opposed, he rejected the Maoist method of "launching political movements." Mindful that the Maoist campaigns of mass mobilization had been destructive to both the Communist Party as well as the national economy, Deng argued instead that "education and persuasion" be employed in the suppression of "bourgeois liberalization."[97]

The Rejection of Bourgeois Democracy

The priority Deng placed on stability also accounted for his rejection of Western democracy, although he did not seem to object to it in principle, maintaining that "We have no objection to the Western countries doing it that way."[98] Deng simply thought that Western democracy was unsuitable for China because it valued the individual over the group. He also found the Western system of governing to be wasteful and inefficient. Deng regarded the American separation of powers, instead of being the theoretical three branches of government, to be "three governments" entirely, with each "branch" pulling the country "in different directions." To Deng, Western democracy was nothing other than unbridled individualism and effective anarchy.[99]

Such a system would be totally unsuited to China because it "would only make a mess of everything." If China were to become a Western-style "democracy," it would achieve neither economic development nor any of the "substance" of democracy. By adopting Western "democracy," China would only purchase chaos and disorder. As Deng put it, "China has a huge population; if some people demonstrated today and others tomorrow, there would be a demonstration 365 days a year. . . . [W]e would have no time to develop our economy."[100]

Socialist Democracy

Rather than mimicking the West, China should have its own brand of "socialist democracy." Although Deng was never clear on what exactly he meant by "socialist democracy," he seemed to be referring to a society in which the interests of the individual, "the part" and the short term were subordinated to those of the collective, the whole, and the long term.[101] It would be a political system where power was the monopoly of a single party, the Communist, who would determine what constituted society's superordinate collective and long-term interests.

That having been said, the one-party dictatorship of Deng Xiaoping has significant features that distinguish it from the single-party totalitarianism of Mao Zedong. For one, there is more personal space in Deng's "socialist democracy"—a result of Deng's abandonment of Mao's utopian ambition to transform and perfect the consciousness of each individual. Deng seemed to have greater confidence in the judgment of the common man. For him, the devolution of authority to the lower levels, including the peasants, was "the height of democracy." He urged his party to have "faith that the overwhelming majority of the people are able to use their own judgment," even conceding that "The masses should have the full right and opportunity to express responsible criticisms to their leaders and to make constructive suggestions. . . ."[102]

While all of this is extremely vague, Deng seemed to draw a clear distinction between thought and behavior which Mao never did. Deng appeared ready to allow individuals the privacy of their opinions, as long as they refrained from directly challenging and attacking the power and rule of the Communist Party. As he put it, "You can reserve your opinions, so long as you don't take part in activities against the Party or socialism."[103]

More intriguing still, Deng seemed to conceive "socialist democracy" to be a work-in-progress rather than a finalized reality. According to Deng, "Democracy is our goal" to be developed "only gradually" and not "in haste" because the country must be kept stable. He seemed to regard democracy as related to the educational level of the masses, holding the possibility that the people would be accorded a greater measure of political participation once their educational level had increased.[104] If this analysis is correct, it could be that Deng envisioned a future when popular participation in government would expand—the result of the country's modernization and growth in the people's income, education, as well as their capacity for rational thought and decision making.

Conclusion

One of the abiding curiosities of the twentieth century must be the phenomenon of Marxist revolutions in societies where Marx and Engels would never expect a workers' revolution to occur. In complete contradiction to the precepts of classical Marxism, "proletarian" revolutions succeeded in underdeveloped societies instead of mature industrial economies.

Beginning with the Bolshevik Revolution in Russia, self-proclaimed Marxist revolutionaries succeeded only in societies where peasants comprised the majority of the population. After the revolutionaries acceded to power, they were confronted everywhere with the vexing conundrum of creating socialism in a primitive economy. On this matter, neither classical Marxism nor Leninism could provide guidance or illumination. It was left to each "socialist" state to improvise a way out of the dilemma.

Under Mao, after an initial period when there was an attempt to impose the Soviet model, the Chinese Communist Party attempted to create socialism with sheer willpower. Mao was convinced that if each individual's consciousness were transformed, the collective enthusiasm and dedication of the masses would create an advanced industrial economy. Instead of being the reflection of the economic base, the superstructure would be the engine of socioeconomic change. Not only did Mao's strategy fail to industrialize China, his ceaseless campaigns against class enemies, real or imagined, took at least 35 million lives, almost destroyed the Communist Party, and brought China to the brink of ruin.

Unlike Mao, Deng clearly recognized the problem of constructing communism in a retrograde economy. He admitted that neither Marx nor Lenin could be expected "to provide ready answers" to questions that arose years after their deaths. For Deng, this meant that after a successful revolution, each country must build socialism according to its own conditions: "There are not and cannot be fixed models."[105]

By returning to classical Marxism's emphasis on the productive forces, Deng managed to transform Marxism into what it never was— a developmental ideology. The central task and focus of his developmental nationalism is the economic modernization of China. Whatever his Marxist persuasion, Deng's ideology, for the most part, is informed by an overriding pragmatism. In order to develop China's retarded economic base, Deng proposed a number of instrumentalities that included privately owned businesses, differential wages, an increasingly unequal income distribution, as well as the importation of foreign capital and technology—all of which is anathema to the committed Maoist.

None of these instrumentalities is regarded by Deng "as an axiomatic, self-justified good."[106] Even the dictatorship of the Communist Party is merely a means to the end of economic development. Deng rationalized that since economic development required order and stability, a one-party system recommended itself.

To the question of why that one party be communist and the political system socialist, Deng had ready answers. One important reason for his insistence on socialism was that, according to Marxist precepts, socialism was the necessary prelude to communism. Despite all the devastation wrought by Mao, and despite having endured three purges himself, communism remained Deng's inspiration and guiding star. "We believe in communism, and our ideal is to bring it into being." For Deng, communism remained the "ultimate goal," for which "countless . . . people laid down their lives." It was the dream that sustained him and the Party even in their "darkest days."[107]

There were other reasons that made socialism attractive to Deng, among which were four essential features that together defined the "essence" of socialism. Socialism's first attribute was "the liberation and development of the productive forces." Deng believed that socialism provided the conditions for a faster development of the productive forces than capitalism.[108] In so doing, socialism would demonstrate its superiority over capitalism, as well as provide the material basis for communism. Deng did grant that socialism's greater capacity to develop the productive forces was not something that could be proven "at the moment" but must await the fulfillment of the third stage of China's economic development, when its per capita GNP had risen to $4,000. Only then would the superiority of socialism over capitalism be "better" demonstrated, and the "correctness" of Marxism be proven.[109]

A second feature of socialism that made it attractive to Deng was the "elimination of exploitation" through the "predominance of public ownership." According to Deng, only socialism could eliminate the greed, corruption, and injustice "inherent in capitalism and other systems of exploitation." As long as "the basic means of production" remained publicly owned, Deng was confident that "no new bourgeoisie" would emerge. In this manner, the socialist system "would remain secure."[110]

A third attribute of socialism was the "common prosperity" it provided—the absence of a "polarization" between rich and poor. Deng insisted that if China were to take "the capitalist road," a few would become rich, including some who might become millionaires. But the rich would altogether amount to less than 1 percent of the population; the "overwhelming majority" of the people would remain in poverty, "scarcely able to feed and clothe themselves." Deng was convinced that while capitalist countries delivered economic prosperity to the few, only socialism could "eradicate" poverty for the many. He concluded that if his economic reforms should result in the polarization between the poor and the wealthy, he would consider those reforms to have been "a failure."[111]

Deng maintained that one of the chief virtues of "socialist democracy" was its greater efficiency. He saw "bourgeois" democracies as inefficient systems that dissipated their energies in constant internal squabbles. Despite its virtues, Deng believed that "socialist democracy's" superior efficiency was contingent on the government being able to keep "to the right policies and direction. . . ."[112] And since the government was the exclusive purview of the Communist Party, everything would hinge on how well that party functioned.

Deng justified the continuing rule of the Chinese Communist Party rule by reinvoking the notion of the "vanguard." The Communist Party, according to Deng, deserved to rule because its members were uniquely possessed of special moral virtues, wisdom and competence. They were selfless beings who only worked "for the good of the people" and who did "not exploit the labour of others." Communist Party members did not "lord it over" or impose their will "by decree" on the people, but kept always in close contact with the masses, inspiring their enthusiasm and representing their will and interests.[113]

According to Deng, Communist Party members dared "to speak the truth and oppose falsehood," always making "a clear distinction" between public and private interests. They did not seek personal favors "at the expense of principle"; they appointed people on their merits rather than by favoritism. Communist Party members were not vainglorious—demanding no "special privileges" no matter how high their positions. They practiced criticism and self-criticism, exposed and corrected shortcomings and mistakes, and always strove for excellence in their work. They were truthful and honest, efficient and quick in their work, producing quality results instead of "empty talk."[114]

More than their moral virtues, Deng demanded that members of the Communist Party be technocrats who could supervise the reformed economy of market socialism, as well as undertake the forward planning of society. They must provide for the training of workers and professionals to meet the country's immediate and future needs, taking into account not only the needs of growing production and construction but also new trends in science and technology. To do all that, Party members must not "be content to remain laymen in science and technology." They must, instead, "dig in and . . . learn the trade" by acquiring scientific knowledge, studying "the objective laws" governing scientific and technical work, and leading the people in "conquering the heights of world science."[115] In all their endeavors, Deng asked that CCP members be effective leaders while, at the same time, "not intervene in too many matters."[116]

In effect, Deng's entire program of economic development was dependent on the membership of the Chinese Communist Party having all the requisite moral virtues and professional competence he demanded. It is the possession of those qualities that would ensure the Party's continuous rule "for a hundred years" as well as the country's long-term peace and stability.[117] All of which meant that, as Deng rightly observed, "If any problem arises in China, it will arise from inside the Communist Party."[118]

Notes

1. *Shijie ribao (World Journal,* hereafter *WJ)* (Millbrae, CA), 15 February 1992, p. 2A.
2. *WJ,* 17 June 1992, p. 12A; and 15 June 1992, p. 2A.
3. *WJ,* 21 October 1992, p. A12; and Wu Yifu, "Guard against the Indiscriminate Use of `Deng Xiaoping Thought,'" *WJ,* 17 January 1993, p. A5.
4. Deng Xiaoping, "On the Reform of the System of Party and State Leadership," *Selected Works of Deng Xiaoping (1975–1982)* (Beijing: Foreign Languages, 1984), 313.
5. Editorial, *WJ,* 17 October 1992, p. A2.
6. Sheila Tefft, "From `Little Red Book' to `Thought of Deng'—China's New Personal Cult," *Christian Science Monitor,* 22 October 1992, p. 1; and Wu Yifu, "Guard against the Indiscriminate."
7. *WJ,* 4 May 1993, p. A12.
8. *WJ,* 23 August 1994, p. A10.   At the height of the Great Proletarian Cultural Revolution, Mao Zedong was briefly credited with having lifted Marxism-Leninism to a new "theoretical" plane.
9. *WJ,* 17 June 1993, p. A12; and 3 July 1993, p. A12.
10. *WJ,* 22 August 1993, p. A9; and 2 August 1993, p. A3.
11. *WJ,* 31 October 1993, p. A9.
12. "Deng's Book a Best-Seller," *San Francisco Chronicle,* 12 November 1993, p. A12.
13. *WJ,* 4 December 1993, p. A14.
14. Editorial, *WJ,* 9 November 1993, p. A2; and 6 November 1993, p. A12.
15. Editorial, *WJ,* 22 August 1994, p. A2.
16. Ibid., and p. A9.
17. See Lowell Dittmer, "Chinese Reform Socialism Under Deng Xiaoping: Theory and Practice," in *China in the Era of Deng Xiaoping: A Decade of Reform,* eds. Michael Ying-mao Kao and Susan H. Marsh (Armonk, NY: M. E. Sharpe, 1993), 3; and Gilbert Rozman, *The Chinese Debate About Soviet Socialism 1978–1985* (Princeton: Princeton University, 1987), 13–14.
18. See the account in Uli Franz, *Deng Xiaoping* (New York: Harcourt Brace Jovanovich, 1988), ch. 5.
19. Deng Xiaoping, "On the General Program of Work for the Whole Party and the Whole Nation," in *The Case of the Gang of Four—With First Translation of Teng Hsiao-ping's "Three Poisonous Weeds"* ed. Chi Hsin (Hong Kong: Cosmos, 1977), 221.   Emphasis added.
20. A good treatment of the Maoist versus Dengist conceptions of productive forces and relations is Michael Sullivan, "The Ideology of the Chinese Communist Party Since the Third Plenum," in *Chinese Marxism in Flux 1978–84: Essays on Epistemology, Ideology and Political Economy* ed. Bill Brugger (Armonk, NY: M. E. Sharpe, 1985), 67–97.
21. Cheng Yueh, "A General Program for Capitalist Restoration—An Analysis of `On the General Program for All Work of the Whole Party and the Whole Nation,'" in *And Mao Makes 5: Mao Tsetung's Last Great Battle,* ed. Raymond Lotta (Chicago: Banner, 1978), 281.
22. There is a convenient collection of some of those articles in English as "Criticize Teng and Beat Back the Right Deviationist Wind," in ibid., 257–397.
23. Deng, "On the General Program," 207, 211–213, 222.

24. Karl Marx, *Poverty of Philosophy* (Moscow: Foreign Languages, n.d.), 122.
25. Karl Marx and Friedrich Engels, *The German Ideology* (Moscow: Progress, 1964), 41.
26. Ibid., 37–38.
27. Marx, Letter to Annenkov, 28 December 1846, in *Selected Works* 2: 442.
28. Friedrich Engels, "Principle of Communism," in *Collected Works* 6 (New York: International, 1976): 348.
29. Karl Marx, preface to *Critique of Political Economy* in *Selected Works* 1 (Moscow: Foreign Languages, 1955): 362–363.
30. Friedrich Engels, "The Peasant War in Germany," *Collected Works* 10: 469–471.
31. Perhaps the most prominent of the European Marxist theoreticians who became anti-Leninists because they understood that a Marxist revolution in any society required the full maturation of the productive forces included Karl Kautsky and Rosa Luxemburg. See Karl Kautsky, *Dictatorship of the Proletariat* (Ann Arbor: University of Michigan, 1964) and Rosa Luxemburg, *The Russian Revolution and Leninism or Marxism* (Ann Arbor: University of Michigan, 1961).
32. On this issue Leon Trotsky was very explicit. See his discussion of the consequences of attempting to build socialism on an impoverished economic base. Leon Trotsky, *The Revolution Betrayed* (New York: Doubleday, 1937).
33. Mao insisted that it was change in the "superstructure" of society, instead of the "productive forces," that generated revolutionary transformation. See Mao Zedong, *A Critique of Soviet Economics* (New York: Monthly Review, 1977), 51.
34. Stuart R. Schram, "Deng Xiaoping's Quest for `Modernization with Chinese Characteristics' and the Future of Marxism-Leninism," in Michael Kau and Susan Marsh, *China in the Era of Deng*, 410.
35. Mary Matossian, "Ideologies of Delayed Industrialization," in *Political Development and Social Change*, eds. Jason L. Finkle and Richard W. Gable (New York: John Wiley and Sons, 1971), 113, 118.
36. Ibid., 120.
37. Deng, "Excerpts from Talks Given in Wuchang, Shenzhen, Zhuhai and Shanghai," 18 January-21 February 1992, and "We are Undertaking an Entirely New Endeavour," 13 October 1987, in *Selected Works of Deng Xiaoping (1982–1992)* III (Beijing: Foreign Languages, 1994): 358, 250.
38. Deng, "We Shall Draw on Historical Experience and Guard Against Wrong Tendencies," 30 April 1987, in ibid., 225.
39. Deng, "We Shall Expand Political Democracy and Carry Out Economic Reform," 15 April 1985, in ibid., 121.
40. Ibid.
41. Michael Sullivan, "Ideology," 71–72.
42. Deng, "Speech at the Third Plenary Session of the Central Advisory Commission of the Communist Party of China," 22 October 1984, in *Selected Works* III: 95.
43. Deng, "Report on the Revision of the Constitution of the Communist Party of China," 16 September 1956, in *Deng Xiaoping: Speeches and Writings* (New York: Pergamon, 1984), 2.
44. Ibid., 29–30.
45. Deng, "Uphold the Four Cardinal Principles," 30 March 1979, in *Selected Works (1975–1982)*, 190; and "Speech at the Opening Ceremony of the National Conference on Science," 18 March 1978, in *Speeches and Writings*, 41.

46. Deng, "Excerpts From Talks Given in Wuchang," 367; and "In Everything We Do We Must Proceed from the Realities of the Primary Stage of Socialism," 29 August 1987, in *Selected Works* III: 248.
47. Deng, "On the Reform of the System," 317–318.
48. Deng, "We Should Draw on the Experience of Other Countries," 3 June 1988, in *Selected Works* III: 261.
49. Deng, "Speech at the National Conference on Science," 40.
50. Deng, "Building a Socialism with a Specifically Chinese Character," 30 June 1984; and "We are Undertaking an Entirely New Endeavour," 13 October 1987, in *Selected Works* III: 73, 250.
51. Deng, "Maintain the Tradition of Hard Struggle," 23 March 1989, in ibid., 283.
52. Deng, "We Must Adhere to Socialism and Prevent Peaceful Evolution towards Capitalism," 23 November 1989, in ibid., 333.
53. Deng, "Review Your Experience and Use Professionally Trained People," 20 August 1991; "With Stable Policies of Reform and Opening to the Outside World, China can have Great Hopes for the Future," 4 September 1989; and "We are Confident that We can Handle China's Affairs Well," 16 September 1989, in ibid., 357, 309, 316, 310.
54. Deng, "We are Confident," and "No One can Shake Socialist China," 26 October 1989, in ibid., 316, 318.
55. Deng, "We are Working to Revitalize the Chinese Nation," 7 April 1990, in ibid., 344.
56. Deng, "One Country, Two Systems," 22–23 June 1984, in ibid., 70.
57. Ibid.
58. Deng, "Maintain the Tradition of Hard Struggle," 282.
59. Ibid.; and "Opening Speech at the Twelfth National Congress of the CPC," 1 September 1982, in *Speeches and Writings*, 86.
60. Deng, "One Country, Two Systems," 70; "We are Working to Revitalize," 345; "We are Confident," 316.
61. Deng, "We are Working to Revitalize," 345.
62. Deng, "Urgent Tasks of China's Third Generation of Collective Leadership," 16 June 1989, ibid., 302.
63. Deng, "We are Working to Revitalize," 345; and "One Country, Two Systems," 70.
64. Deng, "For the Great Unity of the Entire Chinese Nation," 18 June 1986; "Excerpts from Talks;" and "We are Working to Revitalize," in ibid., 164, 366, 345.
65. Deng, "We Must Promote Education in the Four Cardinal Principles and Adhere to the Policies of Reform and Opening to the Outside World," 20 January 1987, ibid., 202.
66. Deng, "A Letter to the Political Bureau of the Central Committee of the Communist Party of China," 4 September 1989, in ibid., 313.
67. Deng, "China Must Take Its Place in the Field of High Technology," 24 October 1988, in ibid., 273.
68. Deng, "Uphold the Four Cardinal Principles," 30 March 1979, *Selected Works (1975–1982)*, 171; and "Speech Greeting the Fourth Congress of Chinese Writers and Artists," 30 October 1979, in *Speeches and Writings*, 79.
69. Deng, "We Shall Draw On Historical Experience," 224.
70. Ibid.; and "Speech at the Third Plenary Session," 95.
71. Deng, "Speech at the Third Plenary Session," 96; and "We Should Draw On the Experience of Other Countries," 261.
72. Deng, "We Shall Speed Up Reform," 12 June 1987; and "Remarks on the

Domestic Economic Situation," 10 June 1986, in ibid., 235, 162; and "Emancipate the Mind, Seek Truth from Facts and Unite as One in Looking to the Future," 13 December 1978, in *Speeches and Writings*, 71.

73. Deng, "We Must Rationalize Prices and Accelerate the Reform," 19 May 1988, in *Selected Works* III: 257.
74. Deng, "Seize the Opportunity to Develop the Economy," 24 December 1990, in ibid., 351.
75. Deng, "Speech at National Conference on Science," 45; "Speech at the Third Plenary Session," 96; "We Must Promote Education," 202.
76. Deng, "Answers to the Italian Journalist Oriana Fallaci," 21 and 23 August 1980, in *Selected Works (1975–1982)*, 333; "Opening Speech at the Twelfth National Congress of the CPC," 1 September 1982, in *Speeches and Writings*, 87.
77. Deng, "Science and Technology Constitute a Primary Productive Force," 5 and 12 September 1988, in *Selected Works* III: 269; "Speech at the National Conference on Science," 41.
78. Deng, "Urgent Tasks of China's Third Generation," p. 303; "Our Work in All Fields Should Contribute to the Building of Socialism with Chinese Characteristics," 12 January 1983, in *Selected Works* III: 33.
79. Deng, "Science and Technology," 270, 269.
80. Deng, "Speech at National Conference on Science," 45–46.
81. Ibid., 43.
82. Ibid., 46, 48.
83. Deng, "Science and Technology," 270; "Excerpts from Talks," 366; "Speech at the Ceremony Celebrating the 35th Anniversary of the Founding of the People's Republic of China," 1 October 1984, in *Selected Works* III: 79.
84. Deng, "Emancipate the Mind," 67.
85. Deng, "In the First Decade, Prepare for the Second," 14 October 1982, in *Selected Works* III: 27.
86. Deng, "Our Work in All Fields," 33; "Make a Success of Special Economic Zones and Open More Cities to the Outside World," 24 February 1984, in *Selected Works* III: 62; and "Emancipate the Mind," 73.
87. Deng, "Excerpts from Talks," 362; and "Interview of Deng Xiaoping by Robert Maxwell on Current Affairs," in *Speeches and Writings*, 97.
88. Deng, "China Will Never Allow Other Countries to Interfere in its Internal Affairs," 11 July 1990, in *Selected Works* III: 347.
89. Deng, "Urgent Tasks of China's Third Generation," 304.
90. Deng, "Take a Clear-Cut Stand," 196, 195.
91. Deng, "The Organizational Line Guarantees the Implementation of the Ideological and Political Lines," 29 July 1979, in *Selected Works (1975–1982)*, 199.
92. Deng, "With Stable Policies of Reform," 307.
93. Deng, "Emancipate the Mind," 69.
94. Deng, "The Overriding Need is for Stability," 26 February 1989, in *Selected Works* III: 277.
95. Deng, "Reform and Opening to the Outside World Can Truly Invigorate China," 12 May 1987, in ibid., 233.
96. Deng, "We Have to Clear Away Obstacles and Continue to Advance," 13 January 1987, in ibid., 200; "Take a Clear-Cut Stand," 196; and "Bourgeois Liberalization Means Taking the Capitalist Road," 130.
97. Deng, "China can Only Take the Socialist Road," 3 March 1987, in ibid., 208.
98. Deng, "Speech at a Meeting with the Members of the Committee for Drafting

the Basic Law of the Hong Kong Special Administrative Region," 16 April 1987, in ibid., 219.

99. Deng, "Take a Clear-Cut Stand," 195.
100. Deng, "The Overriding Need," 277; "Take a Clear-Cut Stand," 196.
101. Deng, "Uphold the Four Cardinal Principles," 183.
102. Deng, "In Everything We Do," 248; "Emancipate the Mind," 66; and "The Present Situation," 242.
103. Deng, "Take a Clear-Cut Stand," 194.
104. Deng, "The Overriding Need," 278; "Take a Clear-Cut Stand," 196; and "We Shall Speed Up Reform," 240.
105. Deng, "Let Us Put the Past Behind Us and Open Up a New Era," 16 May 1989, in ibid., 284, 285.
106. Matossian, "Ideologies," 120.
107. Deng, "Unity Depends on Ideals and Discipline," 7 March 1985; and "Reform is the Only Way For China to Develop its Productive Forces," 28 August 1985, in *Selected Works* III: 116, 141.
108. Deng, "Excerpts from Talks," p. 361; and "Speech at the National Conference of the Communist Party of China," 23 September 1985, in ibid., 146.
109. Deng, "Reform is the Only Way," 141; "We Shall Draw on Historical Experience," 224; and "Take a Clear-Cut Stand," 195.
110. Deng, "Speech at the National Conference of the Communist Party," 146; and "Unity Depends on Ideals," 117; "Speech at the Third Plenary Session," 97.
111. Deng, "China Can Only Take the Socialist Road," 207; and "Reform is the Only Way," 142.
112. Deng, "Speech at a Meeting," 219.
113. Deng, "Speech at National Conference on Science," 52; and "Report on the Revision of the Constitution," 27, 33, 6, 5.
114. Deng, "Speech at the National Conference of the Communist Party," 149; "Report on the Revision of the Constitution," 28; and "Speech at the National Conference on Science," 53.
115. Deng, "Speech at the National Conference on Education," 22 April 1978, in *Speeches and Writings*, 58; and "Speech at the National Conference on Science," 52.
116. Deng, "Help the People Understand the Importance of the Rule of Law," 28 June 1986, in *Selected Works* III: 167.
117. Deng, "Excerpts from Talks," 368.
118. Deng, "Excerpts from Talks," 368.

5

The Dilemmas of Reform

Signs of System Failure

The passing of Mao finally enabled economists of the People's Republic of China finally to publicly discuss the signs of system failure. They felt free to admit that, as early as 1956, "the rate of agricultural growth began declining" and that of industrial growth also "showed a general downward trend."[1] The decline was attributed to the fact that there was little incentive to produce efficiently because enterprises "shouldered no . . . responsibility" since the state provided all fixed assets and productive inputs.[2] Between 1958 and the mid-1970s, total factor productivity declined despite an average annual economic growth rate of about 5.6 percent. More and more resources were needed to produce one unit of output. But increases in the investment in fixed assets only led to waste and overstocked inventories of semi-finished and unsalable finished products.[3] "[M]any producer goods were unsalable and substandard; unit consumption (energy, raw and other materials) in heavy industry was too high."[4]

The problem was compounded by the lack of an objective way to measure economic results or define enterprise optimality.[5] Prices in the planned economy did not reflect "real" costs but were arbitrary decisions made by state bureaucrats. Under those circumstances, enterprise decisions could hardly be anything other than economically flawed.

While the conditions in industry were bad, the situation in agriculture was more serious. Mao had insisted that the production of grain be the "key link" in agricultural policy so that China could be self-sufficient in food production. That prescription led to the neglect of other agricultural pursuits such as cash crops, forestry, animal husbandry, and fisheries. To make more arable soil available for grain production, entire forests were levelled and land reclaimed from lakes, resulting in untold environmental damage.

Despite the herculean effort, whatever increases in grain production were overtaken by the rate of population growth. Mao's dismissal of Malthusian demography as bogus "bourgeois" science indirectly led to the more than doubling of the Chinese population, a growth rate that far outpaced that of the economy. The result was that between 1958 and 1978 the national per capita availability of cotton cloth, food grains, and edible oils decreased by 2 percent, 3.2 percent, and 33.3 percent, respectively.[6] The annual per capita food grains output in 1979 was actually less than that in 1936.[7] For all its claims of having conquered hunger, the government admitted in 1977 that one out of every ten Chinese (or 100 million) lived at the edge of starvation.[8] In 1979, more than a quarter of a century after "liberation," as much as 27 percent of the population still lived at marginal subsistence.[9]

All of which led PRC economists, after Mao's death, to deem "irrational"[10] the entire inherited economic structure of Maoist China. Economic reform had become an irresistible political necessity. Nothing less than a "drastic readjustment" of the entire system was needed.[11]

Although the CCP was now prepared to undertake systemic reform of the economy, the ideocratic nature of the political system meant that reform required some ideological legitimation that was consistent with Marxist canons. That legitimation was provided by Deng Xiaoping's return to classical Marxism's emphasis on the primacy of the "productive forces."

Under Mao, it was the "superstructure" that mattered; everything else was of little consequence. Any reference to the material productive forces was considered heretical. In a reversal of Maoist tenets, the CCP Central Committee in 1984 decisively adopted Deng's insistence that the "relations of production must be adapted to productive forces." More than thirty years after the Communist revolution, China had attained only "the first phase of socialism" wherein the "basic contradiction" remained that between the relations of production and the still-primitive forces of production. China could not transcend the first phase of socialism until it had created a mature economy. But, according to the precepts of classical Marxism, China's material productive forces could grow only in conformity with "objective economic laws."

This meant that there could be no "great leaps" in economic development animated by political enthusiasm. What the Chinese economy required was a set of "productive relations" that would increase productivity, stimulate technological innovation and promote efficiency.[12]

Historically, capitalism has shown itself to be instrumental in the development and modernization of a primitive economic base. The abundance of mature industrial economies might well make work incentives unnecessary, but that was hardly the case in partially industrialized societies such as China. The latter's primitive productive forces required individual and collective material incentives for increased productivity and efficiency. All of which meant that economic modernization necessitated the grafting of capitalism onto the still nascent socialist economy of the People's Republic.

Post-Mao Economic Reforms

The grafting of capitalism began in the countryside—where 80 percent of the population resided—with the reintroduction of material incentives into agricultural production. This was accomplished via the Communist Party's inauguration in December 1978 of a program of rural reforms that began with decollectivization.

Land Reform

Mao's People's Communes were dismantled without fanfare. The gargantuan production units that were conglomerates of agricultural, industrial, military, educational, and commercial functions were replaced by a "contract responsibility system." Family households, the traditional production unit in China, would contract with the state to deliver minimum quotas of produce at state-set prices in return for usufruct land rights. Initially, the contract assured peasants fifteen years of land use; later, the term was extended to at least fifty years. The households were also permitted to sell for profit any surplus they produced in unregulated rural markets; hire a limited number of laborers; diversify their crops; as well as sell or transfer their land rights to others.

Rural reforms began as experiments in select provinces but were quickly expanded throughout China. By the end of 1981, 97.8 percent of the six million production teams in the Chinese countryside were recruited into the new contract system.[13] Agricultural production and income rapidly increased because peasants now had both incentives and opportunities to directly profit from their labor. In the first five years of reform, gross agricultural output grew at a rate of about 7 percent per annum, compared to an annual average of 2.5 percent in the preceding twenty years. Even with crop diversification, World Bank figures had grain production in China increasing by 22 percent between 1979 and 1983.[14] PRC Vice Premier Tian Jiyun in 1992 asserted that, from 1978 to 1984, foodgrains production actually rose by as much as a third (33 percent), from 300 to 400 million tons; cotton production increased almost threefold from 2.17 to 6.26 million tons; and the production of cooking oil rose by 228 percent from 5.22 to 11.9 million tons.[15]

The Revival of Private and Collective Ownership

Another important post-Mao reform was the development of an increasingly dynamic non-state-owned economic sector—collective and privately-owned businesses and industries that began to proliferate in the countryside, towns and cities.

a. *Rural Enterprises.* When the Deng administration freed the rural communes to disaggregate into "household responsibility units," it also permitted those units the opportunity to seek profit in nonagrarian pursuits. Individuals and small collectives were allowed to undertake productive activities for gain in sideline industries; the manufacturing of consumer goods; and the provision of local services. These became the new rural enterprises that grew out of the production teams and brigades of the defunct communes.

By 1994, the number of rural enterprises had grown to more than 20 million, the largest of which number about 500. These large enterprises each employs an average of 1,330 workers and has average fixed assets of 40 million *renminbi yuan*. Altogether, the rural enterprises provided employment to some 100 million people (thereby absorbing some of rural China's surplus labor), accounted for a third of China's foreign exchange-earning exports, and contributed 45.4 billion *yuan* in taxes a year.[16]

Although the rural enterprises are often referred to as rural collective enterprises, that rubric is deceptive in that their ownership is actually quite mixed. Some are owned by individual households; others by a group of households; still others are jointly owned and operated with urban state-owned or collective enterprises, or with foreign investors. 1.3 million rural enterprises (6.6 percent of the total) are joint-stock cooperatives (*gufen hezuo zhi*). These joint-stock cooperatives, together with the individual household businesses, put the number of effectively private rural enterprises to more than 10 million—or half of the total number of rural enterprises in China.[17]

Together, rural enterprises and the contract responsibility system were responsible for a geometric increase in rural income. In fifteen years, from 1978 to 1993, the average per capita rural income expanded by almost seven fold from 134 *yuan* to 931 *yuan*. By 1994, the figure surpassed 1,000 *yuan*.[18]

b. *Urban Enterprises.* In contrast to the rural reforms, reform of the urban sector was not begun in earnest until 1984. In October of that year,[19] the CCP Central Committee admitted that the economic effectiveness of the urban economy was "very low" because the state had "exercised excessive and rigid control" over the industrial sector and had totally neglected the "regulatory role of the market." As a consequence, the urban sector suffered from "irrational" prices, major intersectoral imbalances, overall declines in factor productivity, and distorted wages.

Although urban reforms did not begin until 1984, once they were initiated, they quickly assumed momentum. There are two types of privately-owned businesses in the cities, depending on the source of funding. There are domestic-funded businesses, and foreign-funded or "three-capital enterprises" (*sanzi qiye*). Both domestic- and foreign-funded enterprises are allowed to pursue profits, respond to market signals, and sell in a relatively unrestricted environment.

The domestic-funded privately-owned businesses in China are further subdivided into two types: "individual household" businesses (*geti hu*) and "private enterprises" (*suren qiye*). The two subtypes are distinguished only by the maximum allowable number of employees: an individual household business can employ no more than eight workers; whereas a private enterprise is allowed to have more than eight employees.

In the decade between 1978 and 1988, the number of registered domestic-funded privately-owned businesses grew by a phenomenal 145 times, from 100,000 to 14.5 million.[20] By June 1994, the number of individual household businesses had increased to 18.875 million, employing a total of almost 32 million workers.[21] As for the private enterprises, they numbered 631,000 by the end of 1995, employing some 53 million people. Their total output value of 230 billion *yuan* ($27.6 billion) was 4 percent of the gross domestic product (GDP)—a value that is expected to increase by 50 percent per year to 13 trillion *yuan* by 2000. At that time, the contribution of China's private enterprises to national income may equal that of the state sector.[22]

As for the foreign-funded enterprises, they are subdivided into three types. There are the Chinese-foreign joint investment ventures, Chinese-foreign cooperatives, and wholly foreign-owned enterprises. Official statistics put the total number of all foreign-funded enterprises at more than 170,000 by the end of 1993.[23]

In addition to the private and foreign enterprises, the cities have also seen an expansion of collectively owned enterprises that employed 36.2 million workers by the end of 1992.[24] Altogether, the collective, private, and foreign enterprises have become the most dynamic sector of the Chinese economy, accounting for about 70 percent of the nation's industrial growth—all without a penny of investment from the state.[25] In eleven years, from 1980 to 1991, the proportion of China's GNP which came from the collective economy increased from 23.5 percent to 36.9 percent. By the year 2000, that share is expected to increase to 47.7 percent. As for the private economy, including the foreign-invested businesses, its share of the country's GNP rose from 0.5 percent to 11.8 percent during the same period, and will be 25.1 percent by 2000. [26] Taxes generated from China's private economy already accounted for 11.5 percent of total state revenues in 1994.[26] In some provinces, such as Sichuan, a fifth of provincial-government revenues came from the private sector.[27]

The Open Door Policy

Another important feature of post-Mao reforms was the Party's decision in December 1978 to open the People's Republic to intercourse with the global economy.[28] Once the decision was made, it became apparent that the coastal regions of China were best situated to exploit the opportunities provided by the new policy. In contrast to the interior, the coastal regions had a more developed infrastructure and ready access to imported resources and capital goods. All of which made the coast ideal for the rapid expansion of labor-intensive export production.

Beginning in 1979 and through the 1980s, "special economic zones," "open door cities," and "special open areas" were created along the coast where export-oriented enterprises began to flourish, fueled by infusions of foreign capital, skills and technology. To make them attractive to foreign investors, the SEZs and open areas offered tariff and tax incentives and imitated, in varying degrees, the freedoms of market economies.

The open door policy brought enormous benefits in terms of foreign investment, technology transfer, increased employment and expertise, as well as foreign exchange earnings. By June 1993, according to official statistics, more than 130,000 foreign enterprises were operating in China, representing 146 countries and regions of the world.[30] Foreign direct investment increased from $4 billion in 1989 to $33.6 billion in 1994.[31] China's bilateral trade rose from $20.64 billion in 1978 to $235 billion in 1995, making it the sixth largest trading nation in the world. The dollar value of the PRC's foreign-exchange-earning exports increased 574 percent in thirteen years, from $14.8 billion in 1979 to $85 billion in 1992. By August 1996, those exports had accumulated a foreign reserve of a record $85 billion, providing "a comfortable cushion" for the PRC's further development.[32]

The Limits of Reform

Despite the many capitalist features that were introduced into post-Mao China, important differences still distinguish the People's Republic from market economies. To begin with, state-owned property and enterprises still constitute the core of the Chinese economy. In 1991, the state-owned sector of the economy produced 53.3 percent of China's GNP.[33] This enables the Communist Party to maintain that, despite the introduction of capitalist features, China remains a "socialist market system."

The persistence of the state economy also marks the limits of Deng Xiaoping's reforms. Excluded from reform are fundamental capitalist principles of private property (most importantly, the private ownership of land), and a rational pricing system. These have not been part of Deng's economic reforms because of the threat they could pose to the political monopoly of the Chinese Communist Party. The restoration

of private land ownership, especially of farmland, is anathema to reformist China because it would give a significant measure of autonomy
and power to the people, thereby rendering them much less subject to
the control of the government. The introduction of a rational pricing
system, for its part, would mean the demise of state planning. That, in
turn, would threaten the employment security of the millions who staff
the state and Party bureaucracies. Any major increase in bureaucratic
unemployment could very well breed critical discontent, thereby jeop-
ardizing political stability and the Party's hold on power.

Private land ownership and a rational pricing system thus mark the
limits of reform in China, so that Communist power and rule are
preserved. Those limits also enabled Deng to insist that his reformed
system was still socialist, albeit one "with Chinese characteristics."
Socialism, as he defined it, meant "common property" and the "predominance of public ownership."

The Pricing System

Early in the reform process, both Deng and the Party did recognize
the importance of price reform. They admitted that pricing was "a
most effective means of regulation," that rational prices constituted
"an important condition" for ensuring a "dynamic" economy, and that
price reform was "the key to reform of the entire economic structure."[34]

But the a priori constraints placed on reform meant that meaningful
price and wage reforms proved very difficult to undertake because the
Party was not ready to grapple with the implications of a genuinely
"rational" pricing system.[35] Rational pricing would reveal the intrinsic
inefficiencies of the state-owned and state-run sector.[36] Redundancies
would be evident, and excess and inefficient workers would have to be
dismissed, adding to the general problem of unemployment.

Price reform ultimately settled on a hodgepodge solution. Instead of
a uniform system of rational pricing, a three-tiered pricing system was
instituted. There were the planned prices that were fixed by theoretical, functional, and administrative considerations; prices that were allowed to fluctuate between bureaucratically fixed limits; and market-
determined equilibrium prices. In effect, some prices would be entirely fixed by the state; other prices would fluctuate between given
limits; still others would be the prices determined by market exchange.[37]

All of which rendered uncertain how planning and the market would interact in the national economy to produce rational pricing.

Among the three groups of prices, perhaps the most curious were the administratively fixed or planned prices. Those prices were conceived to be a function of bureaucratic calculation, using the "law of value" as a guide. Making recourse to the Marxist "law of value," PRC economists maintained that government bureaucrats could "rationally" determine the value of a commodity by estimating the presumably "objective" value of the amount of "socially necessary labor" that went into the production of that commodity. In this manner, Party-state functionaries could justify their continued employment for the foreseeable future, as they were needed to determine the prices of inputs and goods in the state sector of the economy.[38]

But using "socially necessary labor" as a direct measure of value and an indirect determinant of price has many problems. To begin with, prices that are the products of state bureaucrats' "measurement" of "socially necessary labor" are, in principle, irrational because they fail to consider market circumstances. Such prices also systematically fail to include the cost of capital necessary in production. The entire notion of "socially necessary labor" serving as the foundation of prices assumes an evident counterfactual—that is, the same capital-labor ratio obtains in all branches of an economy and needs not be part of the calculations.[39] For these reasons, administratively fixed prices can depart significantly from market values. To make up that difference, the state would have to provide price subsidies that constitute a significant drain on the national treasury. In 1989, for example, price subsidies consumed nearly 13 percent of state income in China (37.034 billion *yuan* out of a total of 292.92 billion *yuan*).[40]

The disabling consequences of planned prices were amply discovered in the Soviet Union. There, the effort to rationalize prices by resorting to the Marxist "law of value" was an all-but-total failure. It proved ineffectual in eliminating all the ills of the socialist economy that reform was meant to redress in the first place. Invoking the Marxist "law of value" to determine prices did not rectify the persisting sectoral imbalances, low labor productivity, poor product mix, inferior quality, waste of resources, proliferation of nonperforming assets, and slow turnover of capital.[41] In effect, this kind of "reform" of the pricing system would only reintroduce allocative dysfunctions and distributive anomalies into the Chinese national economy.

The Persistence of State Planning

The fact that a major part of the economy was to continue to be governed by planned prices ensured that the Party-state would remain the critical player in the day-to-day functioning of the Chinese economy. Whatever confusion that was created by a three-tiered system of pricing seemed to have been offset by the promise of security extended to Party cadres and government functionaries, some 36 million of whom reportedly had felt threatened by the reforms.[42] Their insecurity and general anxiety clearly acted as a powerful constraint on system reform.

The daunting character of central-planning reform is evident in the many failed efforts of the Party to adapt China's vast bureaucracy to the demands of the changing economy. As an example, in spring of 1993, Vice Premier Zhu Rongji recommended a major administrative restructuring and downsizing that would mean the dismissal of nearly two-thirds of those in government service. The very prospect of such a hemorrhage of cadre and staff generated an immediate counterproposal by State Council Secretary Luo Gan. Luo's alternative plan involved changes in administrative offices and a reduction in the number of specialized economic departments—but with few dismissals. In the final restructuring, job loss was suffered by less than 1 million state employees.[43] Zhu's proposal became yet another failed effort at reforming the unwieldy bureaucracy. More than ten years after major agricultural and industrial reform had begun, the Communist Party still could not deal with the prospect of alienating its millions of dependents. China was to remain "socialist," operationally defined as "planning" in accordance with the Marxist-Leninist tradition and Deng's own stipulation.

Just as there was a great deal of uncertainty as to what "rational" prices would be, uncertainty also surrounded the character and scope of planning in reformist China. Some PRC economists originally held that planning under the new dispensation could be indicative, wherein broad outlines and general strategies would be provided by the central government, and control would be exercised largely through tax and tariff incentives.[44]

Other Chinese economists insisted that "a socialist country can and must plan its economy" and that the "public sector" must remain in the "dominant position" in the national economy. China was to have a "scientifically" elaborated "single national economic plan" that would be relatively centralized, mandatory, and specific. At the same time, however, China was to avoid an "all-inclusive plan" that set "arbitrary targets" because this method had proved "impracticable" under Mao.[45] State planning must be made compatible with the goal of enterprise autonomy because "an enterprise . . . can usually judge its own needs better than the authorities in charge of allocation" and must, therefore, be given "the freedom to negotiate with its suppliers" in terms of quality and price.[46]

The views of this second group of economists came to be favored by the Communist Party. State planning in reformist China would provide "overall guidance" for "major economic activities." "Major economic activities," however, included such things as "the rate of growth; the balance between the major economic spheres; the scale and regional distribution of capital construction, investment allocation, major projects and the rate of improvement of living standards." "Overall guidance," for its part, included maintaining "balance between finance, credit, materials and foreign exchange. . . ."[47] In effect, the state's "overall guidance" of "major economic activities" would be comprehensive, limiting the range of enterprise initiative in every way. The short- and long-term supply of resources, materials, and capital would be fixed and invariable in its essentials. Under such circumstances, it is hard to imagine how any of the constituent productive units might act autonomously to set prices, decide how much to produce, and distribute goods.

State-Owned Enterprises (SOEs)

Since the "public sector" was to be "in the dominant position" of the economy, the state-owned enterprises were retained. But if the reform of the economy were to be successful in any objective fashion, their performance would have to be improved, not only because of the SOEs' dominance over the economy but because of their notorious waste and inefficiency.

China's SOEs are estimated to number 108,000.[48] According to the government's National Statistics Bureau, anywhere from a half to two-thirds of all SOEs are in the red.[49] To keep them operating requires enormous state subsidies that inflict unsustainable burdens on the national treasury. A PRC economist, Xue Muqiao, estimated the subsidies to total 60 billion *yuan* per year, the equivalent of more than 20 percent of total state revenue in 1989.[50] A more recent account, in 1995, claimed that as much as 60 percent of China's growing budget deficit could be accounted for by the subsidies to shore up losing SOEs.[51]

Given their inefficiency, it is not surprising that the SOEs' share of the national industrial output is shrinking, decreasing from almost 80 percent in the late-1970s to 48 percent in 1995.[52] Non-state enterprises accounted for 93 percent of China's industrial growth in the first quarter of 1994, while SOEs accounted for only 6.6 percent of that growth.[53]

There are few economists in the People's Republic who fail to understand what reform of the state enterprises requires.[54] Although the problem was recognized at the outset of Deng Xiaoping's reforms, it was only in 1986 that a general bankruptcy law was passed which would provide for the closing of losing enterprises. It was hoped that by allowing unprofitable SOEs to close, the system would become more competitive and self-regulating, and increased labor mobility would contribute to overall system efficiency and productivity.

In a market-governed economy, consistent failure to return a profit on investment would condemn enterprises to extinction. But that was not to be the case in the "socialist market economy" patched together on mainland China. Despite the bankruptcy law, "only a handful" of China's losing SOEs actually folded.[55] By the end of 1993, almost seven years after the law's promulgation, only 940 SOEs had actually ceased operation.[56]

The reasons for the impotence of the bankruptcy law are not difficult to understand. Simply put, the leaders of the People's Republic are between the proverbial rock and a hard place. They are aware that inefficient SOEs act as a drag on system efficiency and modernization. But pressing political considerations weigh against closing state enterprises. Even without closing a single SOE, each year there are 10 million new entrants into China's labor force. Add to this number those who are seeking re-employment, and the total number of job seekers swells to 18.6 million a year.[57] In the countryside, the 130 million surplus laborers in 1994 will increase to 200 million by the year 2000.[58] Allowing losing SOEs to go bankrupt would only contribute millions more to the existing "floating population" of millions seeking employment in the already stressed coastal cities.[59] Nor could the new private sector be expected to absorb all who might be released from bankrupt SOEs, as evidenced by the fact that in 1992, only 200,000 former SOE workers secured employment in the private sector.[60] It comes as no surprise, therefore, that 20 percent of 50,000 SOE workers who were surveyed in 1993 by the official National Labor Union opposed meaningful SOE reform.[61]

The reality is that the state enterprises, with 108 million employees, are responsible for the livelihood of three out of every four urban workers in China. When the workers' families are included in the calculation, the total number of those who are dependent on the SOEs for their livelihood swells to about 340 million—a third of China's total population.[62] Assuming that at least half of China's SOEs are unprofitable, their closing would mean that 54 million workers would be threatened with unemployment. When their dependents are included, the number of people who would face hardship increases to 170 million—a figure that is more than 64 percent of the population of the United States!

It is not just SOE managers and workers who are opposed to shutting down losing enterprises, opposition also comes from banks and local governments because of their entanglement in the web of "triangular debts."[63] The SOEs, banks, local governments, and other players are linked to each other in a "steadily spreading gridlock" of intercorporate debt, estimated to total 600 billion *yuan* in 1995—a sum that is the equivalent of a third of China's annual industrial output.[64] In this interlocking chain of debt, if player A were to go bankrupt, it would default on its debt to player B, who would, in turn, default on its debt to player C, and so on. This is why it serves the interest of everyone involved to keep losing SOEs afloat.

There are still more reasons that work against the closing of unprofitable SOEs. To begin with, reducing the role of the state-owned sector in the national economy would mean a corresponding reduction in the role and scope of power of the Party-state. Enterprise bankruptcy would also create special capital loss problems for the economy. Bankruptcy normally constitutes a means of settling accounts between a creditor and his debtors. But in the "socialist market economy" of China which lacks an independent secondary market for the assets of bankrupt SOEs, it is uncertain how a responsible evaluation of enterprise assets might be undertaken.[65] Without an independent secondary market, there would be few ways to salvage those assets. Since the SOEs were established by the state and their continuity assured by subsidies from the state, bankruptcy would mean that the state would have to absorb the losses, unless the government was prepared to see state properties find their way into the non-state sector through improper sale and transfer.[66]

More pernicious still is the fact that not only are there disincentives to closing non-performing SOEs, there are few incentives to make them more efficient by trimming redundant or surplus labor estimated to comprise 30 percent (32.4 million) of all SOE workers. Just the attempt at greater efficiency through rationalizing labor utilization would add greatly to the ranks of the unemployed.[67] Additionally, decentralizing and downsizing SOEs to maximize efficiency could also exacerbate the growing autonomy of local and regional units, in conflict with central power and policies.

The fact of the matter is that political considerations counsel against any meaningful effort to improve the state-owned industries. Almost any genuine effort at reform—be it bankruptcy, downsizing, or restructuring—would increase the number of unemployed and easily create the instability that could threaten the entire program of modernization, not to mention the survival of the Communist Party government. As PRC President and Party Chief Jiang Zemin put it, "We must not force the workers to the streets."[68] This is why, as late as 1995, only about 1,000 Chinese firms had gone bankrupt, "fewer than half of them state-owned and almost all of them small."[69] Given all this, it is not surprising that in 1994, having learned from his failed effort of the previous year to trim the bloated state bureaucracy, Vice Premier Zhu Rongji made very clear that the construction of a "modernized business system atop the state enterprise base" would not be undertaken at the expense of the workers or the state.[70]

Since meaningful SOE reform is politically unpalatable, the Communist Party has sought recourse instead in the "Regulation on the Transformation of State Enterprises," passed by the State Council in 1992 and intended to promote enterprise efficiency. The new rule theoretically separates SOE ownership from management by devolving authority to enterprise managers who are now responsible for profits and losses in exchange for a freer hand in matters concerning personnel, finance, exports, and imports.[71] At the same time, the enterprises could retain a greater share of their profits than in the past. That share was 7.9 percent in 1979, but increased dramatically to 17.6 percent in 1980 and 43.2 percent in 1987.[72]

It was hoped that giving more autonomy to enterprise managers would improve SOE performance. As Vice Premier Zhu put it in a speech in 1995, the problem with state firms is not state ownership per se, but simply bad management.[73] Indeed, a government survey of 2,586 losing SOEs in 1993 found that poor management contributed to the losses of 2,101 enterprises (or 81 percent of the total sample), 33 percent of which (or 697 enterprises) had management as the sole cause for their dismal performance. But improving the quality of managers is not simply a matter of increased autonomy but of enhancing those managers' general education and specific training in modern managerial principles and techniques. Today, only 12 percent of China's SOE managers have a college education, and some 60 percent have only a junior high or lower educational level. Only 13 percent of SOE managers are skilled and a minuscule 0.14 percent can be considered highly skilled.[74]

Another problem is that in an environment in which planned prices distort all judgments and render outcomes arbitrary, the new autonomy of enterprise managers is illusory. As an example, energy costs in China do not reflect market prices because state subsidies reduce the direct costs to consumers. As a consequence there is no incentive to conserve, so that Chinese industries' energy utilization efficiency is very low. China's energy consumption per unit of GNP was six times that of Japan in 1994.[75] Similar distortions afflict the entire system.

There is another problem still. At the same time that the SOEs are expected to reduce waste, enhance efficiency, and maintain quality controls, they are also mandated by the state to meet the social, medical, and sometimes the educational needs of their workers and their families. The SOEs were created not just for productive purposes, they were conceived to be the basic unit for dispensing social welfare.[76] These social welfare responsibilities are enormously expensive and increasingly burdensome in an economy enduring double-digit inflation. To make enterprise managers responsible for profit and loss in such circumstances is not only unfair, but ignores the real problems inherent in a system of irrational pricing and comprehensive state planning.[77]

Given all this, it is not surprising that the effort to reform SOEs through the grant of greater management autonomy has not worked. Official PRC statistics show that the return from SOEs has been dropping steadily, from 11.8 percent in 1985 to 1.9 percent in 1993. Despite the government's efforts at reform, enterprise efficiency has continued to erode throughout the entire period of reform.[78] The situation seems to deteriorate by the year, with SOEs "haemorrhaging even more money" in 1996 than 1995. For every dollar that China's industrial enterprises made in profit during the first six months in 1996, only one cent came from the SOEs.[79] It is very unlikely that the reforms required to render the Chinese economy modern and efficient will be systematically implemented any time in the foreseeable future. As long as the Communist Party remains in power, state-owned assets will remain the established core of China's "socialist market economy," and those assets will continue to be supervised by managers who will, for all intents and purposes, be confined by the parameters of the state plan.

Other Ills of the "Socialist Market Economy"

The politically expedient decision, on the part of the Chinese Communist Party, to graft capitalism onto an established socialist economic core has produced other problems besides an irrational pricing system and deadwood SOEs. These are the ills that are directly spawned from the reforms that have created the jerry-built "socialist market economy" of Deng Xiaoping. Well-meaning though they may be, government reforms sometimes create more problems than are solved because bureaucrats and officials cannot possibly anticipate every nuance and effect of their policy interventions. This has to do with what economists call "the law of unintended consequences"—the best of interventions in an economy often have harmful unintended side effects. "[I]n the long run, the aggregate of decisions of individual businessmen, exercising individual judgment in a free economy, even if often mistaken, is less likely to do harm than the centralized decisions of a government; and certainly the harm is likely to be counteracted faster."[80]

In the case of China's "socialist market economy," the very reforms that were meant to cure the ills of socialism have given rise to unforeseen side-effects that threaten more and more to overcome the entire system. Reform's unintended consequences are social, economic, demographic, ecological, as well as political.

Social Problems

Reformed China is a country of contradictions. Amidst the growing prosperity, an increasing variety of social ills is being spawned. The Communist Party's economic reforms and liberalization were accompanied by a considerable loosening of its totalitarian controls over individual lives. Except for the relatively few political dissidents who openly criticize the government, by and large, life for the Chinese citizen has become measurably freer. But the new social freedoms come at a cost, one of which is an ever-increasing crime rate.

a. *Crime.* Despite periodic anti-crime campaigns, the crime rate increases every year.[81] As a case in point, major crimes of murder, rape, and armed robbery rose by 20 percent from 1993 to 1994.[82] Other crimes have also proliferated. These include prostitution; the illicit sale of drugs and guns; the kidnapping and sale of women and children; smuggling; piracy; and counterfeiting.

In 1993, for example, there were more than 1,740 cases of kidnapping and sale of women and children in Guangxi province. That province ranked second in the People's Republic, after Sichuan, in the incidence of kidnapping.[83] *Newsweek* reported in April 1992 that each year, some 10,000 women and children in Sichuan were kidnapped and sold to northern Thailand's prostitution industry.[84]

As for counterfeiting, more than foreign goods and brand name products are being affected. In 1989, the authorities uncovered 325 cases of fake currency, involving one million yuan. Counterfeit currency circulates in almost every province of China.[85] Criminals regularly disguise themselves as policemen and soldiers in fake uniforms with fake badges and insignia, driving vehicles with stolen official licenses, and armed with unlicensed guns and bullets.[86]

More than that, passengers traveling on China's major railroads are no longer secure, and are subject to robbery by roving bands of peasant bandits.[87] Criminals in uniforms and village thugs have set up private toll gates and checkpoints to fleece motorists. Along the roadways of towns and villages, residents behind boom gates extract "road tax" levies from every passing vehicle.[88]

Theft of public property by citizens seems to have become pandemic. Stolen items include manhole covers in city streets, electricity, railroad cargo, and public facilities such as railway cables, signs, and phones. Between 1992 and 1994, for example, the Weizhou railroad reported the theft of some 3,700 parts.[89]

Even more troubling is the admission by the official Xinhua News Agency that criminal activities have become organized. An internal report of the Public Security Bureau in 1991 recognized that an organized criminal underworld had assumed "embryonic form" and was responsible for as much as a third of all crimes in 1993. Organized crime is already a reality in some parts of China, such as Heilongjiang and Harbin.[90] Criminal groups are described as being tightly organized, led by some of China's newly rich, with large memberships comprised of former prisoners. Some groups are branches of established criminal organizations in Hong Kong and Taiwan; others are indigenous; still others are "joint ventures" between foreign and domestic criminals. Most of China's criminal organizations mimic the secret societies of dynastic China in name, internal structure, as well as rituals.[91] Some groups are so powerful that they are determining the results of local elections and interfering in public affairs and have become, in effect, a second government.[92]

b. *Peasant Unrest*. Aside from crime, China's 900 million peasants who still make up 80 percent of the country's population[93] are growing restive. Although peasant income increased by an annual average of 15.9 percent from 1979 to 1984, the rate of increase decreased to only 3.8 percent after 1990—in contrast to the boom being experienced in the cities. At the same time, the peasants have seen their purchasing power eroded by steep increases in the cost of fertilizers (400 to 500 percent) and food. Government benefits have also been drastically curtailed. Before 1979, for example, 100 percent of rural workers had medical insurance; only 20 percent are covered today.[94]

More than all that, peasant disaffection is fueled by their treatment at the hands of local cadres and officials. To begin with, local governments have been laggardly in paying for the peasants' mandatory grain sales. Those sales are *de facto* land rent exacted by the contract responsibility system. More often than not, peasants are compensated with IOUs instead of cash.

Local authorities have also engaged in extortionist extraction, in contravention of the central government's explicit injunction that taxes on China's peasants could not exceed 5 percent of their income. In addition to national taxes, the peasants must also pay for an increasing array of local taxes and fees. There were fees for those who violated the one-child-per-couple policy; for electricity; for garbage; for rat extermination; for various construction projects; and even for having a dog. One local fee to build an elementary school in Hainan amounted to 6 percent of peasant income. Altogether, in 1991, the average peasant's tax-and-fee burden amounted to 11.8 percent of their income. In some places, the burden was 30–50 percent.[95]

All of which led to a rising incidence of peasant unrest. In 1991, in just one province (Shanxi), there were 110 collective appeals by peasants to higher authorities for a redress of their grievances; that number increased to over 160 in 1992.[96] In 1992, nine provinces experienced over 100 incidents of peasant demonstrations, protests, and attacks on local governments. The situation deteriorated further in 1993. In the first five months of 1993, there were more than 170 incidents of peasant disturbances, including some 50 incidents that involved attacks, burning, and occupation of local government offices; 25 incidents where roads and railways were obstructed; and over 30 cases that involved violence and bodily injuries.[97]

The most serious of the peasant riots took place in 1993 in Renshou *xian* (county) in Sichuan, a major rice-producing province of China. Renshou is situated in an arid but arable region where 93 percent of the population are farmers who must make do with an average per capita arable land availability of only 0.98 *mou* (0.147 acre), and an average per capita income in 1992 of only 470 *yuan*. Chafing under the burden of local fees, Renshou's peasants rioted in January 1993, setting fire to a government vehicle and surrounding local government offices. The riot lasted for more than seventy days, and was followed by an even more serious incident that began in May when peasants attacked cadres, tore down houses, and threw rocks at government buildings. When four peasant leaders were arrested on June 6, hundreds of peasants surrounded the local officials and had to be dispersed with tear gas. On June 7, some 10,000 peasants converged on the local government building; the next day, their numbers grew to 15,000. By that time, the peasants were joined by college students from the surrounding area. What began as a peasant riot threatened to escalate into a student movement as well. The riot finally came to an end only when Beijing acceded to the peasants' wishes by releasing eight of their leaders, abolishing excessive local fees, and dismissing four local officials.[98]

According to a report issued in May 1993 by the State Council, in all these disturbances, peasants not only attacked government buildings but looted state property, taking seeds, fertilizer, farm machinery, tools, and consumer goods. Some of the disturbances had the active participation of local cadres and officials who helped plan and incite the riots. "Anti-government elements" from the cities infiltrated some of the villages and assisted in the planning of riots as well as the creation of illegal autonomous organizations. More than that, peasant unrest was becoming organized and armed. In some areas, peasants had formed their own village committees, militias and courts, openly challenging the government and advocating its overthrow.[99]

Despite Beijing's explicit instruction, after the riots of 1993, reducing local fees and taxes by a half, that instruction is being regularly ignored. This has resulted in continuing conflicts between peasants and officials. Peasants who were unable to pay the extortionary fees have been severely fined, physically abused, and even executed; some committed suicide.[100] Peasant discontent erupted in a major riot that began in August 1996 in Buyunqiao village in Hunan province, where tens of thousands of peasants, joined by students, converged on the village government and held local officials hostage. Thousands of armed police were dispatched to suppress the riot with tear gas, in the course of which "several tens" of people were injured or killed.[101]

c. *Labor Unrest.* At the same time, China's industrial workers are also increasingly restless. Between 1992 and 1993, the number of labor wage disputes rose by 51.6 percent.[102] Hong Kong newspapers estimated that some 200 labor riots and more than 6,000 strikes took place in 1993.[103] The PRC State Council reported that, in just one month in 1994 (April), thirty-three cities in seventeen provinces experienced labor protests that involved gunfire, bombing, as well as organized efforts to overthrow the state.[104] Workers protested against high inflation, reform of the state enterprises, and the Dickensian conditions that are particularly prevalent in privately-owned businesses.[105] The official *China Daily* admitted that one out of every ten manufacturing workers must endure dangerous working conditions. Those conditions were responsible for an average of fifty-four deaths a day in 1993 from industrial fires, poison, and explosion.[106]

Labor unrest seems to be spreading across China. In early 1994, workers who went on strike included 20,000 coal miners in

Heilongjiang; 6,900 workers in a Japanese auto plant in Liaoning; and 300 handicapped workers in Beijing whose demonstration turned violent. A PRC official and labor expert in Tianjin said that "The labor problem is like dry tinder. All it takes is for someone to start a fire, and it will become widespread."[107]

Economic Problems

What makes the assortment of social, economic, ecological, demographic, and political problems particularly challenging is that they are interconnected. China's social problems are, in part, due to its economic troubles.

a. *Inflation.* To begin with, inflation has been a recurring problem since reform began, fluctuating around a national average of about 25 percent per annum.[108] Each period of high inflation has been followed by a government-enforced belt-tightening to cool down the economy by suppressing the flow and availability of capital. Double-digit inflation was one of the grievances that animated the demonstrators at Tiananmen Square and all across China in 1989.

Inflationary pressures stem directly from the mixed economy of "socialism with Chinese characteristics." The growth of the collective, private, and foreign-invested sectors of the economy increased employment opportunities. At the same time, the state-owned enterprises could retain more and more of their profits, part of which went to increased wages and benefits for workers. All of which meant increases in personal income, purchasing power, as well as the amount of money in circulation. But the economy is still one that is dominated by inefficient and underperforming SOEs that do not adequately meet consumer demands. As an example, although the number of Chinese auto plants exceeds the world average, China's national output in numbers of automobile is less than that of General Motors or Toyota.[109] As long as the Chinese economy continues to grow at a high rate while retaining its inefficient state sector, inflationary pressures will probably persist, depressing the purchasing power of fixed-wage earners and creating challenges for government planners.

b. *The Poor.* Aside from inflation, another economic problem is the very poor in China. The World Bank reported in 1993 that more than

100 million Chinese (one-tenth of the population) still endured lives of grinding poverty.[110] Poverty was defined in 1989 by the Chinese government as an average annual per capita income of $54 or less.[111] The World Bank estimated that a third of China's poor lacked basic food and warmth, while the remaining two-thirds lived a "marginal existence."[112]

A particularly vivid portrait of China's poor was provided by a reporter for the *Toronto Global Post* who visited Gansu province in 1989. According to that report, 40 percent of the people in Gansu lacked clothing and food. Some were so poor that a family owned only one pair of pants. Because of the province's aridity, villagers often must rely on water transported in by government vehicles. A local cadre said that in areas that were inaccessible to government vehicles, villagers sometimes had to wash with their urine.[113]

China's problem of enduring poverty is complicated by rural-urban disparities, as well as regional-ethnic inequities. Despite the increased prosperity made possible by the economic reforms, that prosperity is not equally distributed across the country. A recent survey by the Institute of Public Opinion of the Chinese People's University in Beijing found that although only 1.2 percent of *urban* dwellers earned an average annual per capita income of less than 1200 *yuan* (about $144), more than 26 percent of *rural* residents had that low income. The survey also found that 2.8 percent of city residents could claim an average annual per capita income of over 18,000 *yuan* ($2,160)—a level of income which no one in the countryside enjoyed.[114] Not only are China's poor more prevalent in the villages, they are also concentrated in the central and western regions where the minority nationalities reside. Their poverty, when contrasted with the relative prosperity of the dominant Han national group, contributes to the rising discontent and disquietude of China's minorities.

c. *Unemployment and the Mobile Population.* Nor does it appear that the poor could expect relief from the economic reforms. Despite the mushrooming of privately owned businesses since 1979, unemployed workers seem to be finding it more and more difficult to secure work. The percentage of the jobless who managed to find new employment declined from 60 percent in 1991 to 40 percent in 1992.[115] From 1995 to 1996, the number of the unemployed increased by 14.6 percent in counties and townships and by 0.2 percent in the cities.[116]

Government statistics claimed an overall unemployment figure of 200 million or 20 percent of the adult population. This figure of 200 million is deceptive because it does not include China's hidden unemployment—those SOE workers who are not being paid, as well as the estimated 80 million peasants who had left their rural homes to roam the coastal cities in search of work.[117] Those wandering peasants add to China's "floating population" of migrant laborers who altogether may total an astounding 120 million.[118] That mobile population taxes overburdened infrastructures, exacerbates the already alarming rates of crime and general disorder, and is recognized as "a potential source of unrest" by government leaders.[119]

The sizeable number of the unemployed is a powerful constraint on the government's oft-stated intention that it would reform the inefficient state-owned enterprises. Already, some 10 percent of SOE workers are either not being paid on time or not paid at all. Even without closing down unprofitable SOEs, government statistics had the urban unemployment rate increasing from 2.6 percent to 3 percent in 1994. That would mean an additional 5 million unemployed, 1.8 million of whom would require government assistance.[120]

Demographic Problems

a. *Overpopulation.* China's poverty and unemployment are, in part, due to its overpopulation. The population of the People's Republic now exceeds 1.2 billion—22 percent or one-fifth of the world's population—and is increasing by 14 million every year. By 2030, China will have 1.6 billion people. Already, the People's Republic is no longer self-sufficient in grain production and must rely on imports. By that same year, assuming a 1994 per capita grain consumption level, China will require the annual importation of 305 million tons of foodgrains—105 million tons more than the current annual world grain export total of 200 million tons.[121]

b. *Gender Imbalance.* More than simple overpopulation, China's demographics also suffer from a serious gender imbalance, an unintended consequence of government efforts to curb population growth. Beginning in 1979, after decades of Mao's promotion of large families, the Communist Party instigated a population control policy that limits couples to only one child.

But in a culture where sons are still preferred over daughters, couples who are restricted to only one child sometimes resort to the abortion and even infanticide of females. An estimated 12 percent of females never enter the population because of such practices,[122] resulting in a gender birth ratio in China of 114 males to 100 females, a decided deviation from the worldwide average of 105:100. In 1992, a national survey revealed that gender imbalance plagued every province in China. In Hunan, for example, the number of males exceeded that of females by 2.5 million.[123] The nationwide figure could be as much as 52 million in 1993—almost the population of France.[124] In the 25 to 49 age group, the number of males was fifteen times that of females in 1992.[125] By the year 2000, the Shanghai newspaper *Wenhui bao* reckoned that China will have a surplus of 70 million young men who, given the preponderance of young males in criminal activities, could become "a great army of hoodlums" and criminals.[126]

Ecological Problems

China's overpopulation, combined with "a monolithic preoccupation with economic growth,"[127] could only further degrade its environmental conditions. The PRC's grasslands are disappearing from excessive grazing. At the present rate of lumber cutting, China's forests will be totally depleted in seven to eight years. Soil erosion presently affects 38.2 percent of the country's total surface, resulting in an annual rate of desertification of 100 square kilometers, as well as loss of arable land of 19.5 million acres in the past forty years in a country where arable land is already in short supply.[128]

Due in part to its reliance on the indigenous "dirty" coal for fuel, the People's Republic has the dubious distinction of having 5 of the world's 20 most polluted cities.[129] Some 500 Chinese cities have air quality that is "unacceptable" and are no longer visible to satellites. In 1992, the PRC produced 728 million tons of carbon emissions, second only to the United States' production of 1.3 billion tons—this in a country that is not yet fully industrialized! By 2030, China's emissions would reach 2 billion tons.[130] As a consequence, respiratory disease occurs at five times the rate in the United States and is the leading cause of death in China's urban areas.[140]

All across China, from the northeast to the southwest, the country is afflicted with acid rain. A Japanese study indicated that as much as 30 percent of the acid rain that fell on western Japan was traceable to sulfur dioxide emissions from coal burning in China. One Western estimate was that Chinese sulfur dioxide emissions will exceed those of the industrial world by 2035. Production of ozone-eating substances in China could more than double 1991 levels by the end of the decade. In Baotou in China's Inner Mongolian Autonomous Region, the colorless hydrogen fluoride pumped by state-owned industries into the air has left the local population with brittle bones and brittle teeth.[132]

Sixty percent of Chinese cities endure chronic water shortage. Nationwide, there is no proper disposal of industrial toxins, so that, in the case of Shanghai alone, the drinking water of its 13 million residents is contaminated with oil, ammonia, nitrogen, and other potentially dangerous organic compounds. An estimated 80 percent of the country's industrial and domestic waste is discharged, untreated, into rivers.[133] In 1991, about 25 billion tons of industrial pollutants were dumped into China's waterways, creating more toxic water pollution than in the entire Western world. The result is that every river in China is polluted, with at least two rivers (the Huai and the Liao) so polluted that their water is black and odorous.[134]

Altogether, pollution is costing the Chinese economy an estimated $11.87 billion per year or 6.75 percent of the GDP. (The comparable figure for the industrialized nations is 3 to 5 percent of the GDP.)[135] Even more than pollution's economic costs, the grim statistics that chronicle China's ecological damage also "portend a potential disaster of global proportions."[136]

Political Problems

All of these problems will have to be confronted by the successor(s) to Deng Xiaoping who, for all his vaunted economic reforms, neglected to implement meaningful reform of the political system. Deng left behind a political system that is grievously lacking in institutionalization and the rule of law.

a. *Political Succession.* The very fact that Deng, a feeble elderly man[137] who had not occupied any formal political office for years, was considered "the paramount leader" of China is indicative of how power is still determined by personalities rather than formal rules and procedures. The fact that no sinologist can predict with certainty who will securely succeed Deng means that China still lacks an institutionalized procedure to resolve its most critical political task—that of succession as the de facto leader of the Party and state. Nor does it help that at stake is more than the personal succession to Deng. His death on February 19, 1997 also meant the passing away of the founding generation of the Chinese Communist Party. In effect, China now faces both a personal as well as a generational succession problem at a time when communism, as a political system and ideology, is a dying ember in the world.

All of which points to the inherent fragility of this political system. China's misfortune is that it should be fragile at a time when it must confront daunting and possibly intractable problems. And all of these problems will have to confronted and resolved by a party-state that has become weakened, corrupt, demoralized, and geographically fractionalized.

b. *Regionalism.* As part of its effort to free the economy of its productive capabilities, Beijing devolved some of its powers to officials at the lower levels. Once power was devolved, however, the process took on its own momentum. Local and provincial authorities are becoming increasingly independent and defiant of the central government. The signs are increasingly evident.

Rich coastal cities like Shanghai and Guangzhou "operate pretty much as they please." Local-provincial officials regularly shortchange the central government in the taxes they collect. They set their own economic targets, court foreign investors, establish financial institutions such as banks without Beijing's permission or approval, and even raise internal trade barriers against the products of other parts of China.[138]

It is for all these reasons that, in July 1993, Jiang Zemin warned that China would become "a tray of loose sand" and sink into "economic anarchy" if the country were not unified.[139] That same year, in September, an internal Party document held out a bleak prognosis for the country's future. According to that document, if effective measures were not undertaken to suppress the growing local-provincial autonomy, Deng Xiaoping's passing would surely be followed by the disintegration of the People's Republic of China.[140]

c. *Political Corruption.* The growing power of local-provincial governments is accompanied by the increasing moral decay of all levels of government. Political corruption, the abuse of public trust "in the interest of personal and private gain,"[141] has reached alarming proportions. The problem of corruption may be the most destructive of social order and, ultimately, of the political legitimacy of the Communist Party.

China's hybrid economy has given rise to ample opportunities for widespread corruption and malfeasance on the part of government officials and party cadres. Among the many factors that have given rise to corruption, the "irrational price structure" is a major contributor. The failure to fully rationalize the pricing structure in China has created an environment in which corruption is irrepressible.

Deng's "socialist market economy" attempts to accommodate at least two very different pricing systems: planned prices that are predicated on the so-called law of value, and market prices that operate in the non-planned sectors. The problem lies with the state-fixed prices that do not reflect demand and are often lower than market prices. The price differential creates abundant opportunities for bribery, privilege, and personal profit through selective purchase and sale. Party cadres and government functionaries who have access to goods at planned prices can purchase such goods and sell them on the market at equilibrium prices. In the course of that transaction, substantial profits are reaped.

A contributing factor driving up the price differentials between state and market prices comes from the urban private businesses and the rural collective enterprises. These nonstate entities compete at a disadvantage with the state for access to production inputs of raw materials, equipment, and labor. Despite their unprofitability, state-owned enterprises still occupy the "commanding heights" of the economy, hogging all the major resources. In 1992, they accounted for (in revenue terms) 92 percent of power generation; 86 percent of ferrous metals; 72 percent of chemicals; 64 percent of machinery; and 53 percent of textiles.[142] Since the state has priority access to such inputs, the nonstate enterprises must bid up prices to obtain production essentials. Any Party or government functionary who has access to the resources is in a good position to reap personal gain from negotiating with the new entrepreneurs. In the often overheated economy of reformist China, where double-digit inflation is a recurring threat to purchasing power, there is every incentive for government officials and functionaries to supplement their state income with criminal risk-taking. To illustrate, an inflation rate of over 20 percent means that half of what an individual saves disappears after four years.

The irrational pricing system is not the only source of corruption. More seriously, political corruption is an indicator of the erosion of ideology in the Communist Party. Cadres and officials exploit every opportunity for personal gain, behaviors that belie their putative role as the moral vanguards of society. Official corruption assumes many forms. Although the Communist Party had explicitly barred its members from moonlighting in private businesses, the government admitted in 1991 that their numbers were increasing.[143] A popular and widespread form of corruption is the "grey" expenditure: the misuse of public funds and property for private purposes. Public monies are embezzled by officials to invest in private businesses; to speculate in stocks; to construct or purchase homes; or secreted away in personal bank accounts.[144] Public funds, totaling 80 billion *yuan* a year (the equivalent of more than two years' worth of China's outlays for education),[145] are regularly used for officialdom's entertainment—to pay for prostitutes in "dancing halls," for lavish meals in restaurants, and for expenses in nightclubs.[146] In one city alone (Jinzhou in Liaoning province), public funds accounted for 80 to 90 percent of the income of the city's nightclubs, where an estimated 220,000 *yuan* (US $26,400) a day was being squandered by officials.[147]

The most notorious misuse of public funds are the "imperial dinners" that mimic the fares of Chinese emperors. These are elaborate meals that can last several days with menus that include exotic imported animal parts such as Siberian bear paws, Russian deer tails, Mongolian camel humps, and Australian crocodile feet. One restaurant in booming Guangzhou offers three-day imperial dinners with a menu comprised of 108 dishes, some of which are sprinkled with gold dust. The cost of one such dinner, without the gold sprinkles, begins at $3,100.[148] All of this is transpiring while millions of Chinese still live in abject destitution.

Another form of official corruption is the extortionary fees charged by officials for an ever increasing variety of reasons, most of which "often amount to out-and-out bribery." The proliferation of fees charged by rural officials is a prime contributor to the growing peasant disaffection. In the cities, foreign investors are the "fat cows" charged $130 a month for each foreign employee on the payroll and a $1,000 installation fee for each telephone. Reportedly, Fujian provincial government collected about $15 million from investors in 1991 for 6,000 different kinds of fees, donations, and fines.[149]

Even more seriously still is the fact that corruption is corroding the elites of the Party-state. Soldiers and officers of the People's Liberation Army use their clout to speculate in real estate or obtain scarce commodities that are then resold at higher market prices. Some even use military vehicles and naval vessels to smuggle goods ranging from cigarettes to automobiles and airplanes.[150]

The worst offenders are reportedly a select group of political families, collectively referred to as the Big Families or the Princes. These are the children and other relatives of China's living and departed highest leaders—those of Deng Xiaoping, Yang Shangkun, Li Peng, Qiao Shi, Zhao Ziyang, Chen Yun, Peng Zhen, Li Xiannian, Hu Yaobang, Liu Shaoqi, Ye Jianying, Lo Ruixing, and so on.[151] The members of this exclusive club maintain a network of control over trade, commerce, industry, and investment through intermarriage and nepotism.[152] They use their power and connections to speculate in real estate, stocks, imported autos, military weaponry, as well as raw materials such as steel.

Given the pandemic corruption of officialdom, it is not surprising that "economic crimes" appear to have infected everyone in China. State workers "moonlight" in private business ventures on official time. SOEs run taxi fleets, souvenir shops, and supermarkets. Customs officials have created their own clearing and consulting services. The police run their own insurance companies and car repair shops. University professors have branched out into knitwear.[153] Surgeons demand bribes to operate on the sick.[154] Gas and telephone company employees blackmail customers to perform repairs.[155] More and more judges and other court officials are suborned by bribes, without which suspects would be tortured and abused to solicit their confessions.[156] Managers of SOEs waste enterprise resources to improve their own personal circumstances. The outright theft and illicit sale of public assets by almost everyone has become a major problem. According to official estimates in 1993, the loss of public assets amounted to 30 billion *yuan* per year.[157] The theft of electricity alone by households and enterprises cost the government an estimated $2.5 billion in 1988.[158]

A survey conducted in August 1988, employing a sample of 10,000 people in sixteen cities, found that 61 percent believed that Party and government officials regularly misused their power and privileges for personal gain. 46 percent thought that political corruption was the most serious problem in society.[159] Public disaffection at official corruption was one of the precipitants of the 1989 democracy movement that was brought to a sudden and violent end in June in Tiananmen Square. Corruption is no longer peripheral, but endemic, to the system. Beijing admitted in 1994 that corruption had enveloped all of Anhui province. Xinhua News Agency estimated that one out of every five cadres in Anhui (a total of 300,000 officials) had engaged in corruption.[160] To combat the rising corruption, beginning in the 1980s, the Party instigated repeated "Anti-Corruption" campaigns[161] that continue to this day. The very persistence of the campaigns suggests that they have not been successful despite the government's trumpeting that the number of officials disciplined on corruption charges has yearly increased. Those rising numbers, according to some, simply show that the problem is growing, not that it is being curtailed. The attitude of the ordinary citizen in China is one of increasing cynicism. As one man put it, official campaigns to combat corruption are "just a lot of hot air."[162]

Repeated efforts by the Party to deal with the problem have been unsuccessful because those who were disciplined tended to be people who lacked the requisite connections with ranking officials or who ran afoul of powerful political figures, as demonstrated in the case of Beijing Party Chief Chen Xitong.[163] More importantly, the campaigns have had scant success because they did little to address corruption at the very top of the political hierarchy. As one mid-level PRC official put it, "The network of gift-giving and favors involves the families of almost every senior leader. . . . So anyone who tries to move against them immediately runs into resistance."[164]

A survey in 1994 by a Hong Kong consulting firm showed that China was rated as the most corrupt place to do business in Asia.[165] Toward the end of 1993, the Party's Central Committee for Discipline Inspection singled out the "struggle against corruption" as one of the major concerns of the Party. Jiang Zemin identified the corruption that had settled down upon "socialism with Chinese characteristics" as a threat to nothing less than the system's survival. Unless the problem could be resolved, the Party might not have a future.[166] In his speech to the opening of the 1995 session of the National People's Congress, Premier Li Peng warned that "Combatting corruption (is) a matter of life and death for our nation."[167]

Conclusion

Deng Xiaoping's reform of the Chinese economy has enabled the People's Republic of China to shake free of the stagnation of the Maoist years. Without the economic reforms of 1979 and after, which set free the productive and creative energies of the Chinese people, the economy would not have grown at an annual average rate of over 9 percent. But the same reforms have also had their unintended consequences that, together with the persistence of central planning and the state-owned sector, have produced a system that is increasingly beset by major disabilities. Pandemic corruption is only one of many such disabilities.

Jiang Zemin's warning that corruption could be the end of the Party was not without basis. Well into the period of major reforms, the Chinese Communist Party still sought legitimation through the maintenance of an ideological monopoly. However the economy was to be reformed, the political system was to remain securely under the control of the CCP. Deng Xiaoping had justified rule by the CCP by invoking the hoary notion of the Party as "vanguard," whose members were endowed with special moral virtues. The "tidal" corruption that "floods the entire state apparatus, involving those at the centre of power"[168] and affecting the rank and file could only put in question the CCP's claim to moral rectitude and its right to rule.

There are other problems. There has been an alarming increase in general lawlessness and especially in the rate of violent crimes. Criminal gangs have attacked trains everywhere on the mainland. Rogue police and military delinquents rob civilians with frightening frequency. More and more, peasants and urban workers are making their disaffection known in riots and other acts of civil disobedience. Recurring double-digit inflation contributes to the widening income gap between the new entrepreneurs and those surviving on fixed wages. The pressures of unemployment thwart genuine reform of the dysfunctional state-owned enterprises. The problem of surplus labor in the countryside is barely alleviated by the rural enterprises' employment of some 100 million people. The rest spills over as the 120 million-strong "mobile population" who have migrated from the countryside to converge on already overcrowded cities in search of work.

There are those who have dismissed these developments as the inevitable concomitants of the social change and dislocation spawned by rapid economic development which have afflicted other societies in similar transit from tradition to modernity.[169] What has not been generally recognized are a number of serious developments that might very well threaten the future integrity and political continuity of the People's Republic of China. It is to those developments that attention can be profitably turned.

Notes

1. Xue Muqiao, *China's Socialist Economy* (Beijing: Foreign Languages, 1981), 10.
2. Liu Guoguang and Wang Ruisun, "Restructuring the Economy," in Yu Guangyuan, *China's Socialist Modernization* (Beijing: Foreign Languages, 1984), 97–98.
3. Liu Suinian, "Economy Planning," in *China's Search for Economic Growth: The Chinese Economy Since 1949*, ed. Xu Dixin (Beijing: New World Press, 1982), 33.
4. Li Chengrui and Zhang Zhouyuan, "An Outline of Economic Development (1977–1980)," in Yu Guangyuan, *Socialist Modernization*, 9, 10.
5. Liu Suinian and Wu Qungan, *China's Socialist Economy: An Outline History (1949–1984)* (Beijing: Beijing Review, 1986), 407–408.
6. Chu-yuan Cheng, *China's Economic Development: Growth and Structural Change* (Boulder, CO: Westview, 1982), 424.
7. Chu-yuan Cheng, "Economic Reform in Mainland China: Consequences and Prospects," *Issues and Studies* 22 (December 1986): 15.
8. See A. Doak Barnett, *China's Economy in Global Perspective* (Washington, DC: Brookings Institution, 1981), 305.
9. Jan S. Prybyla, "China's New Economic Strategy: Defining the U.S. Role," *Backgrounder* (Washington, DC: Heritage Foundation, 1985), 3.
10. Liu Suinian, "Economy Planning," 34.
11. Xue Muqiao, *China's Socialist Economy*, 11.
12. See the discussion in Luo Rongqu, "An Initial Conceptualization of a Marxist Theory of Modernization," *Social Sciences in China* 9 (June 1988): 53–54; Yu Guangyuan, "The Economy of the Primary State of Socialism," ibid., 66–87; and A. James Gregor, *A Survey of Marxism* (New York: Random House, 1965), ch. 5.
13. Chu-yuan Cheng, "Economic Reform in Mainland China: Consequences and Prospects," paper presented at the Fifteenth Sino-American Conference on Mainland China, 8–14 June 1986, Taipei, Taiwan.
14. See *China: Long-Term Development Issues and Options* (Mission Report of the World Bank) (Baltimore, MD: The Johns Hopkins University, 1985), 44–46.
15. Zhang Zhenbang, "Lun zhongguo dalu di jiti jingji (On Mainland China's Collective Economy)," *Zhongguo dalu yanjiu* (*Mainland China Studies*, hereafter *MCS*) (Taipei) 37 (August 1994): 57.
16. Ibid., 57.
17. Ibid., 59, 57.
18. Song Zhenzhao, "Dalu nongcun di jingji jiegou bianqian yu fazhan kunjing (The Changing Structure and Development Difficulties of Mainland China's Rural Economy)," *MCS* 38 (July 1995): 22.
19. The following discussion is a paraphrase of the decisions of the Central Com-

mittee of the CCP adopted by the Party's Twelfth Central Committee at its Third Plenary Session on 20 October 1984. See *Decision of the Central Committee of the Communist Party of China on Reform of the Economic Structure* (Beijing: Foreign Languages, 1984).

20. Chu-yuang Cheng, *Behind the Tiananmen Massacre: Social, Political and Economic Ferment in China* (Boulder, CO: Westview, 1990), 156–157.

21. *Shijie ribao* (*World Journal*, hereafter *WJ*) (Millbrae, CA), 8 September 1994, p. A19.

22. Lin Lijian, "Dalu `minying jingji' di guoqu, xianzai yu weilai (The Past, Present and Future of Mainland China's `Private Economy')," *MCS* 39 (July 1996): 37–38, 45.

23. *WJ*, 15 April 1994, p. A19.

24. According to the PRC's 1993 *Statistical Yearbook*, as cited in Zhang Zhenbang, "China's Collective Economy," 57.

25. James McGregor, "Two Nations: China's Entrepreneurs Are Thriving in Spite of Political Crackdown," *Wall Street Journal*, 4 June 1991, p. A15.

26. Zhang Zhenbang, "China's Collective Economy," 54.

27. Ibid., 46.

28. "Privatization by Another Name," *Far Eastern Economic Review* (hereafter *FEER*), 13 June 1996, p. 29.

29. See Samuel P. S. Ho and Ralph W. Huenemann, *China's Open Door Policy: The Quest for Foreign Technology and Capital* (Vancouver: University of British Columbia, 1984).

30. *WJ*, 8 September 1993, p. A19; and 23 September 1994, p. A17.

31. Sheila Tefft, "Chinese Shortcuts Getting Longer," *Christian Science Monitor*, 6 April 1995, p. 9.

32. Matt Forney, "Back to the Future," *FEER*, 29 August 1996, p. 40.

33. Zhang Zhenbang, "China's Collective Economy," 54.

34. *Decision of the Central Committee of the Communist Party of China*, 16–17.

35. See the discussion in Lou Jiwei and Zhou Xiaochuan, "The Direction of Reform of China's Price System," *Jingji yanjiu* (*Economic Studies*), no. 10 (1984): 13–20.

36. See the discussion concerning economic planning and the role of the market in the People's Republic in the editorial in *Renmin ribao* (*People's Daily*) (Beijing), 23 November 1992, p. 2.

37. For an insightful review of the discussions among theoreticians in the People's Republic, see *Economic Theories in China, 1979–1988*, by Robert C. Hsu (New York: Cambridge University, 1991), ch. 5.

38. PRC economists have discussed these issues with considerable candor. See, for example, "Challenges to the Conversion of the Management Mechanism which Demand Attention and Solutions," *Economic Management Monthly* (Beijing), 5 October 1991, pp. 33–35.

39. See Alec Nove, *The Economics of Feasible Socialism* (London: Allen & Unwin, 1953), 20–27.

40. Ye Qing, "Tanxi Wang Binggan di caizheng baogao (An Analysis of [Director of PRC Treasury] Wang Binggan's Financial Report)," *Feiqing yanjiu* (*Study of Communist Affairs*) (Taipei), 33 (25 May 1990): 49–50.

41. See the discussion in Nikolai Shmelev and Vladimir Popov, *The Turning Point: Revitalizing the Soviet Economy* (New York: Doubleday, 1989), 166–179.

42. "Controlling Inflation," *AsiaWeek* (Hong Kong), 27 November 1994, pp. 61–62.

43. Lincoln Kaye, "Bureaucrats Beware," *FEER*, 1 April 1993, p. 13.

44. See, for example, Han Zhiguo, "The Commodity Economy: Explorations and

Options from a New Starting Point," *Social Sciences in China* 8 (September 1987): 9–28.

45. Yu Guangyuan, "The Economy of the Primary Stage of Socialism," *Social Sciences in China* 9 (June 1988): 67, 69; and Xue Muqiao, *China's Socialist Economy*, 163.

46. Zhou Shulian, "The Market Mechanism in a Planned Economy," *China's Economic Reforms,* eds. Lin Wei and Arnold Chao (Philadelphia: University of Pennsylvania, 1982), 104, 108.

47. Liu Suinian, "Economy Planning," 45–46.

48. Nayan Chanda, "Withering State: The End is Near," *FEER*, 23 February 1995, p. 48. Another account put China's SOEs at a total of 140,000 in 1994, employing 150 million workers. See *WJ*, 23 September 1994, p. A17.

49. *WJ*, 15 February 1994, p. A12.

50. *Shaonian zhongguo chenbao (Young China Daily)* (Taipei) 17 November 1990, p. 3.

51. Lincoln Kaye, "Fire When Ready," *FEER*, 23 February 1995, 50.

52. Chanda, "Withering State," 49.

53. *WJ*, 23 April 1994, p. A12.

54. See Henry K. H. Woo, *Effective Reform in China: An Agenda* (New York: Praeger, 1991), 234–235.

55. Chanda, "Withering State," 50.

56. *WJ*, 12 November 1996, p. A19.

57. Dong Ruiqi, "Dalu zhuanbian jingji zengchang fangshi zhi yanxi (An Analysis of Changes in Mainland China's Pattern of Economic Growth)," in *MCS* 39 (June 1996): 18.

58. *WJ*, 14 September 1994, p. A12.

59. See Anthony Kuhn and Lincoln Kaye, "Bursting at the Seams: Rural Migrants Flout Urban Registration System," *FEER*, 10 March 1994, pp. 27–28.

60. *WJ*, 15 July 1993, p. A19.

61. WJ, 5 May 1993, p. A12.

62. Chanda, "Withering State," 49. The *Far Eastern Economic Review* put the number of SOE employees at 100 million. See "China in Transition," *FEER.* Another account, by Hong Kong's *Ta Kung Pao* of 11 January 1994, put the number of SOE workers at 190 million. See *WJ*, 11 January 1994, p. A12.

63. Chanda, "Withering State," 50.

64. Lincoln Kaye, "Bursting at the Seams," 51.

65. See the discussion in "Bankruptcy Law," *Mingbao (Ming Pao Daily News)* (Hong Kong) 9 September 1994, p. D3.

66. See *Mingbao*, 8 October 1994, p. B2.

67. Lincoln Kaye, "Bursting at the Seams," 52.

68. *WJ*, 2 June 1994, p. A2.

69. Ibid., 54.

70. *Wenhui bao*, 14 March 1994, p. A2.

71. Lincoln Kaye, "Bursting at the Seams," 52.

72. Chen Chaozhe, "Zhongguo dalu di xiaofei chao (The Growth of Consumerism in Mainland China)," *MCS* 37 (September 1994): 57.

73. Chanda, "Withering State," 49.

74. Dong Ruiqi, "An Analysis," 12. In China, post-high school education is divided between three-year colleges (*dazhuan*) and four-year universities (*daxue*), somewhat similar to the division between community colleges on the one hand, and colleges and universities in the United States.

75. See "Relaxation Brings Disorder, Controls Bring Paralysis," *Hong Kong Economic Journal*, 13 October 1994, p. 5.
76. Chanda, "Withering State," 49.
77. See the discussion in Mu Jianren, "Reflections on Current Theory and Measures," *Jingji yanjiu*, no. 2, 1994, pp. 39–42.
78. Chanda, "Withering State," 48.
79. Matt Forney, "Back to the Future," 40.
80. Quote by Sir John Cowperthwaite, Hong Kong's financial secretary from 1961 to 1971, who is credited with having kept Hong Kong's economy maximally laissez-faire. Editorial, "Market Knows Best," *FEER*, 13 June 1996, p. 5.
81. See Lincoln Kaye, "Disorder Under Heaven," *FEER*, 9 June 1994, pp. 22–26.
82. *WJ*, 21 September 1994, p. A12.
83. *WJ*, 11 April 1994, p. A13.
84. *WJ*, 27 April 1992, p. A2.
85. *WJ*, 17 February 1994, p. A13.
86. *WJ*, 2 June 1994, p. A13; and 14 August 1994, p. A9.
87. *WJ*, 4 September 1994, p. A9.
88. Uli Schmetzer, "Highway Robbery Plagues China," *San Francisco Examiner* (hereafter *SFEx*) 21 May 1995, p. C-12.
89. *WJ*, 4 September 1994, p. A9.
90. *WJ*, 11 September 1991, p. 11.
91. Article in the PRC's *Zhongguo qingnian bao* (*China Youth Daily*), reprinted as "Zhuanjia tantao heishehui (Experts Explore the Criminal Underworld)," in *Xinwen ziyou daobao* (*Press Freedom Guardian*) (Alhambra), 17 February 1995.
92. *WJ*, 22 June 1994, p. A13.
93. Charles Hutzler, "Fuyang Foretells Future of China," *SFEx* 25 February 1996, p. D-2.
94. "Boom-at-a-Glance," *New York Times Magazine*, 18 February 1996, p. 26.
95. Jiang Zhenchang, "Cong Sichuan `renshou shijian' kan dalu nongcun di shehui chongtu (The Social Conflicts of Mainland China's Rural Areas as Seen from Peasant Unrest in Sichuan's Renshou Incident)," *MCS* 37 (February 1994): 75, 73, 76.
96. *People's Daily*, 15 June 1993, as cited in ibid., 75.
97. Jiang Zhenchang, "Social Conflicts," 76–77.
98. Ibid., 71–74.
99. Ibid., 76–77; and *WJ*, 27 June 1993, p. A11; and 17 June 1993, p. A2.
100. *WJ*, 11 November 1996, p. A10. A particularly tragic case was that of Zhou Zaisheng, a Hunan peasant who committed suicide after being fined 50 *yuan* (a fourth of the average annual per capita income of Chinese peasants) for not remitting his peanut tax of 3 *yuan*. See Editorial, *WJ*, 14 November 1996, p. A2.
101. According to the PRC's *Dongfang ribao* (*Eastern Daily*) of 11 November 1996, as cited in *WJ*, 11 November 1996, p. A2.
102. *WJ*, 3 August 1994, p. A12.
103. WJ, 2 June 1994, p. A2.
104. According to Hong Kong's *Zheng Ming* magazine, as cited by *WJ*, 1 June 1994, p. A12.
105. Child labor has returned to China. Young girls, aged twelve to fifteen, are reportedly working in Shanghai textile mills. *China Focus* I (30 September 1993): 7.
106. "Slave-Labor Conditions Support Chinese Transition to Capitalism," *SFEx*, 4 December 1994, p. C-17.
107. *WJ*, 2 June 1994, p. A2. The irony is that it was only in 1994 that the People's

Republic, ostensibly a "workers' paradise" since 1949, finally passed a Labor Act limiting the workday to a maximum of eight hours. The legislation, however, did not include the right to strike. See *WJ*, 16 July 1994, p. A12.

108. See Henry Sender, "Pilgrim's Progress," *FEER*, 9 February 1995, 58.
109. Dong Ruiqi, "An Analysis," 10.
110. *WJ*, 30 April 1993, p. A11.
111. *Zhongguo shibao (China Times)* (Taipei), 11 August 1989, p. 6.
112. According to Hong Kong's *Huaqiao Daily*, as cited by *WJ*, 19 April 1993, p. A13.
113. Report by Huang Lizheng in *Toronto Global Post*, 25 November 1989, as cited by *Young China Daily*, 27 November 1989, p. 6.
114. *WJ*, 15 November 1996, p. A12.
115. *WJ*, 5 May 1993, p. A12.
116. *WJ*, 9 November 1996, p. A14.
117. Hutzler, "Fuyang Foretells," D-1.
118. Kenneth Auchincloss, "Friend or Foe?" *Newsweek*, 1 April 1996, 32.
119. Hutzler, "Fuyang Foretells," D-1.
120. *WJ*, 2 June 1994, p. A2.
121. *WJ*, 23 August 1994, p. A2. A classified CIA report anticipates the slide into chaos and conflict of many parts of the world because, among other reasons, global per capita grain production wil continue to decline, causing food shortages in many countries, including China. David Wood, "CIA Seeks Root Causes of Instability, Social Decay," *SFEx*, 15 October 1995, p. A-14.
122. "Boom-at-a-Glance," 27.
123. *WJ*, 2 August 1994, p. A13.
124. According to the Hong Kong publication, *Zhonghua wenji*, as cited by *WJ*, 17 October 1993, p. A9. *The New York Times Magazine* put the figure at 40 million. See "Boom-at-a-Glance," 27.
125. *WJ*, 21 December 1992, p. A12.
126. Cited by the *San Francisco Chronicle* (hereafter *SFC*), 2 August 1994, p. A11.
127. Tim Zimmerman et al., "China Takes a Deep Breath," *U.S. News and World Report*, 9 September 1996, p. 36.
128. *WJ*, 30 June 1994, p. A11; and 24 July 1994, p. A9. Today, China's average per capita arable land is only two-fifths that of the world average.
129. They are Beijing, Guangzhou, Shanghia, Shenyang, and Xian. *Christian Science Monitor*, 20 April 1993, p. 9.
130. "Boom-at-a-Glance," 27.
131. Zimmerman, "Deep Breath," 36.
132. Ibid., 36–37.
133. Ibid., 37, 36.
134. "Boom-at-a-Glance," 27; and *WJ*, 24 July 1994, p. A9; and 15 August 1994, p. A10.
135. *WJ*, 19 September 1994, p. A13.
136. Zimmerman, "Deep Breath," 36.
137. For at least two years before his eventual death, Deng was in ill health and could neither stand nor walk.
138. *WJ*, 29 June 1994, p. A12; and Auchincloss, "Friend or Foe?" 30.
139. *WJ*, 7 July 1993, p. A12.
140. *WJ*, 20 September 1993, p. A2.
141. Syed Hussein Alatas, *The Problem of Corruption* (Singapore: Times Books International, 1986), 63.

142. Lincoln Kaye, "Disorder," 51.

143. *WJ*, 21 June 1991, p. 10.

144. *WJ*, 15 February 1994, p. A13.

145. *Jiushi niandai (The Nineties)* (Hong Kong), no. 244 (May 1990): 57.

146. *WJ*, 15 July 1993, p. A10; and 15 September 1994, p. A13.

147. An article in *Liaoning wanbao (Liaoning Evening News)*, reprinted as "Yezonghui (Nightclubs)," in *Press Freedom Guardian*, 17 February 1995.

148. Uli Schmetzer, "No More Gold in Fat Cats' Food," *SFEx*, 19 September 1993, p. A-9.

149. Thomas S.S. Dunn, "Straight Talk," *Free China Journal* (Taipei), 22 October 1991, p. 7.

150. Li Zhengzuo, "Gongjun jingshang you `shi buzhun' (Business Involvement by the Chinese Communist Military Has `Ten Prohibitions')," *Zhonggong wenti ziliao zhoukan (Chinese Communist Affairs and Documents)* (Taipei), no. 366 (22 May 1989), 52.

151. *Huafu youbao (Washington China Post)* (Washington, DC) 9 June 1989, p. 6; *Zhongyang ribao (Central Daily News)* (Taipei) 25 February 1989, p. 4; *Young China Daily*, 25 February 1989, p. 7; *WJ*, 9 July 1993, p. A5.

152. Fox Butterfield, "Who Rules Communist China—It's All in the Family," *SFC*, 5 July 1989, p. A22.

153. Uli Schmetzer, "Private Enterprise Breeds Rampant Corruption in China," *SFEx*, 1 May 1994, p. A-22.

154. Ian Johnson, "Venerable Chinese God of Justice Has Work Cut Out For Him," *SFC*, 25 November 1994, p. A20.

155. Schmetzer, "Private Enterprise."

156. According to the PRC's *Guangming ribao (Guangming Daily)*, as cited in *WJ*, 18 November 1996, p. A11.

157. *WJ*, 16 April 1994, p. A13.

158. Some enterprising businessmen in Jiangxi, Zhejiang, and Honan provinces even established special "electric theft services." *Guoji ribao (International Daily News)* (New York) 8 March 1989, p. 11.

159. *China Times*, 13 February 1989, p. 10.

160. *WJ*, 28 March 1994, p. A12.

161. See Chu-yuang Cheng, *Behind the Tiananmen Massacre*, 3, 17, 23–25, 32–34, 91–93, 175, 176, 223–224, 227.

162. Ian Johnson, "Venerable Chinese God."

163. In May 1995, Chen was dismissed from his office and arrested for his involvement in allegedly the largest corruption scandal in forty-six years of Communist Party rule. Reportedly, Chen's censure was due less to graft but more because he was a rival and critic of Jiang Zemin. See Seth Faison, "China's Anti-Graft Drive Grows; So Does Graft," *New York Times*, 10 August 1995, p. A3.

164. Ibid.

165. Johnson, "Venerable Chinese God."

166. See excerpts of Jiang Zemin's speech in *People's Daily* (Overseas Edition), 23 August 1993, p. 1.

167. Renee Schoof, "Chinese Premier Wants Crackdown on Corruption," *SFC*, 6 March 1995, p. A9.

168. A term coined by Syed Alatas, *Corruption*, 64.

169. Professor Thomas Robinson, as an example, articulated this view on 17 October 1993 at the thirty-fifth annual meeting of the American Association for Chinese Studies in Columbia, South Carolina.

6

Reform and Regionalism

Introduction

The reforms initiated by Deng Xiaoping and his confreres transformed more than the economic environment of China. Around a core of state industries, a more liberalized and decentralized system of collective and private enterprises developed with impressive speed. Income and living standards rapidly increased. Foreign trade and investment integrated China into the global economy.

These results were expected by the reformers. But the economic reforms carried with them unintended effects that are transforming the nature of political power in China, with long-term implications that are, at best, uncertain. Among these unintended consequences is the growing phenomenon of *difang zhuyi* (regionalism or localism), which may well lead to the disintegration of the PRC).[1] Beijing's attenuating control over the constituent regions could mark the end of unified Communist rule and the final transformative phase of post-Mao reforms.

All of this is very tentative. In 1994, a study commissioned by the Pentagon estimated a fifty-fifty probability that China would break apart after the death of Deng Xiaoping.[2] The plausibility of such a scenario turns on an understanding of "regionalism" and the available empirical evidence.

Definition

In the uncertain world of social science, definitions are, more often than not, loosely framed and stipulative, serving largely heuristic purposes. The evidence marshalled to support any claim is usually fragmentary and uncertain. As a consequence, the attempt by social scientists to anticipate events is always hazardous and tentative. Nonetheless, China is such an integral component of any calculation concerning Asia's future that an effort to forecast events recommends itself, no matter how problematic the undertaking.

The Chinese employ the expression "*difang zhuyi*" to refer to a form of parochial identification and attachment where the individual's primary loyalty and commitment are not to the nation-state but to subnational units. That subnational unit may be a village, county, province, region, or ethnic group.

The subjective phenomenon of regionalism in the People's Republic finds expression in a number of related behaviors. One indicator is the disposition on the part of subnational government authorities to behave independently of, or in opposition to, the central government (*zhongyang*) in Beijing. By implication, such behaviors suggest a diminution of *zhongyang*'s power and authority. Another indicator of regionalism are the increasing differences and disparities among the constituent politico-geographical units of China. That growing differentiation is the inevitable result of regionalism's particularistic attachments. Those differences may intensify into open hostility and economic protectionism, all of which further corrodes *zhongyang*'s ability to control events. Finally, assessments made by the CCP and its leaders constitute another indicator of regionalism. Their predictions of the likely consequences of unchecked regionalism have become increasingly dire.

Historical Background

Regionalism, like any form of particularistic loyalty, represents a potential threat to the integrity and well-being of the nation-state. Throughout its millennial history, China periodically was overcome by the centrifugal forces now identified with the rise of regionalism. The result was the fragmentation of the Middle Kingdom into two or more contending states.

For more than half of its 4600–year history, China was something less than a unified political state. From the time of the mythic Yellow Emperor (2697 B.C.) to the Revolution of 1911 that ended dynastic rule, China was an integral state for a cumulative 1,700 years or two-fifths of its history.[3] After 1911, the Chinese mainland remained divided until the Communists decisively won the civil war against the Nationalists in 1949, driving the defeated Nationalist forces to the island of Taiwan.

The unity that Communist rule imposed on the mainland was dependent on imperative planning of the national economy, a plan that entailed a corresponding reduction in regional, provincial, and local discretion. But the centralized and essentially autarkic Maoist system produced all the disabilities that brought China to the edge of ruination. Ironically, the post-Mao reforms that were intended to revive the Chinese economy have created the tensions of regionalism that threaten, once again as in China's dynastic past, to undermine national unity.

The Indicators of Regionalism

The seeds of today's regionalism were sown in 1980 by then PRC Premier Zhao Ziyang. In order to make the economy more productive and efficient, Zhao gave greater autonomy to the provincial and local authorities. Throughout the 1980s, Beijing continued to relinquish more and more power to *difang* authorities over such matters as finance, raw materials, capital, wages, prices, economic regulation, and foreign trade.[4]

Growing Regional Autonomy

Over the course of time, the unintended consequences of Beijing's devolution of power began to emerge. *Difang* authorities became increasingly autonomous from the central government; at the same time, Beijing's power correspondingly declined. This burgeoning independence is manifested in a number of ways.

As much as 95 percent of the Chinese national government's income comes from taxes.[5] But *difang* authorities became increasingly disposed to evade taxes, particularly the more affluent southeastern coastal provinces. For example, since the economic reforms began, Guangdong had enjoyed an annual economic rate of growth that was twice as much as the average rate of China's other provinces. Despite Guangdong's prosperity, its tax remittance to Beijing had actually decreased.[6]

Difang authorities were not the only tax evaders. In 1991, Beijing had the greatest difficulty collecting commercial taxes, business income taxes, and customs tariffs—although it was dependent on precisely those taxes for more than half (57 percent) of its total revenue.[7] In the urban areas, private entrepreneurs, foreign enterprises, and the export businesses along the coast were the worst offenders with a 50 to 80 percent rate of tax evasion. Their evasion, according to Beijing, was enabled by the collusion and protection of local and provincial government officials.[8]

Tax evasion seemed to be widespread among the populace. As an example, over 40 percent of households in a Beijing county evaded taxes in 1988. In the countryside, in the five years between 1983 and 1988, the proportion of peasants in a village in Hebei who refused to remit taxes rose from 5 to 90 percent.[9] After the crackdown of the democracy movement in Tiananmen Square in June 1989, Beijing renewed its resolve to combat tax evasion as part of its overall effort to reimpose order and reexert authority. Despite its resolve, taxes owed to the central government by the end of July 1990 actually increased 84.6 percent.[10] In 1996, the government estimated that it was losing more than 50 billion *renminbi yuan* a year because of tax evasion.[11]

Tax evasion has contributed to the increasing erosion of Beijing's fiscal control over the economy, as evidenced in *zhongyang*'s dwindling share of total government revenue. That share was 70–80 percent in the 1950s, falling to 60 percent in the following decade, then to 50 percent and less during the 1980s.[12] By 1994, the central government took in only 30 percent of China's total revenue, while *difang*'s share had increased to 70 percent.[13] When off-budget revenue is included, Beijing's share of total revenue is even less—about 25 percent.[14] More than that, Beijing's revenue income as a proportion of the country's GNP has also steadily decreased since 1978, from 30 percent in 1979 to 19 percent in 1992.[15]

More than Beijing's dwindling share of revenue, it is losing its ability to control the country's capital supply through the increasingly marginalized central bank (People's Bank). Local-provincial banks are determining their own lending policies because *difang* authorities are finding their own sources of capital, enabling the local banks to extend credit and financing at will to local enterprises.[16] *Difang*'s growing capital independence is reflected in Beijing's declining profile in the country's capital investment. In 1989, *difang* authorities were responsible for 90 percent of China's total fixed social capital investment of 410 billion *yuan*; Beijing's share was a minuscule 10 percent.[17]

Difang's growing financial independence probably accounts for its increased disposition to be outspokenly defiant of the central government. For example, in 1990, in a move described as "unprecedented" in the PRC's history, Shandong Governor Zhao Zhihao wrote that Beijing must first consult with local-provincial authorities before policy decisions could be implemented.[18] Zhao was followed, in 1991, by Guangzhou Deputy Mayor Lei Yu's defiant declaration that "our cadres cannot blindly follow Beijing's orders."[19] At the same time, yet another provincial official was quoted as saying: "Beijing, Beijing. . . . Who has time to listen to Beijing? I've got lots of problems, and Beijing doesn't offer me solutions."[20]

More than rhetoric, *difang*'s growing autonomy finds increasing expression in its action. Local-provincial authorities perceive the center as being too preoccupied to oversee their economic concerns and are striking out on their own. More and more, they are making their own decisions. The *Wall Street Journal* observed that China's top leaders are "in some ways making themselves irrelevant" because provincial leaders have taken over the initiative for the country's development.[21]

As examples, in 1991, Liaoning Governor Li Changchun opened a stock market and devised a bankruptcy law for his province.[22] At least seven provincial governments sought the advice of the Chicago grain exchange on how to open commodity exchanges, then proceeded to act on the advice. A corn and soybean exchange was established in Jilin; a peanut and peanut oil exchange opened in Shandong; grain exchanges were founded in Henan, Anhui, and Sichuan.[23]

More troubling still are the emerging signs that local officials are forging ties with organized crime. This was confirmed by an internal document of the PRC's Public Security Bureau (PSB)[24] and corroborated by a Hong Kong magazine, *Asia Inc.* In 1994, the magazine published a detailed account of shady dealings between criminal organizations, the Chinese military, and the PSB itself.[25] To illustrate, military helicopters were used to transport stolen artifacts in a burglary of Honan's provincial museum in 1992.[26] Smuggling, which has become pandemic along China's coastline, is protected by local officials and has their active participation. Enterprises owned or managed by local officials were identified to be among the major smugglers.

Beijing claimed that former government officials, especially those dismissed from the PSB, were responsible for the rising incidence of Chinese piracy in the South China Sea.[27] Those pirates have fired on foreign vessels in the East and South China Seas, including a July 1993 incident involving a Russian transport vessel. According to a report by the International Free Labor Alliance, members of the PRC People's Liberation Army (PLA) were engaged in piracy to supplement their income. For example, in June 1995, a vessel sailing between Hong Kong and Macao was robbed of its cargo by pirates wearing PLA uniforms.[28]

More than piracy, *difang* authorities are hoarding firearms; protecting wanted criminals from prosecution; building on precious arable land; allowing local cadres to moonlight in business; undertaking indiscriminate construction of economic development zones, backed by an equally indiscriminate frenzy of loans from local banks; selling off usufruct rights to state property including local government offices and buildings; jacking up prices on goods, thereby contributing to the country's inflationary spiral; imposing a proliferation of onerous fees on peasants, business people, students, and users of public roads—all in direct violation and defiance of Beijing's explicit rules and injunctions.[29] The unavoidable conclusion from all of this is that local and provincial officials no longer heed either the dictates or entreaties from an increasingly impotent center.

Regional Disparities

A second problem associated with regionalism is that China's economic boom seemed to exacerbate, rather than alleviate, whatever regional disparities and tensions that existed. Reform has widened the economic gap between the coastal regions in the East, and the inland areas of the West where China's minority nationalities are concentrated. That increasing disparity is not simply a result of differences in natural endowment but of government policy.

An integral part of the post-Mao reforms was Zhao Ziyang's "two ends abroad" (*liangtou zaiwai*) coastal- development strategy. That strategy called for a faster pace of economic growth along the coast, a growth that would be based on labor-intensive industry and aggressive foreign trade. Instead of relying on China's hinterland for backward linkages of materials and equipment, both "ends" (imports and exports) of the coastal economy would be oriented to world markets. The Communist Party anticipated that the emphasis on coastal development would lead inevitably to the uneven economic growth of coast and hinterland, but it convinced itself that accrued advantages along the coast would gradually trickle down to benefit all regions.[30]

Beginning in 1979 and through the first half of the 1980s, five "special economic zones," fourteen "open door cities" and five "special open areas"[31] were created along the coast where export-oriented factories began to flourish, fueled by foreign capital, skills, and technology. To make them attractive to foreign investors, the enterprise zones imitated in varying degrees the market freedoms of Hong Kong, offering alluring conditions of low or no taxes; preferential customs; a minimal bureaucracy; as well as a plentiful supply of cheap labor.

These special zones, cities, and areas have become thriving centers of entrepreneurial activity. The SEZs attracted 25 percent ($4.1 billion) of foreign investment in 1989, and accounted for 9 percent ($3.7 billion) of China's total export earnings in 1989 and 15 percent ($8.3 billion) of the country's bilateral trade in the first half of 1991.[32] In 1994, eight coastal provinces and cities were responsible for as much as 93.6 percent ($41.42 billion) of the PRC's value-added exports.[33]

As anticipated, the coastal-development strategy widened whatever gap that already existed between the coast and the inland regions. While the coastal provinces have become prosperous, the hinterland remains the poorest part of China, specifically the western provinces of Yunnan, Guangxi, Guizhou, Sichuan, Gansu, Tibet, Qinghai, Ningxia, Xinjiang, and Inner Mongolia.[34] In 1992, the average economic growth rate of four inland provinces (Shanxi, Henan, Guizhou, Yunnan) was 10.27 percent; the rate for four coastal provinces (Shandong, Jiangsu, Fujian and Guangdong) was 21.91 percent.[35] Overall, *Japan Economic News* estimated that the gap in rate of growth between coast and inland was as much as 200 percent in 1993—and increasing. This would account for the more developed provinces having an average income two to four times that of China's poorer regions.[36] In some cases, the gap is even greater—in 1993, the average annual per capita income of coastal Shanghai and Zhejiang was ten times that of the inland provinces.[37] To make matters even worse for the inland regions, they also must endure a higher inflation rate than the wealthier provinces.[38] Given all that, it is not surprising that the poor regions would feel "left out" of the current boom. At the same time, the more prosperous coastal provinces were "growing so fast" they felt "dragged down by the rest of the country."[39]

In addition to the disparity between eastern and western China and between the coast and the interior, there is also increasing tension between the coastal South (as represented by Guangdong and Fujian) and the coastal North (as represented by Beijing and Tianjin)—a tension that Beijing feared could develop into a "North-South conflict."[40] That tension is fed by widening differences in outlook on property ownership; production methods and enterprises; and openness to the outside world. All of which have resulted in a growing disparity between the North and South in economic productivity and income distribution.

Protectionism

These regional differences and tensions were further intensified because of Beijing's policy of economic retrenchment that began in late 1988. The tightening of credit by the central government led to each region scrambling to shore up falling revenues and protect local jobs. The result was economic protectionism. As one deputy mayor put it: "When the central government is no longer able to look after us, when other provinces and cities blockade our products, why should we open our markets? Wouldn't that be akin to committing suicide?"[41]

Even before 1988, the provinces were already feuding over primary and secondary raw materials of steel, cement, hemp sacks, silkworm cocoons, pigs, and cotton.[42] When economic retrenchment was imposed, simmering protectionist sentiments broke out into the open, beginning in Hunan province. In 1988, Hunan installed "inspection stations" along its railroads to block the transport of foodgrains and pork to Guangdong.[43] From there, the virus of economic protectionism rapidly infected other provinces. Local and provincial authorities quickly adopted an array of protectionist measures, all without the authorization and in contravention to state planning.[44]

Local and provincial authorities undertook the illegal minting of currencies.[45] Goods and commodities from other provinces were boycotted through the outright prohibition of "outside" goods as well as less direct methods that included financial incentives to those who produced, bought, or sold only local products. There were disincentives to discourage patronage of "outside" products, such as a special tax levied on non-native goods and the punishment of violators by withholding business licenses, bank loans, and supplies.[46] *People's Daily* reported that Xinjiang, Hubei, Jilin, and Liaoning imposed restrictions on the import of commodities such as colored TV sets, bicycles, soap, detergent, and wines and spirits from other provinces.[47] Provinces and localities also imposed embargoes on the export of raw materials to other areas. In 1989, for example, the city of Shenyang delivered only 10 percent of the 3,000 tons of cotton it had promised Shandong and Hebei.[48] More than embargoes were imposed, provinces also reneged on their debts and production contracts. In 1989, regions that had contracted with Shenyang to produce coal and aluminum refused to honor their agreements, although Shenyang had invested large sums of capital in the cooperative ventures.[49] Local and provincial enterprises reneged on debts by having their governments restrict the outward flow of capital—all of which worsened the already constricted capital availability in China.[50]

Regional protectionism seems to be continuing, in one form or another, despite the end of economic retrenchment. China's official media have stopped providing details on regional protectionism although the *People's Daily* acknowledged that the practice remained rife. As examples, in 1990, Guizhou banned the importation of bicycles, televisions, and refrigerators from other parts of China; Sichuan had a similar injunction against some nineteen "outside" products. In 1991, Hainan province closed itself off to migrant laborers from other parts of China. In 1993, a report by the PRC State Council asserted that *difang* protectionism affected the production of auto, cotton textiles, color TVs, refrigerators, air conditioners, and processed oil. Protectionism was responsible for the idling of as much as a third of China's cotton and wool textiles industry.[51] Protectionism was also identified to have contributed to the country's grain shortage because of bottlenecks that provinces erected in the national transportation infrastructure which caused tens of millions of tons of foodgrains to rot in 1990.[52]

One PRC official observed that "The current wave of protectionism is the worst in the last forty years. . . ."[53] Freight traffic is frequently stopped and taxed as it moves across inter-provincial borders. Nontariff barriers, in the form of expensive permits or inspections, are rampant. Shipments of grain, cotton, and fertilizer are the most common targets. It was reported that "Boundary disputes . . . are increasing among the provinces, autonomous regions, and counties." China's

Ministry of Civil Affairs acknowledged the occurrence of over 1,000 incidents of border disputes, some involving "bloody fights."[54]

Political Leaders' Concerns

A final set of indicators of regionalism consists of public and private expressions of alarm in Communist Party documents and by its leaders. Those expressions have taken on an increasing urgency.

As early as 1990, Premier Li Peng warned that "Regional protectionism protects backwardness, destroys the country's unified market, obstructs technological progress, and ultimately hurts ourselves."[55] His admonition evidently was in vain. A year later, in June 1991, a conference convened by the State Council in Chengdu admitted that regional protectionism had destroyed the unity and coordination of the national economy.[56] In 1992, an internal Party document identified the situation in six provinces and autonomous regions (Hainan, Fujian, Xinjiang, Tibet, Yunnan, Shenxi) to be "highly volatile" because riots could erupt at any time. One province, Guangxi, was described as "potentially unstable" and containing "hidden dangers."[57] In July 1993, invoking an expression employed by Sun Yat-sen almost a century ago, CCP leader Jiang Zemin warned that if China were not unified, it would become "a tray of loose sand" and would descend into "economic anarchy."[58] This was followed, in September, by another internal Party document that painted an even bleaker picture. The document warned that if the Party failed to undertake effective measures to suppress the "daily increasing" regionalism, anywhere from "a few" to at most ten to twenty years after the death of Deng Xiaoping, China would follow post-Tito Yugoslavia into complete disintegration.[59] This prediction was reiterated a few months later in December 1993 in a government report on national affairs which ruefully recognized that "a weak center and a strong *difang* had become an indisputable reality."[60]

Finally, in January 1994, a book entitled *China's State Capabilities*, published by the Liaoning People's Publisher, admitted that state power in the PRC was "weakening by the day."[61] That same year, in March, a report by the Chinese Social Science Academy asserted that conflicts between the center and *difang* were "unavoidable." The report predicted that, after the passing of Deng Xiaoping, "serious disturbances would erupt in economically strapped areas," culminating in the disintegration of the People's Republic.[62]

The Response From Beijing

The central government in Beijing is clearly alarmed by regionalism and its implications. As early as 1990, it resolved to reverse the trend by attempting to retract the powers it had devolved to the lower levels.

Personnel Rotation

Beijing made first recourse to a long-standing method for controlling regionalism. Since the inception of the People's Republic, local and provincial officials would be regularly rotated to prevent the coalescence of regional identity and local authority. The CCP Constitution mandates a five-year term limit for provincial party committee officials. That precept enables Beijing to change the personnel staffing of provincial party organs by rotating cadres or filling vacated positions with individuals presumably loyal to the center. As an example, in 1990 the governors of Liaoning, Henan, and Hebei, as well as sixteen out of forty secretaries and deputy secretaries in thirteen provincial party committees were all transferred.[63]

This method was deployed not only at civilian officials but at military personnel as well. From the beginning, Beijing ensured that senior officers in the PRC's military regions would be regularly shuffled. In addition to personnel rotation, the division of the People's Republic into seven military regions that do not overlap with natural regional or economic divisions was also intended as a precautionary measure against the rise of regionalism.[64]

Lacking more complete data, it is difficult to determine whether these personnel maneuvers were successful in suppressing regionalism. But Chinese officials and Western observers maintained that the maneuvers, on the whole, have failed at significantly checking the growing regionalism.[65]

What could account for that failure is that Beijing's power over regional personnel selection is far from total, as revealed in the case of Guangdong, a province that was one of the chief beneficiaries of post-Mao reforms, with a reputation as "the most secure of all regional powers in China"[66] and "the leader of the forces against the central government."[67] As the province became increasingly prosperous, central control over the province became a critical test of *zhongyang*'s power. It was Guangdong that, in 1988, originated the "traffic light" (*denglun*) response to Beijing which was quickly adopted by other provinces. Comparing Beijing's directives to traffic light signals, Guangdong advised that "When the light is red, go around it. When the light is yellow, hurry through it. When the light is green, increase your speed."[68]

Much of Guangdong's independence and success are credited to its former governor, Ye Xuanping, to whom Hong Kong has given the moniker of "Emperor of the South." Son of the late Marshal Ye Jianying and a Guangdong native, Ye had occupied leading positions in the province since 1980 before becoming governor in 1985.

Increasingly apprehensive about Ye's power and independence, Beijing endeavored for years to dislodge him from the governorship. In spring of 1991, Ye agreed to leave his office—but on his terms. He consented to leave the governorship for the vice chairmanship of the Political Consultative Committee, provided he could remain in Guangdong as well as choose his successor (then Guangzhou mayor Zhu Senlin).[69] In effect, Beijing failed to dislodge Ye Xuanping from his provincial power base. Ye reportedly threatened to withhold Guangdong's revenue remittance to the center unless Beijing acceded to his wishes.[70] His threat is reminiscent of that made by another powerful political figure. In January 1991, President of the U.S.S.R.'s Russian republic Boris Yeltsin, in a power struggle with Soviet President Mikhail Gorbachev, also threatened to reduce the republic's contribution to the national budget by a drastic 85 percent.[71]

The Seventh Plenum of the CCP-CC

More than the case of Ye Xuanping suggests that the efficacy of the traditional method of personnel rotation is questionable. Since the method has been in practice since 1949, if it were effective in preventing and containing regionalism, the integrity of the People's Republic would not now be threatened. Beijing clearly needs other methods to combat regionalism, one of which was the convening, in December 1990, of the seventh plenum of the CCP's Thirteenth Central Committee.

Beijing hoped to use the occasion of the plenum to decisively check *difang*'s growing power and autonomy. What actually happened was inconclusive, at best. To begin with, the plenum was repeatedly delayed because of resistance from provincial delegates to many of

Beijing's plans.[72] When the plenum finally convened, the delegates could not agree on many issues that were important to Beijing, including the speed of price reform; the return to a more centrally planned economy; the retention rate of *difang*'s revenue income; and the location of new economic development zones.[73] The disagreement was not surprising since the central government had only a minority representation at the plenum of 47 percent of the delegates.[74]

In the end, only one agreement concerning center-*difang* relations was reached by the plenum. Beginning in 1991, all businesses engaged in export must remit an average of one-third of their foreign exchange earnings to the center. This would presumably increase the revenue remittance of the coastal provinces to Beijing, thereby curbing their growing power and autonomy.[75]

The 1994 Tax Reform

That agreement evidently failed to accomplish Beijing's objective of containing regionalism, because three years after the seventh plenum, in 1994, Beijing undertook yet another effort to defeat regionalism. The effort took the form of a revamping of the PRC's tax system.

The existing system was one in which local and provincial authorities would collect the taxes and remit a specified percentage to the central government. Beijing, for its part, would help maintain local-provincial governments by subsidizing, when needed, their expenses as well as providing most of the capital for their industrial and infrastructural development. This arrangement, on the whole, was one that benefitted *difang*. To illustrate, according to available PRC statistics from 1989, local and regional governments remitted an aggregate of 44.7 billion *yuan* in revenue to Beijing but received an aggregate of 56.254 billion *yuan*[76]—a net gain of 11.554 billion *yuan* for *difang*. Despite *difang*'s net gain, this did not mean that every province, county, and village equally benefitted from the arrangement. In 1989, only 55 percent of China's counties requested and presumably received financial assistance from Beijing.[77] For the remaining 45 percent of counties, their arrangement with the center was probably more a burden than a blessing in that they probably gave more to Beijing than they received. China's ten richest county governments, all located in coastal provinces, whose average annual income was over 340 million *yuan*, were probably among this 45 percent.[78]

On 1 January 1994, after much resistance from *difang* authorities, Beijing replaced the existing revenue system with a new dual tax extraction system in which center and *difang* would each collect its own revenue. A National Tax Office would be charged with collecting "national revenue" which includes tariffs, manufacturing taxes, and special consumer taxes (on, for example, cigarettes and alcohol). *Difang* Tax Offices would extract *"difang* revenue," including land-use and land-rent taxes.[79]

Beijing expected that the new system would boost its share of total revenue from 30 percent to a majority share of 60–70 percent. Beijing expected another advantage still. Under the new dual tax system, *difang* authorities would have their own sources of revenue and could no longer count on Beijing's subsidies. Henceforth, the provinces will have to provide for the bulk of their expenditure.[80]

Although the new tax system would presumably ameliorate Beijing's fiscal condition, it is doubtful if the reform could actually combat regionalism. On the contrary, the very abandonment of the old system suggests that Beijing felt it could no longer depend on *difang* authorities to carry out their responsibilities under the old tax system—those of tax collection and revenue remittance. Moreover, by instituting a new system of separate tax extraction, Beijing inadvertently might actually enhance regional autonomy. Not only do *difang* governments now have their own sources of revenue, they also have less reason to be compliant with Beijing because they no longer can count on its handouts.[81]

The new system of revenue extraction may actually hasten the eventuality of a federated or fragmented China. After all, a centralized political system, which is the present nominal configuration of the People's Republic, is one where the central or national government controls political power through the purse. In such a system, subnational governmental units are entirely dependent on the center for its finances. In contrast, a federal system is one where national and subnational governments have separate revenue sources, with each laying claim to distinct and discrete powers.

There is another reason to be skeptical of the efficacy of the dual tax system in combating regionalism. In June 1996, it was reported that Beijing devised yet another plan "to strengthen control over the provinces." Six new Regional Offices (*difang ju*) will be created sometime in 1997 corresponding to the six geographical regions of China: central-east, east, north, northeast, southwest, and northwest. Each Regional Office will supervise the provinces within its purview and ensure that they obey Beijing's injunctions. The secretary of each Regional Office will have the power to dismiss, transfer, or force the early retirement of uncooperative provincial governors and secretaries.[82] All of which suggests that regionalism continues to be problematic.

Beijing's Dilemma

The available evidence, sketchy at best, seems to indicate that Beijing continues to be ineffective at stemming the tide of regionalism. It is not that Beijing does not know how to rein in regional power. Regionalism was an unintended consequence of economic liberalization; it could be eradicated only if the reforms that spawned it were dissolved and China returned to the total-command system of the Maoist era. Thus far, Beijing has failed to combat regionalism; it is loath to employ the only method that will work because the solution to the problem carries intolerable costs.

Simply put, the Communist Party is confronted with a Hobson's choice. If it were to revoke the economic reforms and abolish the special economic zones and cities, the economic modernization of China would be imperiled—assuming that China could modernize through its makeshift system of "market socialism" in the first place. If China were to return to total central planning, its economy would stagnate like the Soviet Union in the 1960s, followed by a slow but inexorable decline as the Soviet economy experienced in the 1970s and 1980s, culminating in negative growth and systemic crisis.

Mindful of the Soviet precedent, the Chinese Communist leadership sees economic development via reform as the only way to preserve political rule. It is convinced that economic failure, compounded by the machinations of the capitalist West, had led to the collapse of communism in Eastern Europe and the Soviet Union.[83]

Unhappily for the Chinese Communist Party, reform of the economy has undesirable costs and unintended effects—among them the problem of regionalism that already has led to economic protectionism by the provinces and may well culminate in the dissolution of China altogether. As one commentator put it:

Contradictions between the center and *difang* will worsen in the future. . . . What the leaders in Beijing worry most about is that the 30 provinces of China will become 30 big princes, that the 300 regions become 300 medium princes, and that China's 2,000 counties become 2,000 little princes—each pursuing its own course of development, presiding over its own territory, becoming in effect independent kingdoms.[84]

Despite the risks associated with economic liberalization, this is apparently the policy to which the Communist Party is committed. As long as Deng Xiaoping was alive, the Party's overriding commitment will remain that of economic development. This was made vividly clear in a 1990 internal Party Document No. 26. In that document, the CCP vowed it would continue with the course of economic reform "as long as there wasn't a Third World War. . . ." More than that, "Even if there were a Third World War. . . as long as it does not take place in China," the Party would "continue to concentrate on economic construction."[85]

The reality is that Beijing has little choice but to continue its reform because China's viability is increasingly dependent on the new economy that reform created. Beijing is addicted to the export revenue brought in by the coastal and other private enterprises. In 1978 before the reforms were launched, exports accounted for only 4 percent of China's GNP; by 1990, they had grown to 19 percent of the GNP.[86] The foreign exchange earnings from those exports are needed to purchase not only the industrial goods, technology and raw materials for economic modernization, but also for the foodgrains to help feed China's population of over 1.2 billion which will increase to 1.3 billion by the year 2000. The income from exports is also needed to repay the PRC's substantial foreign debt, official and unofficial, of close to $125 billion by the beginning of 1996. That debt has more than doubled since 1990 and represents about 95 percent of China's 1996 exports.[87]

The private enterprises are China's export engine as well as the target of foreign investment. Foreign-invested firms in Fujian, as an example, are responsible for more than a quarter of the province's economic output.[88] Privately-owned enterprises are also the most productive of the national economy, despite being a minuscule part (about 3 percent) of the country's total industrial production. In 1990, private enterprises remitted 14.5 billion *yuan* (about $2.78 billion) in taxes and accounted for 70 percent of China's industrial growth. The output of enterprises involving foreign investment, in particular, jumped 56 percent.[89] In 1991, private enterprises provided employment for at least 18 and possibly 40 million people, contributing $9 billion to national income. All of this was accomplished without any capital investment from the state.[90]

In contrast, the state-owned enterprises that still dominate China's industrial production are notably unproductive and inefficient. In 1990, SOE production grew by a scant 2.9 percent, with a third operating at a loss. Those losses required the state to provide $12.5 billion in subsidies and $27 billion in credit.[91] Subsidies to losing enterprises consumed 17 percent of state income in 1990. The secular trend is discouraging. Since 1978, SOE losses increased by an average annual rate of 13.6 percent.[92] In 1991, the $45.89 billion debt accumulated by the SOEs exceeded China's official foreign debt of $45.4 billion.[93] As the *Economist* put it, "All this can be paid for only by taxing the efficient—that is, private—part of the economy."[94]

The Future

All of this provides striking testimony to the fact that China has become so dependent on its private economy that Beijing has little choice but to continue with the present situation. Beijing is compelled to tolerate the increasingly autonomous coastal regions although they are the very forces that may ultimately destroy the Party's grip on power.

In the new reality, Beijing no longer monopolizes power but must negotiate with lower-level officials. This was recognized by Jiang Zemin when he admitted in 1991 that "In economic matters, the days of the center commanding *difang* are gone forever."[95]

More than that, the phenomenon of regionalism is symptomatic of the fragmentation of China into competing interest groups that, thus far, appear to be predominantly arrayed along geo-economic lines. After almost two decades of economic reforms, China has become more pluralistic and differentiated. It is no longer a simple political system monopolized by the central authorities in Beijing. More and more, the center will have to negotiate compromises, broker among competing interests, and share power with regional and local authorities.

The devolution of the People's Republic into a collection of regional "kingdoms" is not improbable. What might contribute to that outcome would be a coalescence of major power groups in each region including Party and government officials, the military, and large private entrepreneurs. Such a coalition could well be capable of pursuing its parochial interests against the center.

It is in this context that a number of developments in recent years become interesting. In July 1990, a high-level meeting of the Communist Party resolved to prohibit all future contacts between PLA enterprises and Taiwan investors.[96] Such a prohibition is indicative not only of Beijing's concern about the potential dangers in such contacts, but also of the fact that contacts are already taking place. An example was the attempt in 1990 by the PLA's Kaili Industrial Company to negotiate a multimillion dollar petrochemicals joint venture with Taiwan mogul Wang Yongqing.[97]

As for a coalition between the CCP and wealthy entrepreneurs, in June 1991, it was reported that increasing numbers of Communist Party members were engaged in private businesses, in direct contravention to the Party's strictures. In one district, the number of CCP members operating private businesses increased 30 percent in five years (1984–89).[98] PRC Vice President Wang Zhen, in a speech in 1991, warned darkly that "some of the newly rich were co-opting leading local party and government officials with promises of shares and honorary titles in their businesses." According to Wang, as much as a third of the 611 rural cadres in a county in Henan province had left the Party to work for businesses owned by newly wealthy families.[99]

All of this is suggestive that coalitions of regional elites may already be in the formative stage. The death of Deng Xiaoping could only accelerate the process. The balance of power between center and *difang* will increasingly gravitate towards the latter. Whether that development would eventuate in China's fragmentation or its peaceful evolution into a *de facto*, if not formal, federation[100] would depend on a number of factors.

Adroit political leadership is an important contingency. The successor(s) to Deng Xiaoping will have to stay committed to economic modernization, as well as possess the skills needed to maintain stability and economic growth, negotiate among diverse interests, as well as calibrate the power balance between *difang* and the center.

The economy is another determinant of the direction that regionalism might take in the future. The Chinese economy has managed, since the reforms began in 1978, to sustain an annual average growth rate of 9 percent. So long as the economic pie continues to enlarge, the provinces will probably be content with the existing political arrangement. But should the economy deteriorate, or if the succession to Deng is fraught with conflict, or if the post-Deng leadership is maladroit, what may result will be the decomposition of the People's Republic of China. Such an outcome would be hastened by a number of developments.

Fragmentation of the Chinese state will be more probable if the affluent coastal provinces attain complete financial independence from Beijing. It is not entirely clear whether their present economic relationship with the center redounds to coastal benefit.

As explained, the 1994 dual tax system created a separate revenue base for the provinces but they will have to be responsible for most of their own expenses. Despite the new system, Beijing would still have to provide for the poorer regions in the interior and especially the west, in the interest of national stability because those regions are heavily populated with minority peoples. It was estimated that 80 percent of the counties in China's five autonomous regions could not manage without Beijing's support. Tibet, in particular, is entirely dependent on the central government. Every Tibetan county operates in the red and must depend on state subsidies for its survival.[101] To continue its subsidization of the poorer regions, Beijing devised a new "capital transfer" plan[102]—a "Charity Fund for the Poor"—to which the wealthier provinces are encouraged to contribute. Reportedly, the plan produces 10 billion *yuan* a year, 80 to 90 percent of which go to subsidize the poor provinces and autonomous regions in Western China.[103]

The coastal provinces, being the heart of China's economic boom, can expect little from the "capital transfer" plan. There are reports that the affluent coastal provinces are increasingly reluctant to contribute towards those subsidies. Under the old tax system, there was much complaining by the affluent cities and provinces that "those who remitted more revenue to Beijing didn't get a fair return."[104] After the 1994 tax reform, Beijing still expected those provinces to contribute generously to the new "Charity Fund for the Poor." Not surprisingly, Beijing's new scheme seems to be meeting strong resistance from the coastal provinces. In 1994, for example, it was reported that Guangdong outright refused to contribute the 16 billion *yuan* ($1.854 billion) that Beijing asked for. In doing so, Guangdong's cadres stated that assisting their own poor, those in the province's northern counties, must be their first priority.[105]

What economic benefits the affluent coastal provinces now derive from Beijing are primarily in the form of infusions of developmental capital. In 1992, for example, Beijing provided a third of Guangdong's overall capital for economic development. (Foreign investors and Guangdong itself each accounted for another third.) In the case of Hainan, in the years leading to 1993, less than a third of its development capital came from Beijing. Foreign sources and other provinces each accounted for a third, with Hainan itself making up the remaining.[106]

If the coastal provinces manage to find their own sources of development capital, their reason to remain subject to Beijing—and to the political arrangement of the People's Republic—becomes less and less compelling. Hong Kong's *South China Morning Post*, in 1994, reported that some local and provincial cadres and enterprises hinted that if they could attract sufficient foreign capital or directly accumulate their own capital without having to subsidize the poorer provinces and regions of China, they would no longer pay attention to Beijing.[107]

It is in this context that the development of a "Greater China"—an increasingly economically integrated regional body comprised of Hong Kong, Taiwan, Guangdong, and Fujian provinces—becomes significant. This will be discussed in the chapter to follow.

Notes

1. Cheng Chu-yuan, *Behind the Tiananmen Massacre: Social, Political, and Economic Ferment in China* (Boulder, CO: Westview, 1990), 196–197.
2. "China's Feuding Regions," *Economist*, 20 April 1996, 28.
3. China was a confederation from 2697 to 1766 B.C., and a feudal federation from 1766 to 255 B.C. In 255 B.C., China was unified by Emperor Qin (*Shi huangdi*). Since that time, periods of unity (a cumulative 1,700 years) alternated with periods of fragmentation (totaling 900 years). Zhang Yufa, "Zhongguo lishi shang difen yuhe (Division and Unity in Chinese History)," in *Fenlie guojia di hudong guanxi* (*Mutually Interactive Relationship of Divided States*), ed. Zhu Songbo (Taipei, Taiwan: Institute of International Relations, 1989), 1–6.
4. Lin Lijian, "Difang zhuyi shili taitou (The Rise in Power of Regionalism)," *Zhonggong wenti ziliao zhoukan* (*Chinese Communist Affairs and Documents*, henceforth *CCAD*), no. 445 (3 December 1990): 19.
5. According to the head of the PRC's Office of Taxation, Chen Xin, as reported by *China Daily*, 23 August 1990. See *Shaonian zhongguo chenbao* (*Young China Daily*, henceforth *YCD*), 24 August 1990, p. 3.
6. *YCD*, 29 November 1990, p. 3; "Gelu zhuhou dizhi zhongnanhai jingshu jingji (The Various Princes Resist the Center's Economic Retrenchment)," *CCAD*, no. 450 (7 January 1991): 49.
7. *Shijie ribao* (*World Journal* or *WJ*), 27 July 1991, p. 11; *CCAD*, no. 437 (8 October 1990): 58.

8. *WJ*, 3 January 1993, p. A9.
9. *YCD*, 22 February 1989, p. 7; *Zhongguo shibao* (*China Times* or *CT*), 13 July 1989, p. 6. It was reported that a group of pig farmers in Jiangxi province urinated on their tax collectors, and kept them confined in a pig pen. See *Guoji ribao* (*International Daily News*), 9 March 1989, p. 11.
10. According to Wang Binggan, director of the PRC treasury, *CCAD*, no. 437: p. 58.
11. You Yifeng, "Dui dalu guoyou zichan liushi zhi tantao (Analysis of Mainland China's State-Owned Property Losses)," *Zhonggong yanjiu* (*Studies on Chinese Communism*) (Taipei), 30 (January 1996): 103.
12. Wang Shaoguang and Hu Angang, "Zhongguo zhengfu qiqu nengli di xiajiang jiqi houguo (The Decline and Implications of the Chinese Government's Extractive Capacity)," *Ershiyi shiji* (*21st Century Bimonthly*) (Hong Kong), no. 21 (February 1994): 8.
13. *WJ*, 11 January 1994, p. A19.
14. Wang and Hu, "Chinese Government's Extractive Capacity," 8.
15. From a study by the Chinese Science Academy reported by Xinhua News Agency, 29 July 1993, as cited by *WJ*, 30 July 1993, p. A12.
16. As cited by *WJ*, 24 July 1991, p. 2.
17. Ye Zhiqiu, "Ji moudun dacheng di zhonggong qizhong quanhui (Chinese Communist Party's Central Committee's Seventh Plenum was Replete with Contradictions)," *YCD*, 20 November 1990, p. 3.
18. Governor Zhao's comment was contained in an article he contributed to *Chinese Economic Structural Reform* (*Zhongguo jingji tizhi gaige*). See Lin Lijian, "Regionalism," 19.
19. *WJ*, 8 May 1991, p. 10.
20. James McGregor, "Two Nations: China's Entrepreneurs Are Thriving in Spite of Political Crackdown," *Wall Street Journal*, 4 June 1991, p. A1.
21. Ibid.
22. *YCD*, 31 May 1990, p. 3.
23. Hong Kong's *South China Morning Post*, 17 April 1991, as cited by *WJ*, 18 April 1991, p. 10.
24. *WJ*, 11 September 1991, p. 11.
25. Ian Buruma, "The 21st Century Starts Here," *The New York Times Magazine*, 18 February 1996, p. 47.
26. *WJ*, 22 June 1994, p. A13.
27. *WJ*, 2 June 1994, p. A13.
28. *WJ*, 12 September 1996, p. A13.
29. See *WJ*, 9 December 1992, p. A5; 20 June 1993, p. A9; 8 August 1993, p. A9; 22 March 1994, p. A13; 8 April 1994, p. A13; 9 April 1994, p. A12; 16 April 1994, p. A12; 1 June 1994, p. A12; 8 July 1994, p. A17; 23 July 1994, p. A12; 14 August 1994, p. A9; 17 August 1994, p. A13; 25 August 1994, p. A13; 1 September 1994, p. A12; and Frank Viviano, "New Map For the 21st Century," *San Francisco Chronicle*, 26 October 1990, p. A16.
30. George T. Crane, "China's Special Economic Zones in 1989: Continuity and Change," paper presented at the 1990 Sino-American Conference on Mainland China, Taipei, Taiwan, June 1990, pp. 3–4.
31. The five SEZs are Shenzhen, Zhuhai, and Shantou in Guangdong province; Xiamen in Fujian province; and Hainan Island province. From north to south, along the coastline of China, the fourteen "open door cities" are Dalian, Qinhuangdao, Tianjin, Yantai, Qingdao, Lianyungang, Nantong, Shanghai,

Ningbo, Yunzhou, Fuzhou, Guangzhou, Zhanjiang, and Beihai. The five "special open areas" along the coast are Liaodong Peninsula; Shandong Peninsula; the Yangtze River delta; the Minnan delta in Fujian province; and the Zhujiang (Pearl River) delta in Guangdong.

32. Li Ping, "Jiang Zemin tan tequ jiangshe ji fan zhiyouhua wenti (Jiang Zhemin Speaks Out on the Establishment of SEZs and on the Anti-Liberalism Problem)," *CCAD*, no. 439 (October 22, 1990): 14; and *WJ*, 30 July 1991, p. 10.
33. Those eight provinces and cities were Guangdong, Shanghai, Fujian, Jiangsu, Liaoning, Shandong, Zhejiang, and Tianjin. *WJ*, 17 April 1994, p. A9.
34. *WJ*, 15 April 1991, p. 11; *YCD*, 10 November 1990, p. 3.
35. *Christian Science Monitor*, 2 April 1993, p. 1.
36. "China's Feuding Regions," 27.
37. *WJ*, 2 September 1993, p. A19; *WJ*, 24 May 1993, p. A12.
38. Li Jian, "Zhonggong jiebukai di jingji nanti (Communist China's Unresolvable Economic Problem)," *Zhonggong dalu (Mainland China Monthly)* (Taipei), no. 330 (February 1995): 25.
39. Nicholas D. Kristof, "China, the Conglomerate, Seeks a New Unifying Principle," *New York Times*, 21 February 1993, p. A6.
40. *WJ*, 29 April 1991, p. 10. See also Li Jinchuan, "Zhongguo di `nanbei wenti' (China's North-South problem)," *Renmin ribao (People's Daily)*, 4 June 1991.
41. Yang Manke, "Baohu zhuyi xingqi, dalu `hejiu bifen' (Protectionism Rises, the Mainland Necessarily Divides after a Long Period of Unity)," *YCD*, 13 September 1990, p. 3.
42. Ibid.
43. *YCD*, 10 November 1990, p. 3.
44. Yang Manke, "Protectionism Rises."
45. The PRC newspaper *Economic Information* reported that some counties in Hubei, Hunan and Jiangxi illegally issued bank notes that amounted to 70 percent of the money circulating in those areas. See Ann Scott Tyson, ibid. This phenomenon was confirmed by Yuan Ruiliang, member of the Overseas Chinese Committee of the PRC's National People's Congress (NPC) and secretary to NPC Vice Chairman Ye Fei. In a conversation with this author on June 26, 1991, Yuan said that in some provinces, state enterprises issued special coupons to their workers which could be redeemed for merchandise in local stores. These coupons are *de facto* currencies.
46. The 8 June 1990 issue of the PRC's *Jingji cankao (Economic Research)* reported that Jilin, Liaoning, Hubei, and Henan have local regulations that permit the sale of only "native" beer, white wine, laundry detergent, bicycles, and color television sets. One province imposed a "local product protection tax" on cement imported from other provinces of 50 *yuan* per ton. Lin Lijian, "Dalu `zhuhou jingji' pingxi (A critical analysis of mainland China's `economy of regional princes')," *CCAD*, no. 431 (28 August 1990), 7–12.
47. Yang Manke, "Protectionism Rises."
48. For example, coal-producing Shanxi province; cotton-producing Xinjiang and Henan; steel-producing Liaoning; and bean-grower Heilongjiang. Lin Lijian, "Dalu `zhuhou jingji'."
49. Ibid.
50. Ann Scott Tyson, "Provincial Wars Over Trade Concern Chinese," *Christian Science Monitor*, 18 October 1990, p. 5.
51. "China's Feuding Regions," 27; *WJ*, 25 July 1991, p. 11; and 15 January 1993, p. A19.
52. *YCD*, 29 October 1990, p. 3.

53. Ann Scott Tyson, "Provincial Wars Over Trade. . . ."

54. *Jiushi niandai (The Nineties)*, no. 252 (January 1991), 81; and "China's Feuding Regions," 27.

55. Lin Lijian, "Dalu `shuhou jingji' pingxi," 7; and Yang Manke, "Protectionism Rises."

56. *WJ*, 26 June 1991, p. 10.

57. "Wider Westen," *Der Spiegel*, August 1992, pp. 166–169.

58. *WJ*, 7 July 1993, p. A12.

59. *WJ*, 20 September 1993, p. A2.

60. *WJ*, 19 December 1993, p. A1.

61. *WJ*, 27 January 1994, p. A12; and 28 January 1994, p. A10.

62. *WJ*, 24 March 1994, p. A12.

63. The thirteen provinces and autonomous regions are Hebei, Inner Mongolia, Liaoning, Jiangsu, Anhui, Yunnan, Tibet, Ningxia, Henan, Guangdong, Sichuan, Xianxi, and Hubei. See Yang Jingzhi, "Zhonggong genghuan bufen shengwei ganbu (The Communist Party Rotated a Portion of Provincial Party Committee Cadres)," *CCAD*, no. 437 (8 October 1990): 40–43. Also Ann Scott Tyson, "China Rotates Leaders to Cut Local Power," *Christian Science Monitor*, 14 November 1990, p. 4.

64. "China's Feuding Regions," 28.

65. Ann Scott Tyson, "China Rotates Leaders."

66. Ye Zhiqiu, "Zhonggong banzou Ye Xuanping difang shili baolei shishou (The Communist Party Fails in Moving Ye Xuanping from his Regional Power Fortress)," *Zhongyang ribao (Central Daily News)*, 2 February 1991; reprinted in *CCAD*, no. 455 (11 February 1991): 58.

67. *YCD*, 10 November 1990, p. 3.

68. *YCD*, 22 October 1990, p. 3.

69. Although Zhu is not a Guangdong native but was born in Shanghai, Zhu had been working in Guangdong since 1952. Chen Jun, "Zhonggong xinren shengshizhang renshi fenxi (An Analysis of Communist China's Newly Appointed Provincial and City Leaders)," *CCAD*, no. 471 (10 June 1991): 49.

70. *The Nineties*, no. 255 (April 1991): 14.

71. *San Francisco Examiner*, 6 January 1991, p. A6.

72. "Gelu zhuhou dizhi zhongnanhai jingshu jingji," 49.

73. Kang Fuxin, "Zhonggong qizhong quanhui zhi taolun jingji yiti (The Communist Party's Seventh Plenum only Discussed Economic Issues)," *CCAD*, no. 450 (7 January 1991): 24–26.

74. *YCD*, 7 January 1991, p. 3.

75. Lin Yuan, "Shenghua waimou tizhi gaige (Deepening the Reform of the Foreign Trade System)," *CCAD*, no. 456 (25 February 1991): 26.

76. Ye Qing, ibid., 50.

77. *YCD*, 31 October 1990, p. 3.

78. Of the ten counties, four are in Jiangsu, four in Zhejiang, and two in Guangdong province. *WJ*, 27 July 1991, p. 11.

79. *WJ*, 12 August 1993, p. A1; 16 November 1993, p. A2.

80. *WJ*, 16 November 1993, p. A2.

81. Less than a year after the inauguration of the new tax system, some local governments began to complain of revenue shortfall. This prompted Beijing to create yet another new system of "capital transfer" (or subsidy) from the center to *difang* in order to "equalize basic services," such as health and education, across the country to compensate for the unequal development among China's

regions, provinces and localities. Beijing's real concern was to prevent social instability and *difang*'s alienation from the central government. *WJ*, 29 August 1994, p. A10.

82. *WJ*, 22 June 1996, p. A14.
83. Li Jian, "Zhonggong qiangdiao 'yi dongou weijian' bimian fuwang (Communist China Emphasizes 'the East European Precedent' to Avoid Its Demise)," *CCAD*, no. 470 (3 June 1991): 13.
84. Wu Anjia, "Zhonggong shishanjie qizhong quanhui zhi pingxi (An Analysis of the Seventh Plenum of the Chinese Communist Party's Thirteenth Central Committee)," *Yazhou yu shijie yuekan* (*Asia and World Monthly*), February 1991, p. 50.
85. Lin Lijian, "Zhonggong dui shiju bianhua di yinyin zhidao (Communist China's Response to Changes in World Conditions)," *CCAD*, no. 436 (1 October 1990): 14.
86. James McGregor, "Two Nations," A15.
87. David Roche, "Faltering Investment Haunts China's Leaders," *Wall Street Journal*, 12 February 1996, p. A14.
88. *South China Morning Post*, 1 April 1991, as cited by *News Digest*, 2 April 1991, p. 2.
89. Cheng Jun, "Chongsheng fazhan shiying jingji (Developing Anew the Private Economy)," *CCAD*, no. 466 (6 May 1991): 24. James McGregor, "Two Nations," A15.
90. *WJ*, 26 June 1991, p. 10; and 15 July 1991, p. 11.
91. *YCD*, 29 November 1990, p. 3. The performance of state enterprises continues to be dismal. In 1991, more than a third (39.5 percent) of them were in the red. *WJ*, 24 July 1991, p. 2.
92. Figures are from an article in the PRC's government periodical, *Qiushi* (no. 8, 1991). See the account by Li Jian, "Zhonggong qitu gaohuo guoying qiye (Communist China Attempts to Revive State Enterprises)," *CCAD*, no. 471 (10 June 1991): 16–18.
93. *YCD*, 15 November 1990, p. 3.
94. "China's Economy: If it Works, it's Private," *Economist*, 30 November 1991, p. 35.
95. "Zhonggong shisan jie qizhong quanhui neng jiejue jingji kunjing? (Can the Seventh Plenum of the CCP Thirteenth Central Committee Resolve Economic Problems?)," *CCAD*, no. 450 (7 January 1991): 28.
96. *YCD*, 1 September 1990, p. 3.
97. Editorial, "Gongjun zuoda weixie taihai jushi (The PLA Threatens the Taiwan Strait)," *Huafu youbao* (*Washington China Post*), 15 June 1990, p. 2.
98. From an account by the *South China Morning Post*, 20 June 1991, citing an article in the magazine *Qiushi*. As reported in *WJ*, 21 June 1991, p. 10.
99. Lin Xiang, "Nungcun zongjiao zongzu shili pengzhang (Religious and Clannish Forces are Expanding in the Countryside)," *CCAD*, no. 470 (3 June 1991): 59.
100. In 1992, a delegation from China's executive branch, the State Council, made a tour of several city and state governments in the United States, including New York, Washington, D.C., and Sacramento. The delegation's explicit purpose was to study the creation, history and functioning of American federalism.
101. *CD*, 30 November 1990, p. 1.
102. See footnote 83 for an account of Beijing's "capital transfer" plan.
103. *1995 Zhonggong nianbao* (*1995 China Yearbook*) (Taipei: Zhonggong yanjiu zazhishe, 1995), section 7, p. 88.
104. *WJ*, 15 June 1992, p. A12.

105. *South China Morning Post* of 3 February 1994, as cited by *WJ*, 22 July 1994, p. A10.
106. *WJ*, 19 June 1992, p. A12; and 27 August 1993, p. A12.
107. *WJ*, 3 February 1994, p. A12.

7

Greater China and the Autonomous Regions

Introduction

Communism, the object of much fear as well as celebration, has proven to be a relatively transient world phenomenon. By the end of 1991, both the Soviet Union and its satellite states in Eastern Europe had fallen. Very little, however, is known concerning the sequence to be expected in the systemic transformation of Marxist-Leninist states.[1] A few states, including Hungary, the former East Germany, and Czechoslovakia, successfully navigated the transition from communism into market-governed democracies. Others, most notably Russia, are suspended in an uncertain limbo of incomplete market reforms and nostalgia for communism. Then there is the former Yugoslavia that, upon its disintegration, descended into the atavistic nationalism of "ethnic cleansing."

In the case of the PRC, its post-communist transformation is already taking place, albeit in a markedly different sequence than its ideological mentor, the former Soviet Union. There, Mikhail Gorbachev attempted political reform without meaningful economic reform. The PRC, in contrast, undertook radical economic reform under the hegemonic auspices of the CCP. Those reforms have transformed the Chinese economy, but they have also created unintended consequences, one of the most serious is that of regionalism. Whether the CCP can control a political environment in which regional, provincial, institutional, and individual interests are increasingly driven by disparate concerns appears to be increasingly problematic.

The problem posed by regionalism is particularly acute in two areas. The first is an emerging geographical entity along China's southeastern coast which many have called a "Greater China." The autonomous regions are a second area in which regionalism poses a direct threat to central authority. These two areas present diverse challenges to the territorial and administrative integrity of the People's Republic. The challenge from Greater China is primarily economic; that of the autonomous regions is ethno-nationalist. Both threats, if uncontained, could eventuate in the dissolution of Communist China.

Greater China

The term "Greater China" refers to a geographical area comprised of the 120 million inhabitants residing in Hong Kong, Taiwan, and the provinces of Guangdong and Fujian along China's southeastern shores.[2] This geographical entity has become economically integrated, and is becoming culturally integrated as well.

Economic integration may be defined as "a process of unification—the means whereby coherence is imposed upon previously separate, even disparate, geographical regions."[3] Two primary indicators of economic integration are multilateral trade and investment. Using these indicators, it is clear that the mainland provinces of Guangdong and Fujian have achieved a remarkable degree of economic integration with Hong Kong and Taiwan.

Trade between Hong Kong and Mainland China

Hong Kong became a British colony in 1842 when the Treaty of Nanjing concluded the Sino-British Opium War of 1840–42. Under British colonial aegis, Hong Kong developed into a vibrant laissez-faire economy as well as a free port.[4] When the Communists assumed power in 1949 on the Chinese mainland, Hong Kong benefitted from the large influx of refugees who supplied the colony with abundant skilled and unskilled labor. Today, Hong Kong takes its place as one of the Four Dragons of Asia. Despite a crushing population numbering 6.3 million residing on only 404 square miles of land, by June 1996, Hong Kong achieved a per capita nominal GNP of $23,200; a per capita purchasing-power parity (PPP) gross domestic product (GDP) of $23,080; and a foreign exchange reserve of $57.2 billion.[5]

From the late-1940s through the 1950s, mainland China was Hong

Kong's biggest trading partner; that situation changed in the 1960s and 1970s, due to the political chaos wrought by the Cultural Revolution. Beginning in 1978, because of the Communist Party's decision to reform and open the mainland's economy to foreign trade and investment, trade between Hong Kong and the mainland accelerated by an annual rate of 39.06 percent between 1978 and 1990. Two-way trade between Hong Kong and the PRC accounted for 27 percent of China's foreign trade in 1989 and 32.4 percent of Hong Kong's total trade in 1991. By 1991, the two had become each other's largest trading partner.[6]

During the period 1978–1990, Hong Kong's imports from China increased by an average of over 31 percent a year, a rate of growth that consistently outstripped that from the rest of the world. Hong Kong's exports to the mainland grew by an even more impressive average annual rate of 124 percent.[7] Before 1978, Hong Kong's exports to China were inconsequential, accounting for only 0.2 percent of the colony's total exports. That share rapidly burgeoned to 11.7 percent in 1985, and 27 percent in 1991.[8]

A considerable portion of Hong Kong's trade with China is conducted with Guangdong and Fujian. The two provinces are hosts to China's first Special Economic Zones that were created in 1979. From 1980 to 1991, Guangdong's exports to Hong Kong grew by 21.2 percent a year. By 1991, 85 percent of Guangdong's exports went to Hong Kong. Its connection with Hong Kong has catapulted Guangdong into being China's foremost exporting province, consistently accounting for more than one-third of total PRC exports since 1986. In 1994, Guangdong exported more than $40 billion worth of goods.[9]

Hong Kong provided a similarly important function for Fujian. In 1992, the colony became Fujian's largest export market. From 1980 to 1985, Fujian's exports to Hong Kong increased by an annual rate of almost 11 percent, accelerating to 28 percent between 1985 and 1991. Altogether, two-way trade between Hong Kong and Fujian accounted for 40 percent of the province's total foreign trade.[10]

Much of the expansion in Hong Kong-PRC trade is due to the colony's increasingly important role as a re-exporter to and from the mainland. Between 1980 and 1985, 31 to 47 percent of China's exports to Hong Kong were subsequently re-exported. That share reached an "astonishing" 86 percent by 1991.[11] In 1994, Hong Kong's entrepôt trade with the mainland totaled HK $868.7 billion.[12] This, perhaps more than anything else, highlights the integration of Hong Kong into the southern Chinese economy.

Nowhere is Hong Kong's entrepot function better illustrated than in the indirect economic transactions between Taiwan and mainland China. It is estimated that, each year, about 25 percent of Taiwanese visitors to Hong Kong are actually destined for the mainland—a fact that elevated Taiwan to the major source of tourists and tourist earnings for Hong Kong.[13] Hong Kong is also a conduit for the exchange of goods and merchandise across the Taiwan Strait. In 1992, almost 49 percent of Taiwan's exports to Hong Kong went to the mainland; nearly 30 percent of what Taiwan imported from Hong Kong actually originated in the People's Republic.[14] This would explain the 21 percent average annual growth rate of Taiwan's exports to Hong Kong since 1989. If this trend continues, Hong Kong will replace the United States as Taiwan's major export market, further signifying Hong Kong's importance as China's entrepôt.[15]

Since 1978, Hong Kong has also become important to China as a direct supplier of industrial goods for the mainland's booming export manufacturing sector that is concentrated in the coastal provinces. Increasingly, Hong Kong is exporting producer goods (machinery and transport equipment) instead of consumer goods to the mainland—further evidence of Hong Kong's economic symbiosis and integration with southern China.[16]

Investment between Hong Kong and the Mainland

Hong Kong's entrepôt function for the People's Republic is not limited to trade. It was estimated in 1996 that over 60 percent, or $76 billion, of foreign investment in China was channeled through Hong Kong.[17] For its part, Hong Kong is itself a major foreign investor in the People's Republic. Not only are China and Hong Kong each other's largest trading partner, they are also each other's foremost outside investor. Direct investment by Hong Kong in the mainland totaled $30 billion by the end of 1993, making the colony the PRC's largest outside investor, accounting for 65 percent of all FDI in China.[18] By the first half of 1995, Hong Kong and Macao together were responsible for 75.1 percent ($196 billion) of all contracted investment in China.[19]

By the end of 1996, China had $42.5 billion invested in Hong Kong. Those investments account for 21 percent of the income of

Hong Kong's insurance industry; 22 percent of the value of its total trade; 23 percent of its bank deposits; 25 percent of its cargo shipment; as well as 50 percent of Hong Kong's tourists to mainland China.[20] The Bank of China is the second largest bank in Hong Kong. The PRC's China International Trust and Investment Corporation owns 12 percent of Hong Kong telecommunications, 12.5 percent of Cathay Pacific, 46.2 percent of Hong Kong Dragonair, and 20 percent of a Hong Kong chemical waste plant.[21] Sometime in the future, Hong Kong also expects to receive 25 percent of the $2 billion that Beijing plans to invest in anticipated oil bases in the South China Sea.[22]

Much of Hong Kong's growing importance as a supplier of industrial goods to China is due to the massive relocation of its manufacturing industries to the mainland. As Hong Kong's economy matured, labor costs and land value became increasingly prohibitive. When China undertook economic reforms in the late-1970s, Hong Kong's labor-intensive manufacturers began transferring their production to the mainland to take advantage of its cheap land and labor. To illustrate, dwellings in Shenzhen, an SEZ in Guangdong, rent for a quarter to a third lower than in Hong Kong.[23] As for labor costs, in 1992, semiskilled workers in Guangdong earned about $100 a month, more than three times the average wage in the rest of China, but "a great bargain" compared with nearly $900 in Taiwan and Hong Kong.[24] By 1996, manufacturing accounted for only about 9 percent of Hong Kong's GDP, a third of what it was in 1980.[25]

Due to Guangdong's geographical proximity and linguistic-cultural affinities with Hong Kong (most Hong Kong Chinese trace their ancestry to Guangdong), the province is a magnet for Hong Kong investors, attracting 54 percent of Hong Kong's FDI and 59 percent of its AFI (all foreign investment) in the mainland.[26] About 80–90 percent of Hong Kong's manufacturing industries had been relocated to Guangdong, creating employment for over 3 million mainlanders. It is for that reason that some have referred to Guangdong as Hong Kong's "industrial belly." Altogether, Hong Kong and Macao entrepreneurs established more than 30,000 enterprises in Guangdong, accounting for 70 percent of the province's total number of registered foreign enterprises and 80 percent of its foreign capital.[27] In the Pearl River Delta alone, Hong Kong investors employ over 2 million workers. The Hong Kong dollar is the currency of choice throughout the province. The economies of Hong Kong and Guangdong have become effectively "inseparable."[28]

Compared to Guangdong, Fujian's intake of Hong Kong capital is less impressive. To illustrate, in 1985–91, Hong Kong invested in the entire province of Fujian a little more than half of what it had poured into Shenzhen, an SEZ in Guangdong.[29] Still, Hong Kong is a major investor in Fujian, accounting for 61.4 percent of the province's total foreign investment.[30] Together, Guangdong and Fujian absorbed as much as two-thirds of Hong Kong's foreign investment in China, providing additional testimony to Hong Kong's economic integration with southern China.[31]

Indirect Trade between Taiwan and the Mainland

In 1948–49, the Chinese Nationalists lost the civil war to the Communists and retreated from the mainland across the Taiwan Strait to the island of Taiwan. In three decades, under the auspices of the Nationalist government, the Republic of China (ROC) on Taiwan became an economic success unparalleled in the developing world. By the late-1970s, the ROC had become economically developed, despite a dearth of natural resources and the mixed blessing of having the world's second densest population. In 1996, Taiwan's 21.5 million people on 14,000 square miles enjoyed a per capita nominal GNP of $12,265; a per capita PPP GDP of $13,235; as well as the distinction of having the world's second largest foreign exchange reserve of $84.7 billion.[32]

After decades of alienation, beginning in 1987, relations between the ROC and mainland China underwent a significant transformation. That year saw the two sides embark on an expanding series of contacts. Since then, an annual average of over 15 million pieces of mail, phone calls, telegraphs, and telegrams have been exchanged across the Strait. Each year, a million residents of Taiwan visit the mainland, infusing at least $2 billion into its economy.[33] Everyday, about 4 billion *renminbi yuan*'s worth of Taiwanese capital (30 to 40 percent of China's total stock capital) circulates in the mainland's stock markets.[34]

Still more significant is the rapid expansion of indirect trade and investment that had taken place since the late-1980s. Those activities remain indirect because Taipei insists there can be no direct mail, transport, commerce, or exchanges of high-ranking officials between Taiwan and the mainland until "mutual trust" is attained. Trust, Taipei maintains, can only be derived when Beijing renounces the use of force against Taiwan and relinquishes its efforts to frustrate and obstruct Taipei's international diplomacy and arms purchases.[35]

The indirect nature of commerce did not prove to be an obstacle. Bilateral trade (mainly through Hong Kong) between Taiwan and the mainland grew from $77 million in 1979 to $14.3 billion in 1993, a phenomenal 185–fold increase in fourteen years. The share of Taiwan's total exports that went to Hong Kong increased from 7.68 percent in 1987 to 21.2 percent ($18.455 billion) in 1993, an estimated 40 percent of which was actually destined for China.[36] By 1994, Taiwan and the mainland had become each other's fourth largest trading partner, their bilateral indirect trade totaling nearly $38 billion.[37]

Indirect Investment between Taiwan and the Mainland

The same forces of rising labor costs and land value that governed the relocation to the mainland of Hong Kong's labor-intensive manufacturing also prompted Taiwan's sunset industries to move across the Strait. The opportunity came in 1987 when Taipei released foreign exchange control and lifted the ban on travel to the mainland. Taiwan entrepreneurs quickly took advantage of the new policy by combining family visits to the mainland with investment ventures. In 1991, Taipei formally authorized what was already transpiring—that is, the "indirect" investment by Taiwan business people in mainland China through the auspices of third parties like Hong Kong. By October 1991, a total of 2,578 Taiwanese enterprises had been registered in Hong Kong, 99 percent of which either invested in or traded with China through Hong Kong.[38]

It is believed that a significant part of the flow of foreign capital from Hong Kong, Japan, the United States, and Southeast Asia into mainland China actually "reflect(s) the activities of Taiwanese firms in disguise."[39] The indirect nature of Taiwan investment in the mainland makes it difficult to accurately estimate its level. But a *Newsweek* account claimed that Taiwan had as much as $24 billion invested in the mainland by 1996,[40] making it the PRC's second largest foreign investor, after Hong Kong.[41] Taiwan-owned businesses on the mainland employ some 5 million workers and are responsible for the indirect employment of another 5 million.[42]

As in the case of Hong Kong, Taiwan's capital is also concentrated in Guangdong and Fujian.[43] Shenzhen tops the list of Taiwan's investment favorites on the mainland, followed by the rest of Guangdong province, Xiamen SEZ (in Fujian), Guangzhou (capital of Guangdong), and Shanghai.[44] Taiwan is the major foreign investor in Fujian, accounting for 44 to 50 percent of the province's FDI (Hong Kong comes second, at 33 percent). Xiamen alone accounts for $1.13 billion of Taiwan capital and as much as a third of all Taiwanese enterprises in the mainland. This prompted Xiamen in 1994 to secure independent law-making powers to create legislation that would particularly favor Taiwan businesses. Xiamen's municipal government plans to enlarge its SEZ to include Kinmen, one of the ROC's offshore islands that is only a few miles away from Fujian's coastline. It is hoped that a Xiamen-Kinmen SEZ would catalyze the creation of a free port in Xiamen, which would be China's first.[45] All of which prompted Fujian officials to openly acknowledge that "they have hitched their fortunes to Taiwan."[46]

In addition to linkages of trade and investment, both Hong Kong and Taiwan (along with Macao) are becoming involved in Fujian's educational endeavors. Between 1979 and 1994, Taiwan, Hong Kong, and Macao together donated 1.2 billion *yuan* towards the education of that province's schoolchildren.[47] A primary school in Xiamen, as an example, was gifted with a classroom full of IBM computers by a Taiwanese businessman.[48]

Economic Relations between Hong Kong and Taiwan

The evidence seems to indicate that the economies of Hong Kong and southern China have become interdependent. The same can be said of Taiwan and southern China. The data on the economic relationship between Hong Kong and Taiwan is more difficult to interpret because of Hong Kong's role as a middleman in the indirect economic transactions between Taiwan and mainland China.

This much can be said: between 1978 and 1988, bilateral trade between Hong Kong and Taiwan increased at an average annual rate of 27.7 percent. Of that, Taiwan's exports to Hong Kong grew at 27.56 percent per year, while Hong Kong's exports to Taiwan increased by 24.02 percent. During the same period, the annual rate of increase of Hong Kong's re-exports (from mainland China) to Taiwan was 30.47 percent.[49] By 1991, Hong Kong had become Taiwan's second largest trading partner, and Taiwan became Hong Kong's fourth largest export market.[50]

Capital flows between Hong Kong and Taiwan were greatly affected by the political uncertainties surrounding the Sino-British negotiations on the future of Hong Kong. As a consequence, Hong Kong's investments in Taiwan fluctuated during 1974–83, decreasing by an average annual rate of 3 percent (a figure that was greatly skewed by a precipitous drop of 40.85 percent in 1983). Taiwan's investment in Hong Kong was similarly affected by the negotiations. Although that investment had been growing by an average annual rate of 54.2 percent between 1974 and 1981, it plummeted to 1.1 percent in 1982 and to 0 percent in 1983.[51]

Investment flows revived when Beijing and London reached an agreement in 1984 that Hong Kong would be returned to the PRC in 1997. Beginning in 1984 and continuing through 1990, Hong Kong's investment in Taiwan increased by an average annual rate of 64.73 percent.[52] By September 1991, Hong Kong had invested $800 million in Taiwan, becoming the ROC's third largest foreign investor (after Japan and the United States).[53] After 1984, Taiwan's investment in Hong Kong also grew at a stable pace.

Greater China and Regionalism

The evidence appears to support the contention that a regional economic body has emerged out of nation-states and colonial residues: the ROC on Taiwan, Hong Kong, and two provinces in the People's Republic. The prevailing political forms seem no longer capable of containing the dynamic economic developments.

All this is the result of political changes in Beijing since 1978. Deng Xiaoping's decision to restore some critical features of a market economy to mainland China carried inevitable consequences, one of which was the opening of Communist China to the transformative influence of market forces that include trade and capital-technology transfers from Hong Kong and Taiwan which have created the economic entity of Greater China.

Greater China is an "iron triangle" of complementary and interdependent commercial and economic partnership which registered the fastest economic growth in Asia in 1991 and is expected to have a GDP equal to France's by the year 2000.[54] In this "iron triangle," Hong Kong provides capital as well as outstanding marketing and financial acumen to Guangdong-Fujian, while the latter supplies Hong Kong with water and foodgrains. Taiwan provides Guangdong-Fujian with capital and technology but relies on Hong Kong as a middleman. Guangdong-Fujian's cheap land and labor enable it to serve as Greater China's industrial manufacturing center, to which Hong Kong and Taiwan's sunset industries have relocated. In this manner, Guangdong and Fujian are enabling Hong Kong and Taiwan to concentrate on developing their high-tech and service industries, thereby upgrading and transforming themselves into post-industrial economies.

The economic dynamism of Greater China has transformed southern China into the PRC's most prosperous and competitive region, where peasant income increased by 100 percent in just six years, between 1985 and 1991. In 1990, Guangdong and Fujian together accounted for 24 percent ($14.8 billion) of China's total exports.[55] In 1995, Fujian exported $9.3 billion worth of goods, ranking fifth in the nation.[56]

Of the two provinces, Guangdong is clearly the dynamo. It leads all of China's provinces in economic growth and wealth, attracting up to a third of all of the PRC's foreign capital since 1979. Guangdong is home to three SEZs (Shenzhen, Zhuhai, Shantou), two open cities (Guangzhou and Zhanjiang), a special open area (the Zhujiang delta), as well as at least one "free trade zone" (in Guangzhou).[57] In 1990, Guangdong exported $10.5 billion worth of goods, about 17 percent of China's total exports. In 1991, Guangdong claimed half (13,320) of the country's total foreign investment projects, $13 billion of foreign capital, more than 20 percent (or 20,000) of registered private enterprises and over 17 percent of all private enterprise workers in China.[58] Not surprisingly, its 1991 average per capita income was almost double the national average. In 1993, Guangdong's GDP grew by an annual rate of 20 percent and its foreign investment by 70 percent. In 1994, the province led the nation in foreign trade, producing some two-thirds of China's total value-added exports for that year.[59]

Shenzhen, an SEZ in Guangdong, ranked first among all Chinese cities in export in 1993, surpassing Shanghai. Shenzhen trades with more than 120 countries and produces most of China's textile products, which have been China's largest export item since 1986, at a total value of $27.1 billion in 1993.[60] Shenzhen's average GNP reached the $2,000 mark in 1991,[61] more than five times the PRC's average per capita GNP.

Given the economic clout of Guangdong and Fujian—which stems largely from their trade and capital linkages with Hong Kong and

Taiwan—it is not surprising that the phenomenon of regionalism is particularly pronounced in these two coastal provinces. Neither province responded to the call from the central government in May 1989 to send garrison troops to Beijing to help suppress the democracy movement. Nor had the two honored the post-Tiananmen national austerity policies.

Guangdong, in particular, is notable for its independence. In 1992, Governor Zhu Senlin repeatedly asked Beijing to devolve even more of its powers to the provinces. That same year, the provincial capital of Guangzhou began horse racing without first obtaining Beijing's permission. Guangdong also broke the central government's monopoly over railroad construction by accumulating its own capital, from local and foreign sources, to construct a high speed railroad.[62]

The trade and investment transfers from Hong Kong and Taiwan have clearly played a decisive role in the growing economic self-sufficiency and political independence of Guangdong and Fujian. The economic clout of Hong Kong and Taiwan is being exerted on other mainland provinces and regions as well. Together with Macao, Taiwan and Hong Kong account for 81 percent of all foreign-invested enterprises in China. In certain areas in southern China, Hong Kong and Taiwan are responsible for as much as 90 percent of total foreign investment. More than half of Guangxi's foreign investment comes from Taiwan and Hong Kong, with Hong Kong being that province's major foreign investor at $1.449 billion. Taiwan, for its part, is the principal investor in Shanghai.[63]

More than just economic integration, there is evidence that mainland China is also becoming culturally homogenized with its Chinese littorals. Along with trade and investment linkages, the popular cultures of Hong Kong and Taiwan have also been exported to the mainland, beginning in the late- 1970s and early-1980s, in the form of music tapes, movies, novels, and television programs. Before too long, mainland audiences became the captives of Taiwan crooner Teresa Teng, Qiong Yao's romance novels, and Hong Kong martial arts movies. Hong Kong's penetration was particularly intense, its pop culture products entering the mainland "through almost every channel and in every format—official and private, legal and illegal, paid and free, print and broadcast, audio and visual, quality and vulgar." At the same time, the mainland's mass culture is also being exported, although the direction of cultural flow is skewed in favor of Hong Kong and Taiwan.[64]

The homogenization of popular culture must be considered another vital component linking Greater China together. As David Shambaugh observed,

> Anyone who walks the streets of Mainland Chinese cities, or even the dusty roads of interior rural villages, cannot help but be struck by the pervasiveness of what might be called a Greater Chinese popular culture; Karaoke bars, MTV, KTV, discos, pornography, rock and rap singers and film stars from Hong Kong and Taiwan have all penetrated the consciousness of mainland China's youth.[65]

All of this has alarmed the leaders in Beijing. Since the late-1980s, Beijing had tried to prohibit the unauthorized importation or broadcast of movies and TV programs from Hong Kong and Taiwan.[66] As an example, an editorial in the *People's Daily* in 1989 decried the pervasiveness of "low-quality cultural products" from Taiwan and Hong Kong, and described the situation as "intolerable." The editorial called for a halt in the flow of such imports because of their "unhealthy" effect on Chinese society.[67] Despite Beijing's efforts, the penetration of mainland culture has only intensified.

Guangdong and Fujian, because of their geographical proximity, are particularly saturated with Hong Kong and Taiwan's cultural exports. The formation of a "Greater Cultural China" can only hasten those provinces' increasingly discrete identity from the rest of China.

Historically, Chinese revolutions tended to germinate in the south because of the latter's great distance from Beijing and its reach. In the nineteenth and twentieth centuries, it was also the coastal south that was the most cosmopolitan in its outlook due to contacts with foreign traders and the outside world. As Wang Xizhe, former Marxist theorist and Democracy Wall activist of the late-1970s, put it, "Step by step, the south is gaining the upper hand. . . . .The issue in the future will be whether the lifestyle and concepts of the south will prevail over those of the north."[68]

As the strength of Greater China increases, Beijing's control over what is now the People's Republic measurably diminishes. Greater China already displays some of the cardinal features of a pluralistic and market-based polity. Taiwan and, in part, Hong Kong both possess functional representative governments. As China's major trading partners and foreign investors, both are carriers of the democratic "virus" and, as such, exercise inestimable influence on the mainland's future development.

Given the fact that Hong Kong will surrender much of its autonomy when it is repatriated to Beijing on 1 July 1997, Taiwan will be the sole unit in Greater China that remains sovereign and independent from Beijing. After 1997, Taiwan will become the linchpin of Greater China. The recognition of the dangers posed by a Greater China that includes a fully democratic Taiwan could well have contributed to Beijing's provocation of the Taiwan Strait crisis of March 1996.[69]

The Autonomous Regions

The formation of "Greater China" is only one piece in the overall picture of a People's Republic where, increasingly, the center does not hold. The autonomous regions[70] on China's periphery are also challenging central authority. Whereas Greater China's threat to the PRC's political integrity is primarily economic, the grievances of the autonomous regions are ethno-nationalist in nature. Those grievances have assumed the form of demands, not only for greater autonomy from Beijing, but for nothing less than secession.

Since its inception, the People's Republic has been a multinational state with one dominant nationality, the *Han* or ethnic Chinese, comprising slightly less than 92 percent of the total population. According to the PRC's 1990 census, the remaining 8 percent (91.2 million people) of the population is made up of 55 minority nationalities who, despite being a numerical minority, occupy 64 percent of China's land area and are concentrated in the economically backward but strategically important border regions.[71] They include the Manchus and Koreans in the northeast; the Mongolians in Inner Mongolia; the Huis in Ningxia; the Uighurs and Kazaks in Xinjiang; the Tibetans in Xizang (Tibet); the Zhuangs in Guangxi; and many smaller ethnic groups in Yunnan and Guizhou.

After the Communist Party assumed control of China, it created a three-tiered system of autonomous political entities for the minority peoples. By 1958, most of today's five autonomous regions (*qu*), thirty autonomous prefectures (*zhou*), and 125 autonomous counties (*xian*) were established. Together, they account for about 64 percent of China's total territory and 78 percent of its minority peoples.[72]

Aside from the ethnic differences that distinguish them from the dominant Hans, China's minorities also endure endemic poverty and a growing gap in living standards from the rest of China. In 1985, the

PRC State Council reported that 142 (or 43 percent) of China's 331 poorest counties were in the minority areas. In 1993, out of the 27 million poor in China (those with less than 200 *yuan* in average annual per capita income), as much as 20 million lived in the autonomous areas.[73]

Of the five autonomous regions of Tibet, Xinjiang, Inner Mongolia, Ningxia, and Guangxi, ethnic conflicts and separatist movements are the most problematic in the first three.[74] The sources for the tensions in those regions transcend ethnicity and poverty. Like the phenomenon of Greater China, the rising nationalisms in the autonomous regions are yet another unintended consequence of Deng Xiaoping's reforms. The increased economic opportunities created by the reforms have attracted entrepreneurial Hans to the minority areas, creating conditions reminiscent of America's "Wild West." Despite those increased opportunities, the autonomous regions lag behind the booming coastal provinces in economic growth. The general feeling among the minorities is that of having been victimized in an unequal race towards prosperity, their resentment further fueled by the channelling of their regions' abundant natural resources out to the coast for processing. At the same time, the minority regions are also experiencing a brain-drain to the more prosperous provinces.[75]

Tibet

Tibet has been described as the region where Beijing "has faced and undoubtedly will continue to face its biggest challenge" because of the international attention and sympathy Tibetans attracted.[76] The history of Sino-Tibetan relations, like most everything else in Tibet, is subject to conflicting accounts.

The Chinese maintain that Tibet has been an inseparable part of China since the thirteenth century from the time of China's Yuan dynasty (1280–1368). In maintaining this, the Chinese conveniently overlook the reversion of Tibet to independent status when the Yuan dynasty fell to the Ming (1368–1644). Thereafter, Tibet was independent for more than 200 years.[77]

Tibetans, for their part, insist that they have "always been a distinct nation" that was effectively independent from 1912 until the Chinese Communist "liberation" in 1950.[78] More than that, Tibetans refer to a Sino-Tibetan treaty of 821 which they claim "clearly" established equality of status between China and Tibet, as well as the frontiers between the two countries.[79] That treaty is carved into an obelisk in front of the Jokhang Temple in Lhasa, Tibet's capital, but "walled out of view by the Chinese. . . ."[80]

Chinese forces under the Qing dynasty briefly occupied Tibet early in the twentieth century. With the fall of the dynasty came Tibet's independence in 1912. But its religious doctrine of non-violence assured it would have no effective army to defend itself against the Chinese Communist takeover in 1950. Although Beijing pledged not to interfere with Tibet's government or society, it proceeded to carve Tibet into six regions, five of which were incorporated into China Proper. The remaining sixth region, half the size of pre-1950 Tibet, was proclaimed an autonomous region in 1965.[81]

Beijing's failure to live up to its promise of non-interference led to mounting tensions in Tibet which culminated in a bloody uprising in 1959 that was brutally suppressed by the People's Liberation Army. Tibet's spiritual and political leader—Tenzin Gyatso, the fourteenth Dalai Lama, believed to be a direct human incarnation of Chenrezig, the thousand-armed, thousand-eyed god of compassion—along with 100,000 of his followers, fled to India where a government-in-exile was formed.

The years after 1959 were difficult ones for Tibet. It was under a military rule from 1959 to 1965. In 1965, the Tibet Autonomous Region was proclaimed, only to be followed by ten years of looting and destruction in the name of the Cultural Revolution.[82] According to the Tibetan exile government, more than six thousand temples and monasteries were pillaged or destroyed; countless monks and nuns were jailed or sent to forced-labor camps; historical records and Buddhist scriptures were publicly burned; much of Tibet's grain output was sent to alleviate food shortages elsewhere in China. Altogether, 1 to 1.2 million Tibetans reportedly died in purges or mass starvation from the grain seizures.[83] By 1966, about 7,000 of Tibet's original 115,000 monks and nuns remained. All of which prompted the International Commission of Jurists to declare the Chinese occupation of Tibet a prima facie case of genocide.[84]

Beginning in 1979, along with the nationwide economic liberalization, the Communist Party also relaxed its control over the religious and cultural lives in the autonomous regions. In Tibet, Beijing condoned a limited revival of Buddhism, believing that "by allowing Tibetans a carefully controlled form of religious expression, they would become happy and content with Chinese rule." Many of the pagodas and monasteries destroyed during the Cultural Revolution were renovated and rebuilt; old festivals were revived; monasteries once again became the heart of Tibetan community. Tibet's borders were opened to the outside world, leading to increased contacts with outsiders, including the infiltration of the teachings of exiled masters in India and beyond.[85]

Ironically, Beijing's liberal policy had an effect opposite than what was intended. A Canadian Tibetan scholar explained that, "As the Tibetans pushed up against the limits of the policy, they realized how cynical the policy really was. . . ." For the Tibetans, their Buddhist religion is a cultural, collective, and national enterprise, which is bound up with the totality of their existence. But it is precisely that all-encompassing nature of Tibetan Buddhism which the Chinese government cannot tolerate.[86]

As part of its new policy, Beijing also initiated a dialogue with the Dalai Lama, maintaining that "everything was negotiable" except that Tibet must remain "an inseparable part" of China. In 1988, the Dalai offered a "middle way," proposing a future in which Tibet would remain part of China but would have wide autonomy in all matters except foreign policy and defense. Beijing denounced the offer as "a disguised form of independence" and reverted to a hardline policy.[87]

Beginning in 1987, Tibet experienced separatist disturbances of varying scale, all spearheaded by monks and nuns, which were put down by the police with live ammunition. On 5 March 1989, large riots broke out in Lhasa which were forcefully suppressed by the Chinese military who reportedly fired on the mob. Estimates were that 469 demonstrators were shot and 3,000 were imprisoned. The Chinese government gave an official figure of twenty deaths.[88]

On 8 March 1989, martial law was imposed in Lhasa which would endure for thirteen months. Since that time, protests have sporadically taken place, mostly in the capital but also in previously unaffected remote areas. In May 1993, the largest disturbance since 1989 occurred in Lhasa, involving 1,500 to 2,000 people and lasting eight to nine hours. The incident began as a protest against inflation and the lifting of price controls on food, but the slogans quickly escalated to the nationalist cry of "Chinese out of Tibet!" The crowd threw stones at police cars, but was quickly subdued with tear gas by machine-gun toting police and soldiers.[89] Amnesty International estimated that by the end of 1994, 628 Tibetans had been imprisoned for their political beliefs, including 182 women and children as young as twelve years old. Many were detained without charges or trials; others were sentenced to two to fifteen years' imprisonment. Confessions were often extracted under torture.[90]

In April 1994, according to the exile government, Beijing deployed 30,000 soldiers or three army divisions to Tibet, bringing the PLA's presence there to a total of 80,000. The International Campaign for Tibet (ICT), a human rights organization based in Washington, D.C., claimed that the number of Chinese soldiers in Lhasa now nearly equaled that of Tibetans.[91] The result, as U.S. Senator Larry Pressler put it, is that "Tibet is an occupied country" where the Chinese army is "omnipresent."[92]

More than the military occupation, ICT also claimed that China has increased its religious persecution, threatening "to smother Tibetan Buddhism. . . ." The rights of monks and lay Buddhists are regularly violated; the few autonomous monasteries have been eliminated; religious practice outside of the monasteries is barred; and "work teams" of state cadres have been dispatched to the monasteries to enforce discipline and identify dissident monks with the help of police interrogators and specialists in torture. Beijing arrogates to itself the supervisory right over the financing, planning and construction of monasteries. It restricts the number of monks at each monastery; mandates a minimum age of eighteen for monks; and requires young Tibetans to gain the permission of the Communist Party before becoming novices. In general, "every kind of attempt by Tibetan Buddhists to revitalize their faith" is being thwarted.[93]

In November 1995, Beijing appointed a six-year-old boy as the eleventh incarnation of the Panchen Lama—a living Buddha second only to the Dalai in religious importance—who died in 1989. In so doing, Beijing followed a 200–year-old precedent from imperial China of appointing Tibetan high religious figures. But Beijing's action was also in contraindication to the Dalai's choice who has since disappeared with his family and is feared to be harmed or under house arrest. In May 1996, in response to the Chinese government's prohibition of public displays of the Dalai's pictures, Lhasa once again erupted in riot, judged to be the most serious in a year. More than eighty individuals were reported to be wounded.[94]

Western scholars and diplomats believe that the sentiment for independence in Tibet is widespread, especially in the cities.[95] The ethnic differences between Chinese and Tibetans are evident. The Chinese language is based on ideographs; Tibetan is alphabetical, based on Sanskrit. China's traditional religion is Confucianism, which is concerned less with the afterlife than with the proper moral code governing hierarchically-ordered human relationships. Tibetan Buddhism, in contrast, evolved from Mahayama Buddhism, with monasteries at the core of social and political life. In short, the two peoples can be said to be "about as similar as apples and asparagus" so that "No Tibetan . . . .would claim to be Chinese."[96]

The ethnic gulf that divides Tibetans and Chinese is made worse by China's traditional regard of minorities and neighboring peoples as "barbarians" of one kind or another. This attitude still persists—if a new brochure issued by Beijing is any indication. Reportedly, the brochure portrays Tibet as in "the last dark ages" before its "peaceful liberation" by the Communist Party who propelled "a primitive society of serfdom into the modern society of civilization." A Tibetan monk gave eloquent expression to his people's collective sense of outrage when he said:

> The reality is that we are part of China. . . . .But even if you are willing to accept this, you get angry by the way China controls us. The Chinese have no real respect for our history or culture. They think we are savages who are lucky to be ruled by China. [97]

Fanning the flames of ethnic discontent is Beijing's aggressive policy of Chinese resettlement in the autonomous region. Although China's minority regions have seen Han in-migration before 1949, Tibet began to experience significant influxes of Hans only after 1950. Since that time, the exile government maintains that "millions" of Chinese have relocated to Tibet, lured by huge economic incentives. Overall, Chinese now outnumber Tibetans by a million; in Lhasa, the ratio is as much as 3:1.[98] To make matters worse, it is the Chinese who seem to have benefitted the greatest from the post-1979 economic reforms. Those reforms have created a growing class of prosperous Chinese officials and traders who are "reaping the benefits of Tibet's development." Left behind are impoverished Tibetans who must endure the price hikes and food shortages that "accompanied heavy Chinese migration" into the region.[99]

More than ethnic discrimination, the Dalai Lama and various international organizations have also accused the Chinese government of exploiting and degrading Tibet's environment. Its forests have been clear-cut to stock China's lumber mills, with potentially disastrous effects on the ecosystem of the entire Asian subcontinent.[100]

An ICT report asserted that, since the early-1980s, China has been producing nuclear weapons and extracting uranium in Tibet. It is believed that near Lhasa may be the world's largest uranium mine. Based on interviews with Chinese nuclear experts, government officials, and eyewitnesses; as well as two field trips and the chemical analysis of native soil samples, the ICT report also claimed that an indeterminate number of natives, especially children, living near uranium mines and No. 9 Science Academy, a secret nuclear city in Qinghai, have become ill or died from radiation contamination.[101]

According to claims made by the Dalai Lama's exile government, China has about ninety nuclear warheads in Tibet, some of which can be fitted on intercontinental guided missiles.[102] Another human rights organization, the International Committee of Lawyers for Tibet, accused the Chinese of using unwitting Tibetans for radiation-tolerance tests and treating Tibet as a dumping ground for nuclear wastes produced in China and abroad. In 1984, China reportedly sold West Germany the right to store up to 4,000 tons of radioactive waste in Tibet for 16 years for a sum of $6 billion.[103]

The account by the Chinese government is entirely different. According to Tibet's Governor Jiang Chunbu, Chinese constitute less than 3 percent of Tibet's total population of 2.25 million, 96 percent of whom are Tibetan.[104] (Almost every Western visitor to Lhasa, however, said that Chinese migrants outnumber Tibetans in the capital.)[105] Rather than Hans dominating the political class in Tibet, the Chinese government maintains that more than 70 percent of the cadres are Tibetan. More than that, 75 percent of Tibet's investment expenditure is borne by the central government in Beijing,[106] which has contributed a total in excess of 20 billion *yuan* since 1950. Tibet has the lowest tax burden of all the regions and provinces of China, with only eighteen varieties of taxes, twenty-three fewer than other provinces. In 1980, Beijing gave the Tibetan government discretionary powers to alter the national tax policy within certain parameters. Tibet's rural and private enterprises are exempted from all taxation until the year 2000. There is no tax on the sale of religious items such as incense; on the products of native industries; on rental income and the sale of staples such as vegetables, fruits, fish, fowl, and eggs; and on the transportation of foodgrains, cooking oil, salt, and meat into Tibet.[107]

An independent Chinese scholar has provided a detailed account of Tibet's economic dependence on the central government, belying its nominally "autonomous" status. According to Xu Mingxu, before 1950, Tibet was an impoverished land with no industries or natural resources, and a population of one million, 30,000 of whom lived in Lhasa, including 4,000 to 5,000 beggars. After 1950, the Chinese government provided every Tibetan with free education and health-care privileges not accorded to the Chinese in the rest of China. Since 1980, Beijing has infused Tibet with more than 1 billion *yuan* a year in subsidies— the product of "the blood and sweat of the Han people." Natives employed in Tibet's state-owned industries not only enjoy free housing, their salaries are two to three times greater than those in comparable positions in Beijing. Tibet's 43,000 monks and nuns are completely supported by the state, and have become "a de facto aristocracy" in the People's Republic. Since 1950, Tibet's population has grown more than 100 percent to over 2.2 million; Lhasa's has increased fourfold to 120,000. Xu asserts that without Beijing's subsidies, only half of Tibet's present population could be supported by the native economy. Today, despite Beijing's financial transfusions, Tibet still must import 25 percent of its foodgrains; its economy remains severely retarded, with industry accounting for only 20 percent of total economic output.[108]

Xinjiang

Xinjiang Uighur Autonomous Region, located in the northwestern corner of China, is the country's largest province. In land area, it is one-sixth of the People's Republic and four times that of France. Xinjiang is strategically situated, bordering on eight countries: Mongolia (which the Chinese still refer to as Outer Mongolia), Russia, Kazakhstan, Kirgizstan, Tajikistan, Afghanistan, Pakistan, and India. Xinjiang contains at least one listening post on Russia and is also the site of Chinese nuclear tests since 1964 in the desert wasteland of Lop Nor.[109]

The autonomous region has been described as "a potential El Dorado." Its crude oil reserves below the Gobi and Taklimakan deserts are believed to be three times the proven U.S. oil reserves and, when tapped, should produce 74 billion barrels of oil to fuel China's soaring economy. Without Xinjiang's oil, China will have to rely on imports for its oil needs. Already, 360 successful wells have been drilled, providing employment for 5,000 workers.[110]

Xinjiang is also known for its jade deposits and other minerals. Beneath the mountain ranges that traverse the region, 122 different minerals wait to be exploited. Gold, silver, and platinum have been discovered. An Australian businessman who has traded with, and seen satellite survey photos of, Xinjiang proclaimed that its mineral resources make Australia's "look just a bit puny. . . ."[111]

Xinjiang's population of 14.6 million is a mosaic of thirteen ethnic groups, most of whom "look more to the Middle East and Turkey for inspiration than they do to Beijing."[112] As a case in point, the Islamic city of Kashgar in southern Xinjiang is 3,500 miles from Beijing but only 150 miles from the border with Kirgizstan. The Uighurs are the majority nationality, numbering 6–8 million; followed by 5–6 million Hans; 1 million Kazaks; the Hui, Mongols, Kirgiz, Tajiks, and Xibe.[113] Muslims (mostly Sunni) make up more than half of Xinjiang's population; the region is also home to China's largest concentration of Turkic-speaking people. Although the Uighurs, Kazaks, and Kirgiz are Turkic-speaking Muslims, there is no full overlap between religion and language. As examples, the Hui are actually Han (and Chinese-speaking) who are considered a distinct nationality because of their Muslim faith. The Tajiks, descendants of subjects of Alexander the Great, are Persian-speaking followers of an Islamic sect led by the Aga Khan. Probably the most exotic of all, the 20,000 Xibe are Manchu-speaking descendants of an army sent in the late- 1700s from northeastern China to help the Qing dynasty guard and colonize the western frontier. Travelling with their wives and children the soldiers arrived with 350 babies born on the year-long trek.[114]

Like Tibet, which the Chinese call *Xijang* (meaning "western store-house"), Xinjiang's name also betrays its double identity. Xinjiang is Chinese for "new frontier" but many of its inhabitants call it "East Turkestan."[115] Long sought by China as a corridor between East and West, Xinjiang was traversed by the fabled Silk Road as early as the second century. Once a part of Turkestan, it was incorporated as a province of China during the Qing dynasty in 1884. But Chinese rule over Xinjiang was uneasy from the very beginning.[116]

Since the early-1900s, there was already talk of a Uighur-led separatist movement that would make Xinjiang an independent nation named Eastern Turkestan. But the independent republics that arose in parts of Xinjiang in the 1930s and 1940s were short-lived.[117] In 1933–34, southern Xinjiang saw a brief attempt to establish an independent "Turkish-Islamic Republic of Eastern Turkestan." In 1944, the Ili valley broke out in an anti-Chinese riot that culminated in the establishment of an East Turkestan Republic, only to be negotiated back into the Chinese fold by the end of 1948 under the Nationalist regime.[118] In September 1949, the governor of Xinjiang, Bao Erhan, broke off relations with the Nationalist government and accepted Chinese Communist rule.[119]

In the early-1950s, Xinjiang's Huis and Kazaks mounted significant armed resistance against Communist rule. But Beijing strengthened its control, creating in 1955 the Xinjiang Uighur Autonomous Region. After that time, by and large, the Chinese government was rarely challenged until the 1980s. Exceptions included a large riot in 1962, and an incident during the Cultural Revolution when Beijing deployed an entire army division to level a Muslim village of 8,000 for demanding greater religious freedom.[120]

As was the case in Tibet, Beijing began to ease on its repression of the minority nationalities in Xinjiang after 1979, only to reap the opposite effect than intended. In 1981, anti-Chinese riots erupted in Kashgar against the decision of the Chinese government to halt the construction of a local mosque. In 1985, a riot broke out in Urumqi when university students demonstrated against the Lop Nor nuclear tests. Another large riot broke out in 1988, probably in response to the Chinese government's extension of the population control policy to the autonomous regions. Although minority couples could have up to two children in the cities and three in the countryside—which was a much more generous policy than the one-child-per-couple restriction for the Han Chinese—the new policy nevertheless intensified the minorities' resentment.[121] A Uighur hotel employee in Urumqi gave expression to that resentment when he said, "There are already few enough of us. If they limit us to two kids, that'll be the end of us."[122]

In April 1990, about fifty Uigurs and Kirgiz were killed by the PLA after two days of riots in Kashgar, Hotan, Kutcha and, most seriously, Baren.[123] Despite the closing of southern Xinjiang to foreign travellers, demonstrations and riots continued until the middle of August.[124]

In June 1991, Hong Kong's *Cheng Ming* magazine reported that "bloody incidents" erupted in two cities in Xinjiang. The first occurred in mid-May when armed citizens occupied a city government for thirty-six hours and exchanged fire with the Chinese military, resulting in more than 140 deaths, injuries, and arrests. The second incident occurred in June when more than 3,000 people surrounded another city government, demanding that they be returned to Soviet rule and that their mayor be democratically elected. In the course of the PLA's suppression of the uprising, some 500 died or were wounded.[125]

In March 1992, a peaceful Uighur demonstration for more religious freedom ended in violence after security forces fired on the crowd, killing several civilians.[126] The following year, in July and August 1993, bombs allegedly set by Muslim separatists exploded in Kashgar. Five men were executed for the attacks, described by the local press as members of the separatist Islamic Reformist Party.

In 1994, it was reported that many separatist incidents took place in Xinjiang, particularly in the south, in which Hans were attacked. Oilfields, mines, and communication lines and facilities were destroyed. Chinese in Xinjiang had to arm themselves and travel in groups to ensure safety.[127]

In 1995, Muslims rioted in Hotan when Chinese authorities removed a popular Islamic imam suspected of fomenting dissent.[128] In 1996, separatists assassinated several people, including two policemen in February and a pro-Beijing Muslim cleric in March. Early in May, nine men, said to be Muslim rebels plotting bomb attacks, were reportedly killed in a gunbattle with police. In late July, Uighur guerrillas attacked a PLA convoy in the Taklimakan Desert. Five days later, in July, Uighur separatists killed twenty Chinese soldiers guarding the border with Pakistan. Uighur exiles in Kazakhstan claimed there had been widespread street fighting in Xinjiang since April, in which 450 PLA soldiers and militia men had died. As much as 1,800 Uighur separatists had been arrested, a figure that was disputed by the Chinese authorities.[129] The official *Xinjiang Daily* cited five violent incidents since early February, as well as police seizures of 2,723 kilograms of explosives, 4,100 sticks of dynamite, 604 guns and 31,000 rounds of ammunition.[130]

Clearly, Beijing's fears of a rise of pan-Turkic and Islamic movements in Xinjiang are not fanciful. There is a new militancy in the alleys of Kashgar and other Uighur cities along the fringes of the

Taklimakan Desert. In the 1980s, much of Xinjiang remained closed to the outside world because of tensions along the Sino-Soviet border. As those tensions gradually eased, and particularly with the dissolution of the Soviet Union in 1991, Xinjiang's border gates were unlocked and travel restrictions were loosened. Xinjiang's officials admitted that political liberalization in the former Soviet bloc has helped "to stir nationalist sentiments against Chinese rule." Exiled Xinjiang separatists returned to disseminate their message of independence, encouraged by nationalist movements in other parts of the world, especially in the newly independent former Soviet republics of Central Asia.[131]

Historically, most of the ethnic disturbances in Xinjiang could be traced to some foreign connection or another. Certainly, the two brief republics in the 1930s and 1940s had the support of foreign governments: the British in the case of the 1933–34 East Turkestan Islamic Republic; Russia in the case of the 1944–48 East Turkestan Republic. Today, it has been suggested that political figures in Uzbekistan, who regard the Uighurs as their "brothers" because of linguistic and cultural similarities, have ambitions to create a pan-Turkic federation that would include Xinjiang.[132] There is also some evidence that the Russian military is selling arms to Xinjiang separatists; extremist currents and illicit small-arms are also coming across the borders from Pakistan and Afghanistan.[133]

After the 1990 riots, Beijing's apprehension concerning Xinjiang's foreign connection greatly increased, which prompted the imposition, in September, of a new set of restrictions on religious activities. Muslim clerics were prohibited from foreign contacts, including receiving donations from outside sources. All preachers must be registered and their sermons regulated. They were required to "oppose national separatism" and were forbidden from teaching the history of Islamic holy wars because this would "incite nationalist hatred." Unruly clerics were threatened with dismissal or arrest. The use of religious writings, recordings, and videos not officially approved was banned, along with unsanctioned mosque construction. Especially targeted are private Islamic schools, some of which were closed for allegedly supporting the separatist movement. Altogether, Beijing closed down fifty religious facilities, halted the construction of 153 mosques, and interrogated more than 12,000 Muslims in Kashgar. The Communist Party also undertook the rectification of ten local CCP organizations in Kashgar, along with its Communist Youth League, the Women's Association and the local militia.[134]

Uighur exiles in the United States said that three issues, in particular, fuel their desires for independence. They are the testing of nuclear weapons in Xinjiang and its effects on the environment; the exploitation of Xinjiang's oil, viewed by the natives as their property; and the massive migration of Han Chinese into the region which is increasingly displacing the natives from their own land.[135]

Uighurs in self-exile in the United States claimed that the Chinese government has been systematically pouring migrants into Xinjiang in order to make Hans the majority. Han immigration into Xinjiang began as a form of military agricultural settlements (*tun tian*) in the 1950s. In the twentieth century, as in the eighteenth, China used the army to colonize Xinjiang. The soldiers organized Production and Construction Corps, comprised of farms, factories, and other enterprises. Their efforts built an economic empire in Xinjiang of 2.2 million people, nearly all of them Hans who answer to Beijing.[136] The migrant soldiers were supplemented by two million urban Chinese youth who were "sent downwards" (*xiafang*) by Mao to lend "a more Chinese flavor" to the autonomous region.[137] More recently, in December 1992, the official *China Daily* reported that 100,000 people displaced by the Three Gorges dam project would be resettled in Kashgar prefecture. That figure is a modest estimate because local officials had agreed to invest $350 million in land and housing development that would provide for the resettlement of 500,000.[138]

The result of the successive waves of Han migration has been a dramatic increase in the Chinese population in Xinjiang. A Western scholar estimated that 250,000 to 300,000 Hans enter the autonomous region each year. Today, Chinese comprise at least three-quarters of Urumqi's residents. In 1949, no more than 4 percent of Xinjiang's population was Chinese; by 1993, however, their proportion had swollen to at least 40 percent, nearly equal to the number of Uighurs. In effect, the number of Hans in Xinjiang multiplied twenty-five times in forty-four years, from 200,000 in 1949 to at least 5 million by 1993.[139]

The heavy influx of Hans predictably has increased ethnic tensions. Hans and the minority nationalities rarely intermarry or work together. The Chinese are better educated and take the best paid jobs in government and industry. They dominate the government bureaucracy that employs many natives but rarely in leading positions. Although the law mandates that Xinjiang's governor must be a Uighur, almost all the natives in government are under Han superiors. Hans run the city and dispense most of the jobs in Urumqi. In Altay, a city spread along a high river valley, as in other Xinjiang cities, Chinese seem to have most of the jobs in the new industries, most notably in the lucrative oil industry where few natives are employed because they lack the requisite skills. Instead, most of the workers are Hans brought in from the oil fields from other parts of China.[140]

All of this has resulted in a conspicuous gap in wealth and living standards between the Chinese and the natives. Chinese women in the factories typically earn more money in two months than a native herdsman can expect to make in a year; the average annual per capita income of oil workers is more than 3.5 times greater than that of the average Uighur peasant (2,680 and 732 *yuan* respectively).[141] The disparity in wealth only feeds the minority nationalities' suspicion that Xinjiang has become a "colony" of China. They are convinced that Beijing's Sinocentric policies are systematically draining Xinjiang of its abundant raw materials to supply the booming factories in the coastal provinces.[142]

Whatever effort that Beijing makes towards providing "autonomy" to Xinjiang's minority nationalities appears to be unsuccessful at assuaging their discontent. Beijing's efforts have included ethnic schools where the teaching is conducted in the group's own language. There is affirmative action in university admission for the non-Hans who are accorded preferential treatment. Natives can use their own languages in newspapers and on radio and television, although Chinese is the official language.[143] There is religious freedom to the extent that all Muslims can freely pray in mosques, although those freedoms have been significantly curtailed since the riots of April 1990.

Expressing, no doubt, his fellowmen's frustration, a Kazak college student complained that "We are being squeezed to death by the Hans. . . .Every year there are more of them. Every month there are new regulations."[144] Another twenty-two-year-old youth in Kashgar admitted that "We don't like Han people. They are not like us: they neither herd, nor ride horses or follow the Muslim faith. We loathe them." A twenty-four-year-old Uighur youth was even more outspoken. After the suppression of the 1990 riots, he professed to be in favor of a war with China. "Even if I were to die in battle, I'll be happy. Xinjiang is Turkestan, it is not China."[145] After comparing Xinjiang to Kuwait in that both had been "invaded by a foreign nation," another young man, a twenty-seven-year-old Kashgar merchant, predicted that "If China were to disintegrate after Deng's death, Xinjiang will be among the first to break away from the Communist Party's control."[146]

Inner Mongolia

Both Inner and Outer Mongolia were a part of China during the Ming and Qing dynasties. In 1921, with the support of the Soviet army, Outer Mongolia declared its independence from China only to become a satellite and dependent of Moscow. In 1924, the Mongolian People's Republic (MPR) was established but was refused recognition by the Chinese Nationalist government in Nanjing.[147] In 1946, the Chinese Communists formally recognized the MPR, who returned the favor when the People's Republic of China was installed.[148] In 1992, upon the dissolution of the Soviet empire, MPR democratized itself into Mongolia. On 30 July 1996, democratic Mongolia conducted its second parliamentary election in which the Democratic Union Coalition won a majority of the legislative seats in the Great Hural, thereby ending seventy years in power of the formerly communist Mongolian Revolutionary People's Party.[149]

In land area, Outer Mongolia is 1.3 times the size of China's Inner Mongolian Autonomous Region (IMAR) but has a population (2.3 million) only one-tenth that of the IMAR. Today, China's Mongolians can be found, not only in the IMAR, but also in Gansu, Qinghai, and Xinjiang. Although Inner Mongolia has the largest concentration of ethnic Mongols in China, numbering 3 million, they constitute a minority 13 percent of IMAR's total population. Hans are the largest ethnic group in Inner Mongolia, at 21 million; other smaller nationalities make up the remaining million.[150]

The fact that Mongols are not a majority nationality in Inner Mongolia probably has made it difficult for them to effectuate any meaningful or significant resistance to Chinese rule. Another reason may be Inner Mongolia's proximity to Beijing—IMAR's capital, Hohhot, is only seven hours by tank from Beijing. From 1949 until the 1980s, Inner Mongolia has had relatively few ethnic disturbances. That, however, does not mean that Beijing is complacent. As one expert put it, "The looming headache of the Chinese authorities is the revival of pan-Mongolism. . . ."[151]

Like Tibet and Xinjiang, Inner Mongolia's minority nationalities were also severely mistreated during the Cultural Revolution. For two years, the Chinese government engaged itself in a campaign to rout a non-existent separatist organization, the Inner Mongolian People's Party. In the course of that campaign, more than 47,000 died and 590,000 were imprisoned. Ironically, by persecuting the ethnic Mongols in the IMAR, Beijing succeeded in creating exactly the demon it feared. Instead of extinguishing the flame of separatism, the campaign sparked the beginning of a genuine movement for Mongolian national liberation in the autonomous region.[152]

In the early-1980s, encouraged by Beijing's more relaxed policy towards Tibet and Xinjiang, Inner Mongolian students began to agitate for greater autonomy. They took their message to the streets and even sent a delegation to petition Beijing. At the same time, activists created a nationalist organization, the Inner Mongolian Revolutionary People's Party, whose rallying cry was "Descendants of Genghis Khan Unite!"[153]

By the end of the 1980s and the beginning of the 1990s, the separatists found new encouragement in the reforms and the subsequent dissolution of the Soviet Union as well as the democratization of (Outer) Mongolia. These events all had a "demonstration effect" on Inner Mongolia's ethnic nationalists. Alert to the potential danger, Beijing quickly reinforced the PLA's presence in Inner Mongolia and along the Sino-Soviet border by a total seventeen divisions.[154]

The Chinese government claims that IMAR separatists have formed several illicit groups with ties to democratic Mongolia, including the Inner Mongolian National Self-Government Committee and the Asian Mongolian Freedom Front. These groups reportedly advocate the independence of Inner Mongolia from Beijing and its unification with (Outer) Mongolia to form a united Republic of Mongolia. Group membership is comprised of university students, intellectuals, and even local Communist Party cadres. The organizations have been active since 1990, distributing propaganda and organizing speeches, symposia, and family reunions. Many of their members have been blacklisted and are under government surveillance. Some scholarly groups have been disbanded.[155]

From 1989 to 1990, Inner Mongolia saw a rash of pro-democracy demonstrations. In May 1991, the Chinese authorities arrested two leaders of the separatist movement, along with many of their followers. They were charged with "attempting to overthrow the leadership of the Communist Party," "fomenting nationalist separatism," and creating a "terrorist atmosphere" within the autonomous region.[156]

From November 1991 to January 1992, large-scale pro-independence protests and riots broke out in many cities across Inner Mongolia. Beijing intensified its surveillance, interrogation, and arrest of activists,[157] secretly sentencing three individuals, two of whom were teachers, to two to eight years' imprisonment for "disseminating intra-Party splittist (separatist) propaganda." Most recently, it was reported that Inner Mongolia's capital and border areas have experienced many anti-Chinese disturbances since November 1995.[158]

Conclusion

The problem of regionalism is most acute in two separate areas in China. The first is the phenomenon known as "Greater China," where China's southeastern coastal provinces of Guangdong and Fujian are becoming economically and culturally integrated with Hong Kong and Taiwan. The second area consists of China's autonomous regions, especially Tibet, Xinjiang, and Inner Mongolia.[159]

The manner in which regionalism expresses itself differs in the two areas. In Greater China, the growing autonomy of Guangdong and Fujian stems from their economic wealth and power, which in turn have been created from the trade and capital linkages the two provinces have forged with Hong Kong and Taiwan. In the autonomous regions, regionalism expresses itself as ethno-nationalism: the desire of minority nationalities like the Tibetans, Uighurs, and Mongolians to secede from the People's Republic. Although China's non-Han peoples constitute only 6–8 percent of total population, they are concentrated in the border regions of China which, though poor, are indispensable to Beijing because of their strategic location. Tibet and Xinjiang are also militarily valuable because they are the sites for the construction and testing of China's nuclear weapons. Finally, the autonomous regions are important because of their natural resources, particularly in the case of Xinjiang's oilfields and Tibet's uranium mines.

To prevent regionalism from becoming a serious threat to its power, Beijing relies on a variegated set of methods. Towards Greater China, Beijing has sought to control the independence of Guangdong and

Fujian with the traditional ploy of personnel rotation—witness the recent transfers of Guangdong governor Zhu Senlin to head the Hong Kong legislature, and of outspoken Sichuan Governor Xiao Yang to oversee construction of the Three Gorges dam.[160] The return of Hong Kong to Chinese sovereignty in 1997 no doubt will also help to contain whatever threats Greater China might pose to Communist Party rule. Finally, Beijing's recent get-tough stance towards Taiwan, when it "test-fired" missiles barely miles away from Taiwan's coastline, sent a clear message that it will not tolerate any move on the part of Taipei to completely sever itself from the historic China and from any prospect of eventual reunification with the mainland.

Towards the autonomous regions, Beijing has not hesitated to use force to squelch even relatively minor ethnic disturbances. Beijing has shown it will use anything within its powers to prevent the breakaway of the autonomous regions, including the surveillance of activists; restrictions on religious activities; arrests and imprisonment; and the use of lethal force by the PLA.

At the same time, the use of force is supplemented with international diplomacy. In recent years, Beijing has been cultivating better relations with its Asian land neighbors. In 1994, Premier Li Peng visited Kazakhstan, Kirgizstan, Tajikistan, and Uzbekistan to develop trade and economic relations. In April 1996 in Shanghai, China, Russia, Kazakhstan, Kirgizstan, and Tajikistan signed an agreement on border and military issues which effectively pledged all parties to peace and non-aggression. In July 1996, PRC leader Jiang Zemin signed joint communiqués with Uzbekistan and Kazakhstan, in which they assured Beijing they would not lend assistance to ethnic separatists in China.[161]

In some cases, Beijing has resorted to "dollar diplomacy"—the employment of financial incentives to dissuade other governments from abetting ethnic secessionists in China. As an example, in June 1996, the PLA gifted Mongolia's military with $360,000 in return for the latter's pledge of non-support for separatist movements in Inner Mongolia and Xinjiang.[162] Beijing is also counting on neighboring governments' apprehension about their own internal stability. For example, Kazakhstan has eschewed support for Uighur nationalists in Xinjiang because it fears that this will give ideas to Kazakhstan's own huge Russian minority who make up over 40 percent of the country's population.[163]

At the same time, towards both Greater China and the autonomous regions, Beijing is also counting on a "pocket- book" appeal to their economic self-interests and pragmatic calculations. Beijing hopes that economic growth will persuade everyone that it is in their interest to stay within the political arrangement of the People's Republic of China. As long as the economy continues to grow at the rate it has since 1979, it would be in everyone's interest to maintain stability.

So long as the Chinese economy continues its dizzying growth, Beijing will have the resources to improve the parlous circumstances of the autonomous regions. Beijing has accorded priority to their economic development in the ninth Five-Year Plan (1996–2000). Increased subsidies, loans, and investment capital will be funneled from Beijing to improve the economies of the minority regions and, through that, dissuade the non-Han peoples from seeking independence.[164]

As for the coastal provinces, as long as they continue to prosper, they will probably not begrudge surrendering part of their wealth to help support impoverished regions such as Tibet. But there is no assurance that this scheme will be effective if the example of Shenzhen SEZ in Guangdong province is any indication. In July 1996, it was reported that Shenzhen outright refused Beijing's request for a 20 percent increase in revenue remission to help the poorer western regions of China. Shenzhen was also resentful that it must bear 70 percent of the subsidies for impoverished Guizhou province, when Qingdao was only asked to contribute 30 percent.[165]

As for Tibet, so long as it continues to be heavily subsidized by Beijing, there will be some incentive to stay within China, although the endless riots and demonstrations suggest that the incentive is weak, at best. In the case of Xinjiang, as long as it continues to do as well economically as it has in recent years with a thriving border trade and increasing foreign investments, keeping Xinjiang intact will appear to be a better bet than uniting with ethnic brethrens in Central Asia. Beijing is counting on people such as a middle-aged Uighur shoe-seller to be the majority opinion in Xinjiang. He reportedly said to a reporter that "I have a good job and a family. As for splittism—that's for people with nothing better to think about."[166] Shirin Akiner, a Central Asia expert at London University's School of African and Oriental Studies, noted that "a lot of Uighurs have benefited from the economic boom and see every reason to stay in China."[167] Xinjiang now has fourteen open ports as well as investment ties with more than twenty countries, including the United States, Britain, France, Kuwait, Saudi Arabia, Hong Kong, and Macao. Xinjiang's economy has grown 10 percent a year since the early-1990s. Its border trade increased more than 32 percent from 1990 to 1991, and a spectacular 150 percent from 1991 to 1992.[168]

As for Inner Mongolia, the fact that its economy is doing much better than independent Mongolia's across the border certainly plays to Beijing's advantage. But the allure of Mongolia's triumphant democratization cannot be underestimated.

Although they are important, simply relying on pragmatic considerations of economic self-interest is not enough. Any country, particularly a multinational state like the People's Republic, requires something more. Eudaemonic legitimation is too fragile a foundation for secure and stable government, more so if citizen expectations exceed economic performance.[169] Political legitimacy must also reside in the inchoate, ineffable, but powerful realm of ideals, feelings, and sentiments. People's hearts, souls, and minds must also be engaged. This will be the subject of the chapter to follow.

Notes

1. See, for example, the discussion in Robert W. Campbell, ed., *The Postcommunist Economic Transformation* (Boulder, CO: Westview, 1994); *Markets, States and Democracy: The Political Economy of Post-Communist Transformation*, ed. Beverly Crawford (Boulder, CO: Westview, 1995).
2. See, for example, Dinah Lee, "Asia: The Next Era of Growth," *Business Week* (11 November 1991): 56–59; and Andrew Tanzer, "Greater China, Greater Profits," *Forbes* (3 August 1992): 84–85.
3. Robert F. Ash and Y.Y. Kueh, "Economic Integration within Greater China: Trade and Investment Flows Between China, Hong Kong and Taiwan," *The China Quarterly*, no. 136 (December 1993): 713.
4. In recent years, however, businesses are increasingly hampered by government. There has also been a sharp rise in government's social spending, resulting in the beginnings of a welfare state. By 1996, overall public spending stood at slightly over 16 percent of GDP (compared with 42 percent for Britain). See Editorial, "Market Knows Best," and William McGurn,"Diminishing Returns," *Far Eastern Economic Review* 5 (13 June 1996): 62–68.
5. "The Bottom Line," *AsiaWeek* (14 June 1996): 64, 63. Purchasing-Power Parity is based on World Bank ratios and takes into account price differences between countries to provide a more accurate picture of national wealth.
6. Li Ming, "Hong Kong's Foreign Trade Role Emphasized," *Beijing Review* (13–19 May 1991): 35; *WJ* (12 April 1992): A1; and *Shaonian zhongguo chenbao* (*Young China Daily* or *YCD*) (7 December 1990): 3.
7. Ash and Kueh, "Economic Integration," 715.
8. Chu-yuan Cheng, "Hong Kong's Changing Economy: New Trends and Future

Viability," *American Journal of Chinese Studies* I (April 1992): 40; Sheryl Wu Dunn, "Hong Kong-China Fence: No Bar to Business," *New York Times* (12 April 1992): L20.

9. *WJ*, 19 September 1994, p. A19.
10. Ash and Kueh, "Economic Integration," 722–723; *WJ*, 13 June 1992, p. A12.
11. Ash and Kueh, "Economic Integration," 715.
12. *WJ*, 16 July 1996, p. A8.
13. *WJ*, 26 February 1994, p. A18; 19 August 1994, p. A6.
14. Ash and Kueh, "Economic Integration," 718.
15. *WJ*, 9 May 1994, p. A15.
16. Ash and Kueh, "Economic Integration," 720.
17. Edward Iwata, "Moment of Truth," *San Francisco Examiner* (hereafter *SFEx*), 30 June 1996, p. C4.
18. Cheng, "Hong Kong's Changing Economy," 41. A more recent account put Hong Kong's total direct investment in China at $77.6 billion by 1995. *WJ*, 29 July 1996, p. A15.
19. *WJ*, 15 June 1996, p. A19.
20. *WJ*, 11 November 1996, p. A16.
21. Murray Weidenbaum, "Greater China: A New Economic Colossus?" *Washington Quarterly* (Autumn 1993): 71–83.
22. Louis Kraar, "A New China Without Borders," *Fortune* (5 October 1992): 125; Teh-pei Yu, "Businessmen and Chinese Bureaucracy: How Taiwan, Hong Kong, and the PRC Work Together," paper prepared for the Twentieth Sino-American Conference on Mainland China, June 1991, pp.8–9.
23. Reuben Mondejar, "Cross-Border Insurance," *Far Eastern Economic Review* (10 October 1991): 70.
24. Kraar, "A New China," 125.
25. William McGurn, "Diminishing Returns," *Far Eastern Economic Review* (13 June 1996), 63.
26. AFI refers to "all foreign investment." Ash and Kueh, "Economic Integration," 733, 734.
27. *WJ*, 25 October 1993, A12.
28. Cheng, "Hong Kong's Changing Economy," 41; Ash and Kueh, "Economic Integration," 743.
29. Ash and Kueh, "Economic Integration," 730.
30. *WJ*, 29 July 1996, p. A15.
31. Ash and Kueh, "Economic Integration", 734.
32. "The Bottom Line," *AsiaWeek*.
33. Editorial, *WJ*, 2 August 1994, p. A2.
34. *WJ*, 20 September 1994, p. A18.
35. For a more detailed treatment of Taiwan-mainland relations, see Maria Hsia Chang, "The Future of Taiwan-Mainland Relations," in *Contemporary China and the Changing International Community*, ed. Bih-jaw Lin (Taiwan, Taipei: Institute of International Relations, 1993), 199–215.
36. *WJ*, 25 July 1994, p. A18; Cheng, "Hong Kong's Changing Economy," 44–45.
37. *WJ*, 12 July 1994, p. A18; and James O'Connor, "Boom Times in Xiamen, Taiwan's Outpost on the Mainland," *San Francisco Chronicle* (hereafter, *SFC*), 15 February 1995, p. A9.
38. *WJ*, 3 November 1991, p. 4.
39. Ash and Kueh, "Economic Integration," 734, 735.
40. Joe Klein, "The Spiritual Power of Democracy," *Newsweek* (1 April 1996): 35.

41. *WJ*, 13 July 1994, p. A16; 2 March 1994, p. A17; Cheng, "Hong Kong's Chang- ing Economy," 45.
42. Barnett F. Baron, "The Chinese Superpower: China, Taiwan, and the Chinese Diaspora," speech at the University of Nevada, Reno, 25 March 1996. Baron is the Asia Foundation's executive vice president.
43. Ash and Kueh, "Economic Integration," 735.
44. Jian Zheyuan, "Xianggang zai liangan jingji jiaoliu de zhongjie diwei (China's Middleman Role in Taiwan-Mainland Economic Transactions)," *Zhongguo dalu yanjiu (Mainland China Studies)* 36 (November 1993): 80.
45. *WJ*, 19 September 1991, p. 10; 3 December 1991, p. A11; 22 March 1994, p. A12; and 2 August 1994, p. A2.
46. Hong Kong's *South China Morning Post*, 1 April 1991, as cited by *News Digest* (New York: Government Information Office, CCNAA), 2 April 1991, p. 2.
47. *WJ*, 14 April 1994, p. A13.
48. O'Connor, "Boom Times," A9.
49. Yu, "Businessmen," 10.
50. *WJ*, 21 December 1991, p. A18.
51. Yu, "Businessmen," 10, 12.
52. Ibid.
53. *WJ*, 21 December 1991, p. A18.
54. According to *Business Week*, 11 November 1991. As cited by *WJ*, 4 November 1991, p. 2.
55. James McGregor, "Two Nations: China's Entrepreneurs are Thriving in Spite of Political Crackdown," *Wall Street Journal*, 4 June 1991, p. A1.
56. *WJ*, 11 June 1996, p. A12.
57. *WJ*, 15 June 1992, p. A3.
58. In contrast, inland Yunnan, Qinghai, Ningxia, and Xinjiang altogether had only 2.6 percent (or 2,500) of China's registered private enterprises. *WJ*, 6 June 1991, p. 11.
59. McGregor,"Two Nations"; and *WJ*, 7 January 1994, p. A19; 17 May 1994, p. A19; and 17 April 1994, p. A9.
60. *WJ*, 9 March 1994, p. A18; and Seven Mufson, "Textile Exports Stream Out of Special Economic Zone in China," *SFC,* 11 January 1995, p. A12.
61. According to an article in the *Economist* (4 October 1991). As cited by *WJ*, 5 October 1991, p. 10.
62. *WJ*, 16 August 1992, p. A10; 3 January 1993, p. A9; and 21 April 1992, p. A10.
63. *WJ*, 1 April 1994, p. A12, and 27 June 1996, p. A19; Barnett Baron, "Chinese Superpower."
64. Junhao Hong, "Media/Culture Penetration of Mainland China by Taiwan and Hong Kong," paper presented at the Thirty-seventh annual meeting of the Ameri- can Association for Chinese Studies, Reno, NV, 10–12 November 1996. See also Thomas Gold, "Go With Your Feelings: Hong Kong and Taiwan Popular Culture in Greater China," *The China Quarterly* 3 (1993): 907–925.
65. David Shambaugh, "Introduction: The Emergence of Greater China," *The China Quaterly* 3 (1993): 659, 658.
66. Hong, "Media/Culture," 8.
67. Editorial, *People's Daily*, 13 December 1989.
68. Sheila Tefft, "Southern China's Activists-Businessmen," *Christian Science Moni- tor* (hereafter *CSM*), 12 April 1994, p. 3.
69. Baron, "Chinese Superpower." For almost two weeks in March 1996, Beijing "test-fired" missiles barely twenty miles from two major ports of Taiwan, and

also conducted war game exercises with live ammunition and a force of 150,000 amassed along the mainland coast facing Taiwan.

70. For background information on the autonomous regions, consult the following: Owen Lattimore, *Inner Asian Frontiers of China* (Boston: Beacon, 1967); John K. Fairbank, ed., *The Chinese World Order* (Cambridge, MA: Harvard University, 1968), 1–33, 180–205; June Teufel Dreyer, *China's Forty Millions: Minority Nationalities and National Integration in the People's Republic of China* (Cambridge, MA: Harvard University, 1976); and Dru C. Gladney, *Muslim Chinese: Ethnic Nationalism in the People's Republic* (Harvard University: Council on East Asian Studies, 1991).

71. *Zhonggong nianbao 1995* (*1995 China Yearbook*) (Taipei: Zhonggong yanjiu zazhishe, 1995), section 5, p. 49.

72. Harald Bockman, "The Brewing Ethnic Conflicts in China and Their Historical Background," in *Ethnicity and Conflict in a Post-Communist World: The Soviet Union, Eastern Europe and China*, eds. Kumar Rupesinghe, Peter King, and Olga Vorkunova (New York: St. Martin's, 1992), 188–89.

73. *WJ*, 13 June 1993, p. A9.

74. On 3 December 1991, at the Thirteenth Plenum of the Eighth CCP Central Committee, Jiang Zemin identified Tibet, Xinjiang, and Mongolia to be three of five areas that displayed significant independent tendencies. The other two are Korea and Taiwan. Reported by Hong Kong's *Jingji ribao*, as cited by *WJ*, 3 December 1991, p. A10.

75. Bockman, "Ethnic Conflicts," 191.

76. Ibid., 194.

77. James D. Seymour, "Zhongguoren kandai xizang wenti di lishixing zhuanlie (A Historic Turning Point in Chinese Perception of the Tibetan problem)," *Zhongguo zhichun* (*China Spring*) (Alhambra, CA), no. 154 (July 1996): 89.

78. "Anti-Chinese Protests Spreading Across Tibet," *SFC*, 23 June 1992, p. A9; and Jeff Greenwald, "Shangri-la's Shackled Spirit," *Image* magazine (of the *San Francisco Sunday Examiner and Chronicle*), 14 April 1991, p. 22.

79. Seymour, "Turning Point," 89.

80. Larry Pressler, "Tibet Under Chinese Thumb," *CSM*, 19 October 1993, p. 20.

81. Greenwald, "Shangri-la," p. 22.

82. Ian Johnson, "Beijing Tries to Lure Chinese to Tibet with Promise of Perks," *SFC*, 26 September 1995, p. A17.

83. "Tibetan Culture Lives On, Despite China's Hard Line," *CSM*, 21 July 1993, p. 4.

84. Greenwald, "Shangri-la," p. 22.

85. James L. Tyson, "Chinese Repression Threatens Tibet's Buddhist Tradition," *CSM*, 21 September 1990, p. 4; and "Tibet: Holiday Resort," *Economist*, 13 April 1996, p. 32.

86. James Tyson, "Chinese Repression." The scholar is Professor Ronald Schwartz of Newfoundland's Memorial University.

87. John F. Burns, "Dalai Lama Finds China's Threats a Subject for Humor and Anxiety," *New York Times*, 6 March 1996, p. A4.

88. Greenwald, "Shangri-la."

89. "Hundreds of Tibetans Protest Chinese Rule," *SFC*, 25 May 1993, p. A8.

90. "China Accused of Horrors in Tibet," *SFC*, 30 May 1995, p. A6.

91. In 1990, Chinese government documents showed a military force of 50,000 troops in Tibet. *WJ*, 25 April 1994, p. A10; and 3 May 1994, p. A12.

92. Pressler, "Tibet."

93. James Tyson, "Chinese Repression."
94. "10 Tibetan Prisoners Throw Chili in Driver's Eyes, Escape," *SFEx*, 25 February 1996, p. A-9; and *WJ*, 31 May 1996, p. A12.
95. "Anti-Chinese Protests."
96. Greenwald, "Shangri-la," 22; Larry Pressler, *op. cit.*
97. Johnson, "Beijing."
98. Bockman,"Ethnic Conflicts," 191; and Greenwald, "Shangri-la," 23.
99. "Tibetan Culture Lives On."
100. Greenwald, "Shangri-la," 24.
101. *WJ*, 19 April 1993, p. A1.
102. *WJ*, 8 June 1993, p. A2.
103. Greenwald, "Shangri-la," 24.
104. *WJ*, 23 May 1993, p. A3.
105. Johnson, "Beijing."
106. "Zhonggong zhaokai disanci Xijang gongzuo zuotanhui (Chinese Communists Convene Third Working Symposium on Tibet)," *Mainland China Studies* 37 (September 1994): 4.
107. *WJ*, 1 September 1993, p. 4; and 31 January 1993, p. A19.
108. Xu Mingxu, "Xijang huoshan guoran chongxin baofa (Tibet's Volcano Is Certain to Erupt Again)," *WJ*, 15 June 1993, p. A5. See also his *Xijang wenti: lishi, xianzhuang yu weilai (The Tibetan Issue: History, Present and Future)*, Papers of the Center for Modern China, Somerset, NJ, October 1991, no. 12.
109. *YCD*, 23 October 1990, p. 3.
110. Thomas B. Allen, "Xinjiang," *National Geographic* 189 (March 1996): 43.
111. Uli Schmetzer, "China's El Dorado Seethes With Unrest," *SFEx*, 15 April 1990, p. A16.
112. "Beijing Dispatches Troops to `Silk Road' Outpost," *SFC*, 10 April 1990, p. A19.
113. Schmetzer, "China's El Dorado."
114. Bockman, "Ethnic Conflicts," 194; and Allen, "Xinjiang," 13, 34, 24.
115. The Turks are divided into two tribes: the western Turks settled in Turkey and Iran; the eastern Turks, mostly Muslim, are found in Kazakstan, Kirgizstan, and Xinjiang.
116. Ann Scott Tyson, "Beijing Rebukes Ethnic Unrest," *CSM*, 18 April 1990, p. 4.
117. Allen, "Xinjiang," 13.
118. Bockman, "Ethnic Conflicts," 187, 188.
119. Bi Yingxian, "Zhonggong yu zhongya guanxi (Communist China's Relationship with Central Asia)," *Mainland China Studies* 7 (September 1994): 9.
120. *YCD*, 3 May 1990, p. 3.
121. Ann Scott Tyson, "Beijing."
122. J. H. Chao, "Chinese Influx Irks Muslims," *SFEx*, 27 December 1992, p. A2.
123. Schmetzer, "China's El Dorado."
124. *YCD*, 15 September 1990, p. 3.
125. *WJ*, 29 June 1991, p. 10.
126. Chao, "Chinese Influx."
127. *WJ*, 14 August 1994, p. A9.
128. Allen, "Xinjiang," 13.
129. *WJ*, 11 July 1996, p. A12; 12 July 1996, p. A12; and 16 July 1996, p. A10. Beijing maintained that only "several thousands" were arrested. *WJ*, 13 July 1996, p. A14.
130. Anthony Davis and Sangwon Suh, "The West Gets Wilder," *AsiaWeek*, 14 June 1996, p. 32.

131. "Beijing Dispatches Troops to `Silk Road' Outpost"; and Bockman, "Ethnic Conflicts," 192.
132. Bi, "Zhonggong," 10.
133. *WJ*, 28 June 1996, p. A12; and Davis and Suh, "West," 32.
134. *WJ*, 15 August 1993, p. A2; *YCD*, 19 October 1990, p. 3; 23 October 1990, p. 3; and 30 October 1990, p. 3. The new religious restrictions were also imposed on the Tibetans as well as Chinese Christians.
135. Allen, "Xinjiang," 40.
136. Ibid., p. 24; and Bockman, "Ethnic Conflicts," p. 191.
137. Schmetzer, "China's El Dorado."
138. Chao, "Chinese Influx."
139. Allen, "Xinjiang," 22.
140. Ibid., p. 27.
141. Ibid., p. 18; and *WJ*, 24 April 1993, p. A14.
142. Ann Scott Tyson, "Beijing."
143. Allen, "Xinjiang," 27.
144. Schmetzer, "China's El Dorado."
145. *YCD*, 23 October 1990, p. 3.
146. *WJ*, 15 August 1993, p. A2.
147. Cheng Tiejun, "Waimeng minzhucao dui zhongguo dalu di chongji (The Impact of Outer Mongolia's Democratic Movement on Mainland China)," *China Times*, 16 February 1990, p. 7. Under pressure from Stalin, the Nationalist government briefly recognized the MPR immediately after the Second World War but quickly reversed itself. In July 1996, a legislator of the Nationalist Party on Taiwan proposed that the Republic of China on Taiwan formally recognize the now democratic Mongolia.
148. *WJ*, 10 June 1991, p. 10.
149. The Coalition won forty-eight out of the seventy-one contested seats for the seventy-six-seat parliament. Voter turnout was an impressive 87.3 percent. Foreign poll observers, including former U.S. Secretary of State James Baker, attested to the election's free and fair character. Scott Hillis, "Mongolian Democrats Claim Victory," *SFC*, 1 July 1996, p. A12.
150. Bockman, "Ethnic Conflicts," 194; and *WJ*, 10 June 1991, p. 10.
151. Bockman, "Ethnic Conflicts", p. 194.
152. Cheng Tiejun, "Outer Mongolia."
153. Ibid.
154. Ibid.
155. *WJ*, 10 June 1991, pp. 1 and 10.
156. Ibid.
157. The reports were denied by Beijing. *WJ*, 25 March 1992, p. A12; and 3 April 1992, p. A12.
158. *WJ*, 29 March 1992, p. A10; and 28 June 1996, p. A12.
159. Trouble may also be brewing in China's three northeastern provinces, formerly Manchuria, which reportedly have "not forgotten [they were] sovereign, most recently from 1932 to 1945." Johann Fink, "In East Asia, Many Peoples Seek Statehood," *CSM*, 19 September 1991, p. 19.
160. *SFC*, 12 February 1996, p. A8.
161. *WJ*, 25 April 1994, p. A10; and 6 July 1996, p. A2.
162. Reported by Bangkok's *Asia Times*, as cited by *WJ*, 28 June 1996, p. A12.
163. Davis and Suh, "West," 34.
164. *WJ*, 1 July 1996, p. A20.

165. Hong Kong's *South China Morning Post*, as cited by *WJ*, 9 July 1996, p. A17.
166. Chao, "Chinese Influx."
167. Davis and Suh, "West," 34.
168. *WJ*, 24 December 1992, p. A10; Davis and Suh, "West," 34; and Bi, "Zhonggong," 11.
169. Leslie Holmes, *The End of Communist Power: Anti-Corruption Campaigns and Legitimation Crises* (New York: Oxford University, 1993), 52.

8

The Appeal to Nationalism

The Problem

By altering Marxism-Leninism-Maoism into a developmental nationalist ideology, Deng Xiaoping provided the rationale and legitimation for the economic reforms that have transformed China in less than two decades. But the reforms also spawned unintended consequences that more and more threaten the future of the People's Republic of China. Among them, the problem of regionalism qualifies as one of the most pernicious.

"Turning and turning in the widening gyre, the falcon cannot hear the falconer; Things fall apart; the center cannot hold. . . . "[1] The coastal provinces, made prosperous by foreign trade and investment, are increasingly independent from Beijing. The autonomous regions, harkening to the call of ethno-nationalism, have made their separatist desires unambiguous. Across the broad expanse of continental China, the ancient forces of centrifugalism once again threaten to break through the dikes.

The disinclination of the coastal provinces and the autonomous regions to remain inside the political system of the People's Republic is intensified by ideological erosion. Fewer and fewer in the CCP and among the people still believe in the god of communism. Without the legitimation and fixative qualities of ideology, the Party would no longer function as an integral national organization. Under those circumstances, there would be even less reason for provincial and local officials to maintain their primary attachment to Beijing.

There is increasing evidence that both the Party and its ideology are in parlous circumstances. To begin with, China's premier ideologues appeared to have been contaminated by "spiritual pollution." In July 1991, it was announced that the Institute for the Study of Marxism-Leninism and Mao Zedong Thought would be dissolved because it "had become a hotbed of capitalist thought." Beginning in the late-1980s, according to Beijing, reformist thinkers made the institute their "main camp." Nearly 13 percent (nine out of seventy) of the institute's associates had been involved in the 1989 democracy movement.[2]

The erosion of ideology is reflected in the dissension within the ranks of the Party. A survey conducted in July 1987 revealed that only 57 percent of CCP members were proud of their membership. Less than a third (30.26 percent) of all respondents in the survey had "a good image of the Chinese Communist Party in their minds." Whereas 66.74 percent of all respondents thought that China needed a reform of the political system, an overwhelming majority (80.27 percent) of CCP members held that belief.[3]

Given the discontent within the Communist Party revealed by the 1987 survey, it should come as no surprise that two years later, about 800,000 CCP members actually took part in the 1989 democracy movement. As reported by Hong Kong's *Cheng Ming* magazine in 1991, the Party's internal investigation revealed that between May and July 1989, over 90,000 CCP members turned in their membership cards; 8,000 cadres resigned from their work posts; more than 300 Party organizations proposed to dissolve, reinstitute, or change the name of the CCP. After the violent suppression of the democracy movement at Tiananmen, 27 percent of Party organizations did not return to normal operation. For over a year, some 2.4 million CCP members expressed their disaffection by withholding their dues.[4] All of which prompted then PRC President Yang Shangkun, in a speech in October 1991, to warn that the Party was in danger because "Some of our comrades are beginning to have doubts about socialism and are worried about its future in China."[5]

Aside from the corrosion within the Communist Party, the rise in the number of religious converts in officially atheistic Communist China is also suggestive of a decline in ideological belief and commitment. The number of religious believers in China was estimated by the Party to be one-tenth of the population in 1991.[6] Excluding religions such as Buddhism and Daoism which do not have formal conversion rituals, official government figures in 1991 had the number of Muslims, Catholics, and Protestants in China at 17 million, 3.5 million, and 4.5 million, respectively. Those figures meant that, since 1949, the number of Muslims had grown by 112 percent; Catholics 30 percent; and Protestants by 543 percent. The actual number of Christians in the People's Republic is actually much higher than the official figures because many of them remain covert in underground churches. According to unofficial estimates made in 1992, when those covert Christians are included, China's Catholics and Protestants actually numbered 12 million and 63 million, respectively. Beijing is particularly troubled by the increase in the number of Christians because they are identified as a conduit for the West's "peaceful evolution" of China away from socialism. Among the Christians, Beijing has special reason to be concerned about the Protestants. Not only is the religion popular among young people, the number of new converts exploded after the 1989 Tiananmen incident.[7] As a case in point, according to PRC Vice President Wang Zhen, the number of Protestants in Henan province increased 250 percent in eight years, from 40,000 in 1982 to more than 100,000 by 1990.[8]

Compounding the problem is the fact that the Party seems to be losing out to religion in its relative ability to attract followers. In 1990, in one village in Henan, three times as many people were converted to Catholicism than were recruited into the Communist Party (813 versus 270).[9] Surveys of 500 Shanghai university students, conducted by the PRC's Central Institute of Education and Science, found that the percentage of students who "believed in communism" fell precipitously from 60 percent in 1982 to only 2.95 percent in 1989. At the same time, the percentage who "believed in religion" rose from 8 percent to 41.8 percent. Even more alarming to Beijing is the fact that some members of the ostensibly atheistic Communist Party are Christian.[10]

Despite the parlous state of the Party and its ideology, if all else fails, Beijing could still depend on force to compel compliance from breakaway provinces and regions. The military would be the last instrument that could be used to preserve the integrity of the People's Republic—provided that the People's Liberation Army retains its institutional and ideological coherence.

After the violent suppression of the student demonstrators at Tiananmen Square on 4 June 1989, Beijing labored at convincing the Chinese people as well as foreign observers that the PLA—the instrument employed in the suppression—remained a patriotic and unified institution. The truth suggests a somewhat different picture.

In the first place, the PLA's high command was divided over how to deal with the students. Reportedly, the commanders of the Thirty-eighth and Twenty-eighth Armies balked at using force against their own people.[11] Armies from China's border regions had to be brought in to do the job, in the course of which thousands of unarmed civilians were crushed by tanks or killed by soldiers with AK-47s. It was maintained that conflicts between the PLA's Twenty-seventh and Thirty-eighth Armies were symptomatic of "deep divisions within the army that could have threatened . . . the leadership as a whole."[12]

In the fallout after the bloody events at Tiananmen, at least twenty officers at the division level and above, as well as thirty-six officers at the regimental or battalion level were investigated for dereliction of duty. Between June 1989 and September 1990, thirty PLA officers fled the country.[13] In November 1990, a special internal investigation implicated 4,200 members of the PLA, an unspecified number of whom were described as skeptical of the Party's leadership and of socialism's putative superiority. The PLA maintained that some of its members were in contact with "illicit" organizations; wrote and distributed "reactionary" leaflets; sold intelligence to foreign agents; and attempted to flee from the country.[14]

The PLA's troubles had predated the Tiananmen incident. It was reported in 1991 that, since 1987, more than 600 cases of a "political nature" involving young officers had been brought before the military's highest court. Thirty-five "conspiratorial" and "reactionary" groups were identified; some 400 PLA members were implicated, including two colonels, four lieutenant colonels, seven majors, and twenty-nine lieutenant commanders.[15]

In July 1991, a mainland Chinese magazine, *Vanguard* (*Qianshao*), reported that young officers had formed secret organizations within the PLA and were awaiting the right opportunity to instigate a coup. The government uncovered one such covert group in the Fuzhou military region and captured about forty escaping officers. There had also been an increase in military sabotage. PLA dissidents set fire to a satellite and missile base in Qinghai, which killed more than 250 people. Four of the conspirators were captured, and the military division that was assigned to the base was transferred to Hubei. In general, unrest was reported to be on the rise within the PLA, particularly in Tibet and Xinjiang.[16] In the case of Tibet, "nominally communist" local officials were identified to be secretly loyal to the Dalai Lama and were acting as his "internal agents."[17]

One of the prime indicators of ideological decay must surely be corruption by Party and government officials. In China today, corruption has corroded the Party, the government, and even the PLA. From top to bottom, members of the Party, state and military are engaged in bribery, smuggling, and flagrant misuse of public funds. Repeated efforts to control and eliminate the abuses have been ineffective. Premier Li Peng admitted in 1995 that corruption was imperiling national stability.[18]

Corruption has contributed to the increasing delegitimation of Communist Party rule which, in turn, exacerbates the ideological and spiritual vacuum. Today, the regime in Beijing is described as having "no ideology that captivates the world, no legitimacy to secure its rule at home."[19] The moral decay of government is a microcosm of the anomie, lawlessness, and nihilism in the larger society. As a prominent Chinese journalist put it,

In Russia, there's no state, but there is a society. . . . Here it's more like the reverse. . . . There's nothing to hold us together. It's only a question of time before everything falls apart.[20]

The Turn to Nationalism

Classical Marxism conceived economic classes to be the real and fundamental units of human society. Nations and states, in contrast, were held to be artificial constructs wholly manufactured by the ruling class to dupe the workers. Though Marxist, the Chinese Communists had never hesitated to exploit nationalism when it suited their purpose. Mao Zedong himself recognized the tactical value of nationalism. Maintaining that nationalism, communism, and imperialism were the three "isms" in the world and that nationalism was originally "the rear base of imperialism," Mao nevertheless affirmed that nationalism could become "our rear base" if it was opposed to imperialism.[21]

During China's war with Japan in the 1930s and 1940s, nationalism indeed became the Chinese Communist Party's "rear base." The CCP successfully aligned itself with the anti-Japanese sentiments of the Chinese people, and rapidly multiplied its membership and expanded its base in northern China.[22] The CCP's exploitation of nationalism as its "rear base" targeted, not just the Japanese, but also the western colonial powers. As a case in point, for years, the Chinese Communists made a particular issue of a sign that was hung outside a park in the foreign section of pre-communist Shanghai, which allegedly was inscribed with the stinging words CHINESE AND DOGS NOT ALLOWED. The infamous sign became a vivid symbol to the Chinese of the contempt and abuse that the foreign powers had heaped on China for a century, beginning with the Opium War. In 1994, a mainland Chinese magazine, *Shiji* (*Century*), revealed that the Chinese Communist Party had fabricated the entire account.[23]

Just as it had appealed to nationalism in the past, the CCP today is turning to nationalism as a panacea for its many problems. The *Economist* observed that, "With communism discredited and democracy distrusted, China is in search of a new ideology . . . [and] nationalism may be filling the gap."[24] In the twilight of Deng Xiaoping's rule, the Party is actively promoting and encouraging a resurgent Chinese nationalism so as to extend its lease on power. Amidst the centrifugalism, ideological vacuum, and eroding legitimacy, the Communist Party is appealing to nationalism as a last resort and the only glue that could keep intact the People's Republic of China.

On Nationalism and Related Concepts

Nationalism has proven its primordial power time and again through the centuries. Today, its potency is vividly illustrated across the world: in Bosnia and Chechnya, Tibet and Sri Lanka, the West Bank and Northern Ireland. As a concept, however, more often than not, it is poorly defined and understood. As Walker Connor put it, the study of nationalism is an "Alice-in-Wonderland world" where "slipshod and inconsistent terminology remain the bane. . . ."[25]

Any effort at conceptual clarification must begin with distinguishing *nation* and *nationalism* from related concepts. To begin with, *nation* is analytically distinct from *state*, although the two may empirically overlap. Nor is *nationalism* the synonym of *patriotism*, although both sentiments may coexist in fact.

The effort to distinguish *nation* from *state* must begin with Max Weber. Weber consigned *nation* to the category of *Gemeinschaft*—a community based on a sentiment of solidarity. The *state*, in contrast, was an example of *Gesellschaft*—an association developed consciously for specific purposes.[26] Thus, *nation* refers to a community of solidarity, but it is also something more. There are many human groups or collectivities, such as clans and tribes, which are also communities but are not considered nations. Weber had insisted that *nation* could only be defined in relation to the state. What makes a particular community a nation is its intimate relation to statehood. The latter refers to a government that claims authority over a defined territory.

For the purpose of this exposition, *nation* is defined as a biologically reproductive[27] collection of people who feel that they belong together, constituting a community, but who also demand their political expression in the acquisition of statehood. A nation, therefore, is a subjective phenomenon in that its very existence depends on sentiments and perception. But it has an objective foundation in that the feelings of solidarity and community stem from having certain objective attributes in common. Those attributes may be a common race, ethnicity, territory, and culture (the latter is inclusive of language, religion, customs, political values, and experience). None of these commonalities, by itself, is necessary for nationhood or nationalism, but it is intuitively evident that the greater the number of shared traits, the more likely that feelings of solidarity would be correspondingly enhanced.

On an affective level, the word *nationalism* refers to the sentiments of love, identification, loyalty, and commitment to the people who constitute one's national group. The word *patriotism*, in contrast, refers to the loyalty and commitment an individual gives to her government or state. The distinctions between *nation* and *state*, and between *nationalism* and *patriotism*, are recognized by the Chinese. In Chinese, nation is *minzu* (people-clan) and nationalism is *minzu zhuyi* (people-ism). The state, in contrast, is *guojia* (country-family) and patriotism is *aiguo zhuyi* (love-country-ism).

Nationalism may also refer to an ideology that promotes the values and interests of the nation "to a position of primacy, subordinating or even excluding from consideration other loyalties or beliefs."[28] More often than not, the nationalist ideology conceives of the nation as possessing "distinct claims to virtue" that may be used to legitimate aggressive action against other national groups.[29] It must be said, however, that neither nationhood nor nationalism *logically* entails such outward aggression.

The relationship between nation and state is one of symbiosis. A nation can better secure its well-being if it has its own state—its own territory and government. It is only through the possession of land and territory that a nation can maximally secure its economic means of survival and livelihood. And it is only through having its own government that a nation can best protect itself from external aggressors, as well as preserve its collective identity and culture.

But the state also needs the nation. A state can best survive if it harnesses the solidarity feelings of the national community in support of its power. The more the state can associate itself with the nation and identify with national sentiments, the greater the state's reservoir of good will and legitimacy.[30]

Given the symbiotic relationship between nation and state, the temptation is always present for vulnerable states to rouse the sleeping giant of nationalism to serve their own interests by blurring the analytic boundaries between nationalism and patriotism. The nation becomes synonymous with the state, with the most fervent nationalists also the most loyal statists. In such cases, nationalism becomes equated with *etatism* or *statism* (*guojia zhuyi*)—an ideology that elevates the state and the collective to a position of supremacy, commanding the highest loyalty from the individual citizen.

States that are not comprised of a single nation and are, in reality, multinational empires are particularly prone towards *etatism*. Such is the case with the People's Republic of China. Today, as in the days of the dynasties, China is a multi-ethnic empire where the majority Hans rule over smaller minority nationalities. For a multi-ethnic state, nationalism by any of the constituent groups would be highly divisive. Instead, as a PRC scholar recommended, the appropriate ideology should be *guojia minzu zhuyi* (state-nationalism), which he defines as "a form of nationalism that is in accord with the interests of the state." "The interests of the state," in turn, are defined as "the collective interests of all the nationality groups that comprise the country."[31]

But the concept of *state-nationalism* fails to address the political mechanisms that would determine the collective interests of the constituent national groups. In political systems that lack democratic processes to identify those collective interests, it would be the Rousseauist state that presumes to speak for the "general will." In effect, what is presented as *state-nationalism* is nothing other than simple *etatism*. Furthermore, in the one-party state of the People's Republic, where government is the monopoly of the Communist Party, *etatism* becomes essentially *partyism*—the authoritarian rule of the Chinese Communist Party. So, when the CCP celebrates the Chinese "nation" and stokes the passions of Chinese "nationalism," what is actually being invoked are *etatism* and *partyism*, and the interests that are actually being served are nothing other than the Party's own interests of prolonging its rule.

The New Chinese "Nationalism"

The Chinese Communist Party is clearly cognizant that the country's political integrity is more fragile than at any time in its history. In a talk in 1992, Deng Xiaoping drew a contrast between the contemporary situation and the past when he explained that China managed to hold itself together even through the tumult of the Cultural Revolution because of the personal charisma and authority of "prestigious leaders" like Mao Zedong and Zhou Enlai. But the situation is different today. If China were to descend into chaos, there would be civil war "with blood flowing like water" and the country fragmenting into separate kingdoms.[32]

Deng's imminent death promises to make the national situation even more brittle. Although nationalism has always been a feature of Chinese Communism, it clearly was secondary to the class-focused ideology of Marxism-Leninism-Maoism. Today, though, the Party no longer engages in the rhetoric of class struggle, and state-nationalism is all that is left of its official ideology.

It is in this context that the resurgence of nationalism as *etatism* in China becomes intelligible. Amidst the gathering storm of centrifugalism, social instability, and political decay, the Chinese Communist Party has turned to state-nationalism as its panacea. As various Western commentators observed, "left ideologically bereft by the global collapse of communism,"[33] China's leaders have only a "visceral nationalism to fall back on as their justification for holding on to power."[34]

The immediate catalyst for Beijing's renewed attention to nationalism was the 1989 democracy movement. After the violent suppression of the student demonstrators at Tiananmen Square, the Party initiated a "campaign of national unity" in which the youth were singled out for "patriotic education." Calling the democracy movement a "counter-revolutionary rebellion" that had the "black hands" of foreign enemies behind it, the Party urged the Chinese people to unite under its leadership or the country would descend into chaos.[35]

More than young people were targeted for "patriotic education." In

September 1994, the CCP's Propaganda Department issued the "Fundamental Principles on Implementing a Patriotic Education" for all the people. In November 1995, the Party published the *Selected Works for Instruction in Patriotic Education*, a volume that contained the writings and speeches of Mao, Deng, as well as Jiang Zemin on the subject of patriotism.[36] According to the *People's Daily*, the book was specially intended "to fill an ideological vacuum" among the 800 million peasants of China who were enjoined to "love their country" and not to "forget the humiliation of foreign aggression".[37]

Beijing's nationalist campaign reached a high point in 1995 during the fiftieth anniversary of the end of the Second World War. According to one account, "Television news was laced with segments on heroic fighter pilots, and newspapers were stacked with articles detailing the wartime violence committed by the Japanese."[38] Busloads of Chinese schoolchildren arrived each day in Nanjing to tour the museum commemorating the victims of Japan's Rape of Nanjing—those three days in November 1937 when some 300,000 Chinese men, women, and children perished at the hands of the Japanese Tenth Army. The museum's director admitted that the purpose of the exhibit "is to provide patriotic education for children and young people, and not to let them forget history. . . . We intend to use patriotism as a unifying force because China needs stability. . . ."[39]

The campaign of national unity continues to this day. Jiang Zemin instructed his Party to rebuild itself (*dangjian*) "under the new banner of nationalism"[40] and urged that the masses, especially the young, be "deeply inculcated" with the values of "patriotism, collectivism and socialism."[41] An "open letter" from the Propaganda Department of Qingdao's Municipal Party Committee called on all citizens to strengthen their "patriotism."[42] Banners all over Shanghai proclaim: "We love our motherland! We work to make our country great and rich!"[43]

As part of its campaign of national unity, the Chinese government is promoting a revival of traditional culture, harking back to the time of China's legendary first emperors: *Yan Di* (2838 B.C.) and *Huang Di* (Yellow Emperor) (2698 B.C.).[44] Institutes and scholarly associations to study Chinese civilization, "the culture of Emperors Yan and Huang" (*Yanhuang wenhua*), have sprung all across China—almost all with government support.[45] Publications on the subject appear with regularity, so that the entire country is in the grips of a "national study fever" (*guoxue re*).[46]

The new cultural renaissance is aimed at forging a common national identity out of the more than 1.2 billion people of China. Instead of seeing themselves as Han, Tibetan, Uighur, or Mongolian, it is argued that all the inhabitants of the provinces and autonomous regions of the People's Republic constitute a "Chinese nation" (*zhonghua minzu*). This "Chinese nation" is a large nation-family (*minzu dajiating*) of "mixed bloodlines" (*hunxue*), the result of thousands of years of interbreeding and cultural-political assimilation by the more than fifty constituent "blood" groups. It is even asserted that recent scientific studies of bloodtypes in China established that all the bloodlines are traceable to a single origin: Emperors Yan and Huang. Even the peoples of farflung Qinghai and Tibet, it is claimed, are genetic descendants of the Yellow Emperor, who was not simply the ancestor of the Han people. In other words, in the Chinese civilization family, the distinction between the Han core and the border peoples is that of varying levels of cultural attainment (*wenhua shang di xianjin yu luohou zhibie*) rather than race (*zhongzu*).[47]

More than the determinant of lineage, the "Chinese nation" is bound together by the powerful adhesive of culture and civilization. Membership in the "Chinese nation" hinges on one's "acceptance or assimilation into the Chinese culture, regardless of blood."[48] It is claimed that China's entire traditional way of life was founded by the two legendary emperors. Emperor Yan is credited with discovering medicine and especially farming, the backbone of the Chinese economy for millennia. For his part, the Yellow Emperor is believed to have created the code of human relations—the moral foundation of Chinese society—as well as housing, clothing, the written script, porcelain, the compass, and some hundred other technologies and handicrafts. This ancient culture that traces its origins to the first emperors kept the "Chinese nation" together in times of crisis and transition, enabling Chinese culture to become the world's oldest continuous civilization.[49]

Today, it is argued, a cultural revival is needed because Chinese traditional culture is "the spiritual bond of the Chinese nation" (*Yanhuang wenhua shi zhonghua minzu di jingsheng nuodai*). Only an appeal to the ancient traditions could keep the People's Republic unified. More than that, the commonality of culture also induces overseas Chinese to contribute their wealth and talent for China's economic development. Their common cultural identity will enable Chinese all over the world to survive in an increasingly competitive global environment dominated by regional trading blocs.[50]

As part of the renascence of Chinese civilization, ancestor worship is being revived. The PRC government has embraced historical relics, such as the Great Wall, that once were considered symbols of feudal oppression. In April 1995, a mausoleum reputedly built for the Yellow Emperor was refurbished with $700,000 in donations from local and overseas Chinese. The mausoleum was promoted by *China Daily* as "a place for all Chinese people to worship their ancestors."[51]

China's ancient morals and practices, long vilified by the Communist Party as feudal and hopelessly retrograde, are now recommended as virtues. Jiang Zemin has taken to peppering his speeches with Confucian sayings.[52] Party ideologues now admit that, for forty years, due to the overweening influence of "leftist" thinking, the Communist Party had been excessively critical of China's traditional culture and, in so doing, overlooked the functional value that tradition has for contemporary society. It is now recommended that select elements from Chinese tradition be retained if they serve the interests of economic development and social stability.[53]

The classic Confucian virtues are now recognized to be both timeless as well as timely. Those virtues include *ren* (charity), *li* (propiety), *xiao* (filial piety), and the proper conduct of "the five human relations"—all of which enhance social stability. In particular, the virtues of "collectivism" (*zhengti jingsheng*) and "patriotism" (*aiguo zhuyi*) that are putatively part of the "Chinese moral tradition" must be resurrected to combat the rampant corruption, materialism, hedonism, and "extreme individualism" of contemporary society. The meaning given to "patriotism" is especially interesting. More than love for society, nation, and the state, patriotism is understood to mean "loyalty to the prince" (*gongzhong*).[54]

Although the new nationalism clearly serves the Party's purpose, it has spontaneous roots in the Chinese people's understandable pride in the measurable progress they have achieved in nearly two decades of economic reform. Economic success has fostered a new collective sense of confidence. The result, as the *Wall Street Journal* put it, is "a new, self-reassuring nationalism stoked by Chinese government rhetoric and actions. . . ."[55]

The indicators of this new nationalism are appearing with increasing frequency. China's rising pride is reflected in its determination to be "the No. 1 power in Asia." Towards that objective, the city of Chongqing has announced plans to construct what will be Asia's tallest building. Hainan island is building Asia's biggest zoo with more than 5,000 animals.[56] And the Three Gorges Dam, when constructed, will be the world's largest dam.

The evidence seems to indicate that the new nationalism is widespread among the Chinese populace. Since 1991, up to 10,000 people a day attend the flag-raising ceremony in Tiananmen Square, "a polished, goose-stepping affair."[57] Among the general population, three groups are identified to be particularly prone towards the passion of state-nationalism. They are: (1) the administrators, teachers, and public sector workers who are most dependent on the state for their immediate survival and succor; (2) the youth; and (3) the armed forces. The latter two groups, through their education and training, are especially inculcated with the government's worldview and ideals.[58]

Such is the case in China today. State employees, young people, and the members of the military are the most imbued with patriotic nationalism. As an example, delegates to China's 1995 National People's Congress reserved their greatest applause for nationalist themes at the end of Premier Li Peng's speech when he spoke of the imminent return of Hong Kong to Chinese rule, the anticipated eventual reunification with Taiwan, and a Chinese foreign policy that "would not allow foreign interference."[59]

Former PRC envoys to the United States, Canada, and Australia were among the authors of a policy paper prepared by an official Beijing think tank which "practically exudes with national pride." National pride is also palpable in the words spoken by Wang Yongming, an official at Beijing's Xicheng District Communist Party School, who said that China's potential for making progress is "endless" because it is "a great country, with . . . a long history."[60] National pride is also evident among Chinese economists in Beijing, who have been described as convinced that China is "returning to its normal position of eminence," that of being "No. 1" in the world.[61]

As for Chinese youth, they are not the generation who had agitated for democracy during the 1980s. Today, Chinese students are less inclined to place the blame for everything with the Communist Party government. Instead, they have impressed many with their "strong patriotism—some call it nationalism" and are more likely to think as Lei San, a twenty-two-year-old student at Nanjing University. "I think China should first become stronger," said the computer science major, "then we can concentrate on building democracy."[62]

The new nationalism is even flourishing in the hearts of exiled dissidents who are among "the quickest defenders of China's accomplishments" despite their disagreement with the repressive political system. Even the overseas Chinese are not immune from nationalism's primeval power. "As China's economy thrives, the 55 million or so Chinese abroad take ever more pride in the country's transformation." Dozens of Hong Kong Chinese, whom Beijing named "affairs advisers" in the run-up to 1997, have opposed Governor Christopher Patten's democratic reform and, to demonstrate their loyalty to the regime in Beijing, surrendered their U.S. or British passports.[63]

The Potential for Aggression

If the new nationalism in China were simply a matter of national pride and confidence, it would not pose a potential problem for the world outside of the People's Republic. But the resurgent Chinese nationalism has a decidedly reactive flavor. As Hong Kong legislator Christine Loh remarked, "If you don't bear a grudge against China's historical oppressors, then you don't *ai guo* (love your country) enough."[64] For more than a hundred years, beginning with the Opium War, the Chinese people endured the humiliation of foreign invasions and defeats. As a consequence, the collective memory of China's "trauma of defeat" is "like dry tinder and can easily be inflamed."[65]

The flame of reactive nationalism is assiduously fanned by the Chinese leadership, who is seizing every opportunity "to harp on China's past humiliations and present glory."[66] The government publishes an encyclopedia of abuses by foreign powers since the 1800s.[67] In April 1996, the Chongqing city government forbade stores to sell Japanese and German World War II warship models and confiscated about 250.[68] This was followed, in June, by a ban against some 2,000 businesses having names with "Western-sounding color" because they were "undermining national culture."[69] New restrictions—a maximum of forty minutes of foreign movies during prime time—were imposed on Chinese television in order to fight "a slide in cultural values."[70]

Beijing's national unity campaign places special emphasis on arousing the Chinese people's "consciousness of suffering . . . by channeling anger against the West." Many Chinese are convinced that the West, in particular the United States, is engaged in a systematic effort "to contain China or to prevent its rise as a great Asian power."[71]

Former U.S. Ambassador to China James Lilley characterized Chinese nationalism as "a type of anti-Americanism. . . . We are seen as the ones who frustrate their legitimate rights."[72]

Foreign businessmen in China have sensed a recent anti-foreign backlash in Beijing's investment policy. The preferential treatment that was extended to foreign investors in the 1980s is being scaled back. The government's overriding message is that calls for democracy and human rights can bring disunity and disorder, "opening the door to foreign aggression and new humiliation." Scenes of turmoil in the former Eastern-bloc nations are broadcast extensively on China's national network and have convinced many Chinese that a strong, one-party government is essential for national stability.[73]

Chinese reactive nationalism is particularly intense among the youth, those forty years old or younger, and among the intelligentsia. Although none of them is old enough to have personally experienced humiliation at the hands of the imperialist powers, the youth are the most antagonistic towards the West, especially the United States. A poll taken by a PRC newspaper, *China Youth Daily* (*Zhongguo qingnian bao*), in July 1995, found that 87.1 percent of Chinese youth regarded the United States as the most unfriendly towards the PRC. The following month, in August, another survey found that 94.2 percent of young people approved of the "anti-imperialist, anti-hegemonist" Mao Zedong, while only 48.7 percent approved of the reformist Deng Xiaoping who had opened China's doors to interaction with the West. Clearly, the Chinese are profoundly ambivalent about the United States, an ambivalence that was manifested in another random survey taken in July 1995 which found that America, at a plurality of 35 percent, was the country of choice for Chinese to visit or emigrate.[74]

A more recent example of reactive nationalism in China was the publication, in June 1996, of a book entitled *China Can Say No* (*Zhongguo keyi shuobu*). The book has been described as anti-Western, anti-American, and imbued with an "extreme nationalism." It became an instant bestseller—its first print-run of 50,000 copies sold out in a few days. Collectively authored by five thirty-something intellectuals, including a journalist, a university professor, and a poet,[75] the book's tone has been described as "both self-pitying and bellicose." It asserts that there is a "grand conspiracy" by the West, along with Japan and Vietnam, against China, who have formed an "Anti-China Club" to oppose the PRC's "sovereign rights" over Taiwan and the South China Sea. The Chinese government and people are criticized for being unduly influenced by the West, particularly the United States and its "cultural imperialism." The C.I.A. is accused of attempting to destroy China's social order by, among other methods, disseminating literature encouraging Chinese youth to have sex. Chinese women came under special criticism for their "infatuation" with Western fashions and Western men. Hollywood is the main instrument of America's "cultural invasion." Through its movies and a proliferation of other products, Hollywood infects Chinese society with the virus of violence and individualism. American companies, such as Motorola, are charged with selling inferior technology to China. To retaliate against Washington's insistence on Chinese recognition of U.S. intellectual property rights, the book favors a boycott of American wheat and other goods. It is also proposed that the United States compensate China for its "great inventions" of paper and gunpowder with a "user's fee." Finally, after criticizing Beijing's foreign policy for being "too weak," the authors recommend that the People's Republic, "when conditions necessitate," employ force to "reclaim" Taiwan. The feelings of the Taiwanese in this matter are immaterial because as the leading author, Song Qiang, put it, "Taiwan is part of China, just as two plus two equals four." The authors also urge that an alliance be formed with Russia to resist "American imperialism" and its efforts to "contain" China.[76]

China Can Say No might be dismissed as reflective of only its authors' opinions were it not that, in September 1996, it was reported that the book had the affirmation and support of the Communist Party's top leadership. The government is financing a television series based on the book, at 150,000 *yuan* per episode. A second volume of the book was published in October 1996.[77]

More than being reactive, the new Chinese nationalism is irredentist. Along with their new sense of confidence and pride, the Chinese appear ready to resume their historic status as the Middle Kingdom. A Western diplomat in Beijing described China as "maturing" and in the process of "defining its own sphere." Beijing perceives that the world has moved from a bipolar to a multipolar system after the Cold War, and China intends to be a significant actor in the new world.[78] Another commentator observed that, unlike Germany and Japan who have the capabilities but lack the will or self-confidence to act abroad, China is "a thoroughly traditional great power" that is growing rapidly but uncertainly into a world system "in which it feels it deserves more attention and honor." "In coming years, China's ambitions are bound to expand."[79]

How Beijing conceives of the historic Middle Kingdom has troubling implications for the rest of the world. In the course of China's millennial history, its borders have ebbed and flowed, peaking during the Mongol (Yuan) and Manchu (Qing) dynasties. Traditionally, the Chinese empire was conceived to comprise "China Proper," "Outer China," and the tributary territories. "China Proper" is the cultural heart of China and the core of Han settlement. "Outer China" is comprised of buffer territories ruled directly from China Proper but inhabited almost entirely by non-Han peoples. This buffer zone historically included all or parts of Xinjiang, Inner and Outer Mongolia, Manchuria, Tibet, and at times, northern Korea and northern Vietnam. During the Yuan dynasty, "Outer China" expanded to include all of Korea, Central Asia, the Ukraine, Iraq, Iran, Burma, and all of Vietnam. Outside this buffer zone were China's traditional tributary client states, considered to be voluntary parts of the Chinese empire who were allowed to have their own rulers as long as their foreign policy were in accord with China's. Among China's traditional clients were the peoples of Southeast Asia, Taiwan, Korea, the islands in the South China Sea, the East China Sea and most of the Bay of Bengal.[80]

Government-issued maps of China used in PRC school textbooks[81] show *three* borders for China: the current boundaries; those in 1919; and the borders in 1840 at the time of the Opium War. Each alienated section is labeled and Chinese students are taught how the land was taken. Of the three borders, those in 1840 are the most expansive and include, within them: the Russian Far East; Sakhalin Island; the western half of the Sea of Japan; the Korean peninsula; the Yellow Sea; the East China Sea; the Riukiu Islands; Taiwan; Hong Kong; the South China Sea; Vietnam; Laos; Thailand; Cambodia; Burma; Malaysia; the Andaman Sea and Island; Nepal; Bhutan; Kirghizstan; part of Kazakhstan; Russia's Altay and Sayan Mountains; and Mongolia.[82]

If this map is any indication, irredentism may be an integral component of Beijing's promotion of Chinese state-nationalism. Today, a giant digital clock in Tiananmen Square counts down the hours until Hong Kong's "glorious return to the motherland" on 1 July 1997.[83] As for Taiwan, Beijing's recent saber rattling in the Taiwan Strait, not only "sent a frisson of fear through the region"[84] but enjoyed immense popular support on the mainland. Public opinion polls in the PRC showed that a majority supported the government's policy of "liberating" Taiwan by force as well as its aggressive and uncompromising attitude toward the United States.[85]

The new assertive Chinese "nationalism" is also being felt in the South China Sea, a potentially oil-rich region that is claimed by all the Southeast Asian countries, as well as Taiwan and the PRC. Notwithstanding its oft-expressed preference for peaceful negotiations to resolve rival claims, Beijing has not hesitated to press its territorial claims over the South China Sea by force. As one commentator observed, Beijing's "actions undermine its rhetoric."[86] PLA naval ships have been cruising the Sea and building armed outposts on its islands and coral reefs. In 1974, the Chinese captured the Paracel Islands from a South Vietnamese garrison. This was followed in 1988 by the capture of six atolls in the Spratly group from Vietnam. Beijing's latest move, in February 1995, was to set up a garrison on Mischief Reef inside the Philippines' 200–nautical-mile exclusive economic zone.[87]

In April 1992, in a talk on naval strategy, PLA Navy Deputy Commander Zhang Xusan declared that "Now is the time for China to alter its naval strategy to reclaim the rich natural resources of the South China Sea!"[88] Earlier that year, in February, the South China Sea was formally designated as part of the People's Republic when China's national legislature passed a Territorial Waters Act (TWA) declaring that the PRC's "sovereign territory" includes all the territorial and maritime space adjacent to the Chinese mainland, as well as the airspace above. Specifically named territories include Taiwan, Diaoyutai, Penghu Islands, the Spratly Islands, and the Paracels. Article 14 of the TWA specifies that the PLA Navy has the right to pursue and dispel any foreign vessel found within Chinese territorial waters.[89]

All this has clearly alarmed China's neighbors. The rise of a more assertive China is now described as "the main challenge to stability in East Asia."[90] Chinese belligerence is "a nightmare" for Japan because of the latter's strategic dependence on shipping lanes that run near the coast of China and through waters claimed by Beijing.[91] José Almonté, national security adviser to the president of the Philippines, referred to China's rising nationalism as "ominous." A senior Vietnamese diplomat privately admitted to his country's fear of China's growing power.[92] That is not surprising, given the 1979 Sino-Vietnamese war over contested border territories, not to mention Vietnam's history of 1,000 years of Chinese rule that began in 111 B.C.

Already the world's fourth largest, the PLA's budget has grown every year since the end of the Cold War. By the early-twenty-first century, China's military capabilities are expected to override those of other countries in the Asia-Pacific region. It is this rising concern about China by its neighbors that has led to increased arms spending across the Asian-Pacific region, with the biggest increases in Japan, South Korea, Taiwan, Thailand, and Singapore.[93] It does not help that recent Chinese government documents allegedly referred to the South China Sea as its *"shengcun kongjian"*[94] (which translates as "living space" or more ominously, in German, as *Lebensraum*). PLA Commander Liu Huaqing, in April 1989, identified the seas to be the loci for future conflicts between China and other countries. According to Liu, China is both a continental as well as a sea power. For the People's Republic of China, the "vast expanses" of its seas not only are "natural barriers" of national security but constitute the "living space" that could ensure China's development and survival.[95]

Irredentist nationalism serves multiple purposes, one of which is to provide China with needed land and resources, including energy. Beijing is under enormous pressure to maintain an accelerated rate of economic growth if it hopes to achieve the goal it has set for itself of a gross national product of $2.16 trillion by 2010, six times the 1993 figure. To do that, China will have to sustain an annual economic growth rate of over 10 percent.[96] It will have to vastly improve its existing infrastructure as well as increase power generation. Demand for gasoline, fuel oil, and other refined products has already outstripped domestic production,[97] so that, beginning in 1994, China has become an oil importing nation. Control over the oil deposits in the South China Sea, estimated by Beijing to contain more than 12 percent of the world's unmined oil and natural gas reserves,[98] therefore is not simply a question of extending power but of fueling Chinese industry and feeding people in the next century. As one Sinologist put it, "So if there is oil in the South China Sea you've got to have it. . . [because the Chinese] don't have a lot of spare change to give out."[99]

In addition to the volatile situation in the South China Sea, controversy has also reheated between China and Japan over the ownership of tiny islands in the East China Sea which the Chinese call Diaoyutai and the Japanese the Senkakus. Although the dispute is decades old, the issue took on an urgency in July 1996 when Tokyo extended its exclusive economic zone over the islands. At the same time, a Japanese right-wing group took substantive action by erecting a lighthouse on one of the islands. Though uninhabited, the islands are surrounded by rich fish stocks and potentially rich gas and oil deposits.[100]

Such is the power of nationalism that the dispute has mobilized Chinese from disparate communities, igniting a grassroots movement in communist China; capitalist Hong Kong, Macao, and Taiwan; as well as the overseas Chinese community in the United States and Canada. Demonstrations in San Francisco and Vancouver on 22 September 1996 drew over 4,000 and 20,000, respectively.[101] Even Wang Xizhe and Liu Xiaobo, dissidents well known for their opposition to the Chinese Communist Party, called for the use of military force to reclaim the islands.[102]

Japanese coast guards were dispatched to the islands in late September to turn away two groups of Chinese protesters, in the course of which, a Hong Kong activist drowned in the stormy sea after leaping overboard to symbolically claim the waters for China.[103] His death drew over 50,000 mourners to a candlelit vigil in Hong Kong. On 1 October, the PRC's National Day, Premier Li Peng demanded that Japan back off its claim to the Diaoyu Islands. In so doing, Li became the highest-level PRC official to speak out on the issue.[104]

Chinese irredentism is, for the moment, confined to Hong Kong, Taiwan, the South China Sea, and Diaoyutai. But there is no logical reason why Chinese irredentist ambitions should remain restricted to those four areas. In 1993, a CCP Military Affairs Commission meeting to determine China's military strategy and objectives after the Cold War concluded that, although a new world war was unlikely, medium- and small-scale limited wars were unavoidable. China's military objectives in the future, in order of importance, were to be "First, eastern and southern China's coastal waters; second, the South China Sea; third, the Sino-Indian border."[105]

Altogether, Beijing currently has outstanding unresolved border and territorial disputes with at least ten countries. They include Japan (over the Diaoyu Islands); Taiwan (over the Pratas Island in the South China Sea, presently occupied by Taiwan); Vietnam (over the Paracel Islands in the South China Sea, occupied by China since 1974); Brunei, Malaysia, Philippines, Taiwan, and Vietnam (over the Spratly Islands in the South China Sea, six atolls of which have been occupied by China since 1988); the Philippines (over the Mischief Reef in the South China Sea, occupied by China since 1995); India (over two border areas still disputed and left unresolved after the Sino-Indian border war of 1970); and in Central Asia, with Kazakhstan, Kirgizstan, and especially Tajikistan.[106]

Future PRC behavior regarding China's "lost territories" will depend entirely on practical considerations. These include the PLA's capabilities; Beijing's calculations as to the probability of success in employing force; the success or failure of international diplomacy; and conditions internal to China that might provoke the regime to use external aggression as a quick but effective way of galvanizing domestic unity. Those internal contingencies include population pressures, resource deficiencies, political fragmentation, and social unrest.

It is this potential for Chinese "nationalism" to turn virulent that is a cause for concern. The *Far Eastern Economic Review* reported that "nationalism with a chauvinistic, authoritarian cast" is gaining credibility within China's elite intellectual circles and their influence "is making itself felt within the halls of power."[107] Many former liberals in the People's Republic are now disillusioned with the West, because of the failure of the 1989 democracy movement and the personal experiences some of them encountered in the West. Those intellectuals are now turning inward, to embrace a new "cultural conservatism".[108] They are convinced that neither liberal democracy nor communism is suitable for China. Instead, some are looking to totalitarian dictators for their heroes. Adolf Hitler is "idolized" for pulling Germany out of its post-World War I doldrums, and Mao Zedong is recalled with "nostalgia"[109] as a "genius" and "godlike" figure.[110] Farmers in an impoverished county in Shanxi province have spent close to $17,000 of their own money to build a grandiose temple to Mao.[111]

A scholar of nationalism noted that aggressive or virulent nationalism seems to be correlated with at least two conditions. The first is "the trauma of defeat" at the hands of some other national group(s). A second condition is political authoritarianism and an illiberal conception of human beings wherein the individual is not conceived to possess inalienable rights, nor is there a conviction that "all nations can develop together in a positive sum game." Universalism is held to be a "febrile myth." Instead, the conviction is that "one should think with one's blood. . . ." As a consequence, nationalist quarrels are transformed into Darwinian zero-sum struggles.[112]

The new "nationalism" in the People's Republic of China meets both conditions. The "trauma of defeat" is amply supplied by China's

historical humiliation at the hands of the Western powers and Japan—
a history that the Communist Party repeatedly reinvokes to its people.
China's social, political and economic conditions also lend themselves
to the rise of extreme nationalism. Although private businesses and
entrepreneurs have proliferated since 1979, there is no concomitant
growth of a civic culture that could inoculate society against a repeat
of the mass mayhem and violence that were pandemic during the
Cultural Revolution. The political system remains unreformed and authoritarian. The *Weltanschauung* of the Communist Party and even
non-party intellectuals is that of an increasingly competitive global
environment of dwindling resources where nations are locked in a
social Darwinian struggle for survival.[113] And it is in that competitive
environment that the People's Republic has set for itself the goal of
economic development while burdened with a fifth of the world's
population.

The combination of China's illiberalism and historical trauma, as
one commentator observed, may well result in the alchemy of "communism and extreme nationalism into fascism."[114] Michael Mann
warned that mild nationalism is characteristic of democracies, whereas
"democracy perverted" is the breeding ground for aggressive "exclu-
sionist" nationalism—that particular brand of nationalism that is capable of committing atrocities against all persons conceived to be
beyond the pale.[115] The Chinese Communist Party, in resorting to
irredentist reactive nationalism as its panacea, may well come to dis-
cover that the cure is worse than the disease. For nationalism is a
double-edged sword: It is useful in rallying support for the regime but,
once opened, the Pandora's box of nationalism may prove difficult to
contain.

Notes

1. W. B. Yeats, "The Second Coming," in *A Little Treasury of Great Poetry*, ed.
    Oscar Williams (New York: Charles Scribner's Sons, 1947), 450.
2. *Shijie ribao (World Journal*, hereafter *WJ*), 20 July 1991, p. 2.
3. An article on the first public opinion survey conducted in July 1987 of the
    political psychology of PRC citizens, in *Baixing Semi-Monthly*, Hong Kong, no.
    188 (16 March 1989), pp. 9–10.
4. *WJ*, 7 July 1991, p. 7.
5. *WJ*, 10 October 1991, p. 2.
6. "Dalu qingnian xinqiu zongjiao weiji (Mainland Chinese Youth Seek the Com-
    fort and Identity of Religion)," translation of a Reuters news dispatch, in

Zhonggong wenti ziliao zhoukan (*Chinese Communist Affairs and Documents*, hereafter *CCAD*), no. 453 (28 January 1991): 55.

7. *1995 Zhonggong nianbao* (*1995 China Yearbook*) (Taipei: Zhonggong yanjiu zazhishe, 1989), section 7, pp. 60, 61.

8. Lin Xiang, "Nungcun zongjiao zongzu shili pengzhang (Religious and Clannish Forces are Expanding in the Countryside)," *CCAD*, no. 470 (3 June 1991): 58.

9. Ibid.

10. *1995 China Yearbook*, section 7, p. 60.

11. A. James Gregor, "The People's Liberation Army and China's Crisis," *Armed Forces and Society* 18 (Fall 1991): 19.

12. Leslie Holmes, *The End of Communist Power: Anti-Corruption Campaigns and Legitimation Crises* (New York: Oxford University, 1993), 156 (footnote 11) and 154.

13. Ibid., 19.

14. Report by the PLA's investigative work conference on military discipline, 26–30 November 1990. Lin Jing, "Gongjun zicheng jilu gongzuo wenti yenzhong (The PLA Admits to the Gravity of its Disciplinary Problems)," *CCAD*, no. 470 (3 June 1991): 54.

15. *Baixing Semi-monthly*, no. 236 (16 March 1991); and Qiang, "Zhonggong junfang dongtai di jianyao shuping (A Summary of Communist China's Military Activities)," *CCAD*, no. 465 (29 April 1991): 1–2.

16. *WJ*, 7 July 1991, p. 1.

17. Nicholas D. Kristof, "Tibetan Official Calling for Purge," *San Francisco Chronicle* (hereafter *SFC*), 15 February 1993, p. A8.

18. Renee Schoof, "Chinese Premier Wants Crackdown on Corruption," *SFC*, 6 March 1995, p. A9.

19. Fareed Zakaria, "Speak Softly, Carry a Veiled Threat," *New York Times Magazine*, 18 February 1996, p. 37. Zakaria was the managing editor of *Foreign Affairs*.

20. As related to Nicholas D. Kristof, "China, the Conglomerate, Seeks a New Unifying Principle," *New York Times*, 21 February 1993, p. 6.

21. Mao Zedong, "Talks at the Beidahe Conference (Draft Transcript)," 17–30 August 1958, in *The Secret Speeches of Chairman Mao*, ed. Roderick MacFarquhar, Timothy Cheek, and Eugene Wu (Cambridge, MA: Council on East Asian Studies, Harvard University, 1989), 401.

22. See Chalmers A. Johnson's classic work, *Peasant Nationalism and Communist Power: The Emergence of Revolutionary China* (Stanford, CA: Stanford University, 1962).

23. *WJ*, 12 April 1994, p. A13.

24. "China: Saying No," *Economist*, 20 July 1996, p. 30.

25. Walker Connor, "The Nation and its Myth," in *Ethnicity and Nationalism*, ed. Anthony D. Smith (Leiden: E. J. Brill, 1992), 48.

26. Kenneth Thompson, *Beliefs and Ideology* (Chichester: EllisHorwood Limited, 1986), 59.

27. This criterion would exclude non-reproductive groups such as the "Queer Nation" or the "feminist nation" from being considered as true nations.

28. Robert Tombs, "Introduction," in *Nationhood and Nationalism in France*, ed. R. Tombs (New York: HarperCollins *Academic*, 1991), 3.

29. Michael Mann, "A Political Theory of Nationalism and Its Excesses," in *Notions of Nationalism*, ed. Sukumar Periwal, (Budapest: Central European University Press, 1995), 44, 55.

30. Thompson, *Beliefs*, 59, 60.
31. Li Xing, "Lun guojia minzu zhuyi gainian (On the concept of state-national-ism)," *Minzu yanjiu (Nation Studies)*, Beijing, no. 4 (1995): 10, 13, 14.
32. Deng Xiaoping, "Excerpts from Talks Given in Wuchang, Shenzhen, Zhuhai and Shanghai," 18 January-21 February 1992, in *Selected Works of Deng Xiaoping (1982–1992)* III (Beijing: Foreign Languages, 1994), 362; and "Interview of Deng Xiaoping by Robert Maxwell on Current Affairs," in *Deng Xiaoping: Speeches and Writings* (New York: Pergamon, 1984), 97.
33. Nayan Chanda and Kari Huus, "China: The New Nationalism," *Far Eastern Economic Review* (hereafter, *FEER*), 9 November 1995, p. 20.
34. Editorial, "Stay Back, China," *Economist*, 16 March 1996, p. 15.
35. Chanda and Huus, "New Nationalism," 20; and Patrick E. Tyler, "China's Campus Model for the 90's: Earnest Patriot," *New York Times*, 23 April 1996, p. A4.
36. Dong Liwen, "Lun zhonggong di aiguo zhuyi (On Communist China's Patriotism)," *Gongdang wenti yanjiu (Studies in Communism)* (Taipei) 21 (August 1995): 26.
37. "China Prints Book to Educate Farmers," *SFC*, 28 November 1995, p. A11.
38. Chanda and Huus, "New Nationalism," p. 21.
39. Tyler, "Earnest Patriot."
40. George Wehrfritz, "China: Springtime Perennial," *Newsweek*, 10 June 1996, p. 17.
41. Quotation by Jiang Zemin, in *Dangdai sichao (Contemporary Thought)* (Beijing), no. 1 (1995). Note the order of the three "isms." *Dangdai sichao* is a "leftist" publication that is reputed to represent the cutting edge thinking on China's new "nationalism."
42. "Zhi quanshi shimin di yifeng gongkai xin (An Open Letter to All Citizens)," published by the Qingdao CCP Municipal Committee's Propaganda Department, 21 March 1996.
43. Ian Buruma, "The 21st Century Starts Here," *The New York Times Magazine*, 18 February 1996, p. 31.
44. Deng Luoqun, "Dangdai yanhuang wenhuare di xingqi jiqi shidai yiyi (The Revival and Historical Relevance of the Culture of Emperors Yan and Huang)," in *Dangdai sichao*, no. 6 (1994): 56.
45. Chen Xi, "Zhongguo zhishi fenzhizhong di minzu zhuyi (Nationalism among Chinese Intellectuals)," *Beijing zhichun (Beijing Spring)*, Woodside, NY, no. 39 (August 1996): 39.
46. See Song Xiaoqing, "Jingdai `guoxue re' di xingshuai (Rise and Fall of Modern-Day `National Study Fever')," *Wenhua yanjiu (Cultural Studies)*, Beijing, no. 1 (1996): 55–60.
47. Deng Luoqun, "Emporers Yan and Huang," 57, 59.
48. Zhou Weizhou, "Rujia sixiang yu zhongguo chuantong minzu guan (Confucianism and China's traditional conception of nation)," *Minzu yanjiu*, no. 6 (1995): p. 66.
49. Deng Luoqun, "Emporers Yan and Huang," 58, 59.
50. Ibid., 60, 61. It is interesting how Deng's ideas mirror those of Joel Kotkin's *Tribes: How Race, Religion and Identity Determine Success in the New Global Economy* (New York: Random House, 1993).
51. Chanda and Huus, "New Nationalism," 21.
52. Ibid., 21.
53. Luo Guojie, "Hongyang zhonghua minzhu youliang daode chuantong (Widely Publicize the Chinese Nation's Excellent Moral Tradition)," *Dangdai sichao*, no. 4 (1994): 2–4.

54. Ibid., 4–6.
55. Marcus W. Brauchli and Kathy Chen, "Nationalist Fervor," *The Wall Street Journal*, 23 June 1995, pp. A5 and A1.
56. Ibid., A5.
57. Chanda and Huus, "New Nationalism," 21.
58. Mann, "Political Theory," 55.
59. Schoof, "Crackdown," A9.
60. Brauchli and Chen, "Nationalist Fervor," A1, A5.
61. Chanda and Huus, "New Nationalism," 21.
62. Tyler, "Earnest Patriot."
63. Brauchli and Chen, "Fervor," A1, A5.
64. "Shades of Loyalty," *Economist*, 13 April 1996, p. 80.
65. Liu Xiaozhu, "Jingti jiduan minzu zhuyi zai dalu qingqi (Beware of the Rise of Extreme Nationalism on the Mainland)," *WJ*, 3 April 1994, p. A6.
66. Chanda and Huus, "New Nationalism," 21.
67. Ibid., 20.
68. *China News* (Taipei) 12 June 1996, p. 4.
69. *SFC*, 24 June 1996, p. A8, citing the official *China Daily* of 23 June. Also banned were business names containing "vulgar, feudalistic, bizarre and absurd content."
70. *SFC*, 25 June 1996, p. E3.
71. Tyler, "Earnest Patriot."
72. Brauchli and Chen, "Fervor," A5.
73. Chanda and Huus, "New Nationalism," 20, 22–23, 21.
74. *WJ*, 9 July 1996, p. A10.
75. *WJ*, 9 July 1996, p. A10; and 3 July 1996, p. A12.
76. "China: Saying No"; *WJ*, 8 July 1996, p. A2; and 26 June 1996, p. A12.
77. *WJ*, 12 September 1996, p. A12.
78. Brauchli and Chen, "Fervor," A1.
79. Zakaria, "Speak Softly," 37, 36.
80. "The Dragon Awakes," *Browning Newsletter* 20 (21 February 1996): 5. This is an investment newsletter for stockbrokers, published in the United States.
81. This map is included in a PRC textbook, *A Brief History of Modern China*, published in Beijing in 1954. See "The Dragon Awakes," 4.
82. "The Dragon Awakes," 4.
83. Chanda and Huus, "New Nationalism," 21.
84. "Terrific Pacific," *Economist*, 20 July 1996, p. 29.
85. "Against the Wind," interview of Liu Binyan with Kari Huus, in *FEER*, 9 November 1995, p. 26.
86. Thomas L. McNaugher, "Is the United States Ready?" *The Brookings Review* (Fall 1994), 16.
87. Nayan Chanda, Rigoberto Tiglao, and John McBeth, "Territorial Imperative," *FEER*, 23 February 1995, p. 14.
88. Ding Zongyu, "Lun zhonggong yu nanhai zhoubian guojia lingtu di fenzheng (On Communist China's Territorial Dispute with the South China Sea's Neighboring Nations)," *Studies in Communism* 21 (April 1995): 43.
89. "Zhonghua renmin gongheguo linghai ji pilianqu fa (The People's Republic of China's Territorial Waters and Adjacent Territories Act)," in *1989 Zhonggong nianbao* (*1989 China Yearbook*), section 6, pp. 36–37.
90. "Terrific Pacific."
91. Steven Butler, et al., "Refocusing in Asia," *U.S. News and World Report*, 22 April 1996, p. 49.

92. Chanda and Huus, "New Nationalism," 22.
93. "Asia's Arms Racing," *The Economist*, 3 February 1996, p. 29.
94. Chanda and Huus, "New Nationalism," 22.
95. *1995 China Yearbook*, section 6, p. 41.
96. Lin Chung-cheng, "Spread the Risk," *Free China Review* 46 (March 1996): 52.
97. Craig S. Smith and Mary Scott, "Demand for Refineries is High in China," *Wall Street Journal*, 26 December 1995, p. A4.
98. Ding Zongyu, "Territorial Dispute," p. 41.
99. Quote by Andrew Nathan, in Chanda and Huus, "New Nationalism," 22.
100. "Japan Blocks Taiwanese from Islands," *WJ*, 24 September 1996, p. A13.
101. *WJ*, 23 September 1996, p. A1.
102. *WJ*, 1 October 1996, p. A2.
103. "In an Ocean of Controversy," *Time*, 7 October 1996, p. 30.
104. "China Premier Warns Japan on Islets," *SFC*, 1 October 1996, p. A14.
105. Ding Zongyu, "Territorial Dispute," 47.
106. See map on "Boundary and Territorial Disputes in East Asia," in *United States Security Strategy for the East Asia-Pacific Region* (Washington, DC: Department of Defense, February 1995), 19.
107. Kari Huus, "China: The Hard Edge," *FEER*, 9 November 1995, p. 28.
108. Chen Xi, "Chinese Intellectuals," 39–42.
109. "Rotten Roots," *The Economist*, 3 February 1996, p. 30. See the many articles lauding Mao in *Dangdai sichao*, no. 1 (1992): 60–62; no. 1 (1994): 26–27; no. 2 (1994): 60–64; and no. 3 (1994): 2–10, 61–62.
110. See the positive regard for Mao in a book that was first published in 1994 in the PRC and became an instant bestseller. Wang Shan, *Disanzhi yanjing kan zhongguo* (*Looking at China Through the Third Eye*) (Taipei: Zhouzhi wenhua, 1994), 45, 48–62, 87, 89–90, 116, 120.
111. Rod Mickleburgh, "He's Back: China in Grips of a Mao Revival," *San Francisco Examiner*, 22 September 1996, p. A-16.
112. John A. Hall, "Nationalisms, Classified and Explained," in Periwal, *Notions*, 18, 19.
113. Chen Xi, "Chinese Intellectuals," 40.
114. Liu Xiaozhu, "Extreme Nationalism."
115. Mann, "Political Theory," 62–63.

9

Conclusion

In 1957, the annual average per capita income of Communist China was $58. Twenty years later, by the time of Mao's death in 1976, it had increased to only $139. In contrast, during the same period, Taiwan's average per capita income rose by 753 percent from $149 to $1122.[1] By the late-1970s, the PRC was still mired in economic underdevelopment, whereas the Republic of China on Taiwan had become a newly industrialized country.

Those statistics suggest that Mao's tenure in power was deleterious to the Chinese economy and to its modernization. After three decades of Maoist socialism, mainland China's average annual per capita GNP in 1978 was only $253, making it one of the poorest countries in the world, on a par with Haiti and the Central African Republic.[2]

Under the leadership of Deng Xiaoping, however, China is in the process of fulfilling the historic project of economic development. In the words of *Newsweek*, Deng's reforms have "raised more people from poverty to near prosperity in a shorter time than any society has ever done."[3] By 1994, China's average per capita GNP had multiplied ten times to $2,500. This was accomplished by sustaining an average real economic growth rate of 9 percent a year between 1978 and 1994. At that rate of increase, the GNP will double in eight years so that by 2025, not only will China be the largest economy in the world, it will have become the world's new superpower, "the diva of the next century."[4]

An Autopsy of Maoism

An examination of the negative impact of Maoism on China's economic development must begin with the Chinese Communist Party's selection of Marxism-Leninism as its guiding ideology. That choice could not be more inappropriate and less helpful for an underdeveloped society. In 1965, at a time when American sinologists were celebrating the accomplishments of Maoism, Geoffrey Hudson of Oxford University observed that Marxist ideology "furnished no workable solution to the problem of developing retarded nations." Nothing in the ideology provided "a key whereby the necessary consequences of backwardness can miraculously be avoided."[5]

Marxism-Leninism was never a developmental ideology; it had little to offer in the form of either guideline or recipe for economic development. Worse than that, the primacy that the ideology placed on class struggle could not be more destructive of economic construction. Early in the twentieth century, Sun Yat-sen had recognized the destructive nature of Marxism. He pointed out that because industrialization took place within the framework of the nation-state and required the coordinated effort of all the people, nothing could work more against the objective of national development than a preoccupation with class struggle which pitted countrymen against countrymen.[6]

It took Mao to exacerbate whatever aspects of Marxism-Leninism that were already inimical to the economic development of a backward society. Mao's radical reconception of class membership to be contingent on an individual's thoughts, together with his insistence on practice as the necessary means by which each individual consciousness could be transformed, led him to a program of continuous revolution. The resultant, unceasing mass campaigns were thoroughly destructive of social order and stability, the prime requisite for industrial development. The cumulative impact of constant strife and turmoil was a Chinese economy that suffered a variability four times that of the Philippines or Taiwan in a similar time period.

Another inherent disability of Marxism-Leninism is the command economy of central planning where the market is abjured in favor of the arbitrary decisions of government bureaucrats which are then implemented by local cadres. In the case of China, not only were the bureaucrats and cadres often untrained in economics, in their zeal to curry favor with superiors, they would fabricate statistics to present a deceptively rosy picture of the economy's performance. Those statistics were then incorporated by the central planners to formulate the next five year plan. In this manner, mistakes were compounded by more mistakes, producing catastrophes on the scale of the famine that followed the Great Leap Forward in which at least 15 million Chinese starved to death.[7]

By eliminating the market, the command economy invites precisely this kind of gross miscalculation, what economists call "the law of unintended consequences." That is, the best of interventions in an economy often have harmful unintended side effects. In a free economy, in contrast, the aggregate of decisions by individual businessmen exercising their individual judgment, in the long run, is less likely to do harm than the centralized decisions of government. Even if mistakes are made, whatever harm that is done is likely to be counteracted faster.[8]

To add to an already error-prone system, the political counterpart of the command economy was installed in the form of totalitarianism. Despite the fact that Marxism-Leninism-Maoism contained no "absolute knowledge capable of predictable results which could possibly justify a totalitarian system",[9] the CCP centralized all power in itself, convinced that it was in possession of dialectical "scientific" truths. Private property was eliminated through the purge of rural landlords and urban entrepreneurs in the campaigns of the early-1950s; competing parties and dissident views were suppressed. The result was a system even more prone to error, where public policy was the exclusive domain of a single party and, often, of one man. But the supreme leader and his colleagues, more often than not, were untutored in political economy. Instead, other considerations had governed their rise to the top of the political hierarchy: those of political ruthlessness, personal charisma, ideological rectitude, and *guanxi* (personal connections).

In the totalitarian system, the elevation of ideology to the level of sacred dogma artificially constrained and delimited the range of policy choices and solutions to problems. In the case of the People's Republic, capitalism and private ownership, competing parties, and heterodox ideas were all abjured. As a consequence, policymaking in Maoist China could not have been a rational process governed by considerations for pragmatism, creativity, or efficiency. As Hudson put it, "Where leaders are irremovable and failures, or responsibilities for them, can be concealed by political censorship, the consequences of error tend to be greatly magnified and perpetuated."[10]

Constant uncertainty, turmoil, and upheaval did not provide an environment conducive to the attainment of the other preconditions of economic development—those of capital accumulation and investment, innovation and social cooperation. Initially, the abolition of private property was justified by the CCP to effectuate control over all investments for rapid industrialization. Indeed, for much of the 1950s, the command economy did facilitate the rapid progress of China's heavy industrial development, although that was accomplished at the expense of agriculture and consumer goods production.

But, beginning in the second half of the 1950s, Mao's determination to realize utopia disrupted the process. In his quest for a great leap forward into communism, a radical ethic of absolute egalitarianism and an organizational infrastructure of communes were imposed on China. Egalitarian distribution of wages was a disincentive to work hard. Harebrained schemes to convert peasant backyard furnaces into steel mills resulted only in the colossal waste of resources. The insistence on ideological orthodoxy, together with Mao's war on intellectuals, stifled creativity and innovation. Economic autarky closed China's doors to foreign capital and technology, as well as international aid. Whatever social cooperation that was marshalled by Mao's personal charisma and his employment of Stakhanovite role models[11] was thoroughly obliterated in the chaos of the Great Proletarian Cultural Revolution that plunged China into a living hell of cannibalism[12] and a Hobbesian war of all against all.[13] When the Great Helmsman finally passed away in 1976, bringing the Cultural Revolution decade to closure, the wonder was not that the country was still poor and underdeveloped but that there was still a China.

Economic Development under Deng

In 1994, the *Financial Times* of London observed that "Deng Xioping's role in liberalizing the Chinese economy made him the world's most significant political leader of the second half of the 20th century."[14] Arguably, Deng's greatest accomplishment was to transform Marxism-Leninism-Maoism into a developmental nationalist ideology. Returning to classical Marxism's emphasis on the productive forces, Deng rationalized economic reforms that would have been anathema under Mao by maintaining that socialism could not be constructed with poverty.

To motivate people to work harder, radical egalitarianism was eschewed in favor of an appeal to material incentives through such reforms as the rural contract responsibility system, privately owned businesses, rural enterprises, and differential wages. Harder and more diverse avenues of work resulted in the increased accumulation and availability of domestic surplus capital. At the same time, foreign capital, skills, and technology flowed in from the open door policy. Economic autarky was abandoned for an aggressive export-led international trade strategy, putting to good use China's comparative advantage of low labor costs. In this manner, the People's Republic earned the foreign exchange to pay for the technological imports needed for industrial development. Intellectuals were no longer viewed as unregenerate class enemies and were even accorded a measure of respect and consideration, provided they refrained from overtly opposing Communist Party rule. The treatment of intellectuals, along with allowing Chinese students and scholars to study abroad, were all conducive to innovation and creativity.

All of this was anchored on an absolute insistence on order and stability. The elements of Maoism that had fostered chaos and disorder were eschewed. The effort was made to replace Mao's charismatic rule with eudaemonic legitimacy. Mao's one-man rule and the attendant cult of personality were explicitly rejected in favor of the more stable arrangement of a collective party leadership.[15] Under Deng, the Communist Party no longer resolved factional disputes with extraprocedural violence.[16] Instead, intraparty conflicts have been managed without fratricidal bloodletting so that the institutional integrity of the Party as well as social stability could be preserved.

Most importantly, the Party rejected Mao's formula of a continuous revolution. Instead of mass campaigns that so easily degenerated into anarchic mayhem, the Party would rely instead on "solid, systematic measures" of "exhaustic persuasion" and "calm discussion" to effectuate political change and education.[17] In this manner, a recurrence of the ruinous Cultural Revolution might be averted. When spontaneous mass movements did occur, as in the 1989 democracy movement or the uprisings by minority nationalities in the autonomous regions, the government would not hesitate to suppress them with lethal force. All in the interest of order and stability, without which capital accumulation and investment, innovation and social cooperation would all be jeopardized.

The success of Deng's ideology for economic construction is rooted in its predominantly pragmatic approach to problems. As such, Dengism conforms to Mary Matossian's prescription that an ideology of delayed industrialization advocate and adopt whatever instrumentality that promotes economic development and that strengthens the nation.[18] Deng's ideology also displays the transformative capacity that S. N. Eisenstadt recommended.[19] Deng made Marxism sufficiently porous to incorporate the notion of "an initial stage of socialism" in which capitalist reforms could be used to develop the economy. Under Deng's leadership, the Communist Party government has also decentralized and devolved its power, displaying the weaker authority structure that offers less resisting power against change and innovation.[20] Finally, Dengism also meets W. W. Rostow's "propensities" criteria.[21] It recognizes the importance of science; it is receptive to innovation. And as the motto "Getting Rich is Glorious" demonstrates, Dengism has no lack of a propensity to seek material advance.

That having been said, Deng's reforms are not without their flaws. At the same time as it commended Deng for his achievements, the *Financial Times* also noted that "his failure is on almost as grand a scale as his successes. . . ."[22] The reforms have unintended consequences that, together with the toxic legacy from the Maoist era, present China with a daunting array of problems. Those problems, if left unattended or mismanaged, could well turn the world's next superpower into an exploding supernova.

The Threats to Economic Development

In the seventeen years since the economic reforms began, the People's Republic has clearly demonstrated an impressive economic growth capacity. But economic growth is not economic development. Although development entails growth, growth does not automatically result in development. Economic growth refers simply to an increase in GNP; economic development is something more. It is the structural transformation of an economic system resulting in the quantum and sustained increase of productive capacity.

Today, after seventeen years of economic growth, the People's Republic, though developing, cannot yet be considered developed. Unlike an industrialized society, most of China's population still reside in the countryside; only 21 percent of the population lived in cities in 1985.[23] China's average per capita income is less than that of many Eastern European countries, not to speak of its neighbors in East Asia.

According to the World Bank, it will take China ten to fifteen years to attain the present economic level of Thailand.[24]

For China to transform growth into development will require not only that the GNP continues to grow but also the structural transformation of a still agrarian economy into one that is industrial-manufacturing. The majority of the labor force must be shifted from farming to manufacturing, and from labor-intensive to capital- and technology-intensive production. Investment must be channeled to the construction of a physical and human infrastructure that subtends and enables industrialization. This means an extensive and efficient ground and air transportation system; a communications system of mail, telephone, telegraph, fax, and internet; and an energy supply system that provides the oil, natural gas, coal, and electricity to fuel the modern industrial economy. As for the human infrastructure, China's industrial development requires that mass literacy and educational levels be elevated; the percentage of skilled labor be expanded; investments in research and development, and in science and technology, be increased; and mass healthcare, including potable water, be provided—all in order to produce the educated, skilled, and healthy workforce of an industrial society.

Notwithstanding its high growth rate since 1979, the economic development of the People's Republic is not assured. Today, China finds itself mired in an interlocking maze of problems that, singly or collectively, threatens its future.

Threats to Capital Accumulation and Investment

To begin with, recurring double-digit inflation erodes the individual's income and buying power. More than that, rising prices also promote a disposition to consume instead of save.

A bloated political bureaucracy requires salary support from state revenue that could be better used as investment capital for infrastructural development. Despite Deng Xiaoping's reiterations on the need for political reform, including the streamlining and downsizing of the bureaucracy, little if any effort was actually undertaken. Between 1978 and 1990, growth in the number of government employees far surpassed that of China's labor force. Those employed at all levels and agencies of government increased by 98.1 percent, while the total labor force grew by 29.1 percent.[25]

That bloated bureaucracy's primary function is to administer, maintain and preserve the command economy. The retrograde system of planned prices, price subsidies, and subsidies to state-owned enterprises act as a powerful drag on the generation and accumulation of surplus domestic capital. Price subsidies consume state revenue that could be put to more productive use.[26] The state-owned sector, if anything, has only become more inefficient and deficit-prone since the economic reforms began.

Chinese government accountants conceded that, even without including subsidies, SOE losses for the first time exceeded profits in the first quarter of 1996. Total profits, by some 68,700 SOEs, fell by 88 percent from the previous year. Enterprises that had been operating at a deficit for an extended period of time now numbered 12,000; of those, 10,000 were considered moribund.[27]

Subsidies to floundering SOEs now exceed the taxes those enterprises return. Although the SOEs produced only a third of China's total industrial output by the mid-1990s, they consumed roughly three-quarters of the government's industrial investment. That investment is being poured into an increasingly expanding black hole. Official statistics indicate that government investment in SOEs had increased by more than 640 percent from 170 billion yuan in 1985 to 1,100 billion yuan in 1995. Despite those increases, "China's state sector is in worse shape now than at any time in its . . . years of economic reform." Net losses in the state sector eclipse the entire equity of China's banks, making debt write-off impossible. The threat of unrepaid loans driving banks to insolvency prompted Moody's, in September 1996, to lower credit ratings on eleven Chinese bank affiliates in Hong Kong.[28]

According to one estimate, SOEs absorb and distort the allocation of over 70 percent of China's resources. The retainment of the "moribund" state sector means that about two-thirds of China's massive 40 percent savings rate of national income, as well as most of the country's skilled human resources are presently wasted.[29]

Beijing's response to this, instead of moving resolutely to reform the dysfunctional state sector, has been protectionist. In July 1996, the national government announced it would limit competition for ten Chinese beer makers, including the struggling Tsingtao Brewery, to curb foreign domination in that market. Guangdong province also moved to protect the domestic producers of household goods, including cars, computers, and air conditioners, by limiting imports.[30]

Another problem that could affect capital availability in the future is China's increasing dependence on imported foodgrains. The introduction of the contract responsibility system in agriculture led unsurprisingly to a burst in farm productivity. By the mid-1980s, however, agricultural production seemed to have reached a stasis, but the Chinese population still grew by 14 million per year. At the same time, because of over farming, housing construction, desertification, toxic contamination, and soil erosion, China was losing 5 percent of its arable land per year, totaling 19.5 million acres in the past forty years. The loss of arable land is particularly problematic in the case of China where only 11 percent of the land surface can be cultivated, so that China's per capita availability of arable land is only a third of the world average. All of this accounts for China having to begin to import foodgrains to augment its domestic supply. If this trend continues, assuming a per capita grain consumption at the 1994 level, China will require, by 2030, the annual importation of 305 million tons of foodgrains.[31]

Those foodgrains will have to be paid out of the PRC's current foreign reserves of $85 billion. Impressive though that figure is, those reserves will also have to used to pay off China's foreign debt. That debt is estimated to be at least $105 billion of foreign government debt; when other state-sector debts are included, China's total foreign debt is probably closer to $125 billion.[32]

China's foreign reserves will also have to be used to import needed raw materials. In the future, China will have to rely increasingly on imports because of its inadequate store of natural resources, a situation that is exacerbated by profligate waste—a disposition that is bred and encouraged by the socialist economy.

Although China has 22 percent of the world's population, its store of natural resources is far below the world average. China has 7 percent of the world's arable land and fresh water; 3 percent of its forests; 11 percent of its coal reserves (and that 11 percent is of the highly polluting "dirty" variety); and only 2 percent of the world's oil reserves. It is estimated that in order to maintain an economic growth rate of 8 to 10 percent, China's demand for natural resources will outstrip domestic supply by more than 20 percent by the year 2000.[33]

All of which means that China's foreign reserves will probably become increasingly depleted by debt repayment and the purchase of imported foodgrains and raw materials. There will be correspondingly less for the importation of advanced technology for economic development.

Threats to Innovation

The more relaxed policy towards intellectuals, including allowing students and scholars to study in the industrialized democracies, has definitely enhanced China's innovative capacity. But this is purchased at a cost.

To paraphrase Deng Xiaoping: by opening China's windows to the outside world, some flies may be let in. Those "flies" are the ideas of representative government and individual rights and liberty which inspired the 1989 democracy movement and which, in the eyes of the Communist Party, constitute a direct threat not only to its power but also to social order and stability. Although the Chinese government succeeded in suppressing the movement, it alienated the very stratum of the population it relies on for innovation—China's intellectuals. The latter include the approximately 40,000 students and scholars who were in the United States at the time, a majority of whom chose to stay in America when given the opportunity by the Bush administration.

In a country where those with university education and specialized skills already comprise a small percentage of the population, the permanent loss of tens of thousands of potential innovators to the United States is a substantial brain drain that China can ill afford. But the problem of China's brain drain transcends the loss to the United States. Altogether, only about a third of the more than 220,000 Chinese students who have gone to study abroad since 1979 actually returned. To compound the problem, those who left also tended to be China's best and brightest. To illustrate, in 1995, the top five postgraduates in physics and all eight postgraduates in physiology and biophysics at Beijing University left China to pursue work or study abroad. Sixty percent of recent architecture graduates from Qinghua University, another top school, also went abroad.[34]

The loss of so many with advanced education and training to other countries is particularly problematic because China has so few of them to begin with. In 1980, only 1 percent of the PRC's college-age population was enrolled in colleges and universities. By 1992, after twelve years, that proportion increased to only 2 percent, a figure that compares poorly with other developing countries, not to speak of developed countries. As a case in point, the comparable figure for India, another developing country, was 32 percent in 1992.[35] The small percentage of university enrollment among China's college-age population meant that only 1.4 percent of the total population had a college-level or above education in 1990, compared to 13.9 percent in the Soviet Union in 1989; 14.3 percent in Japan in 1980; 32.2 percent in the United States in 1991; and 37.4 percent in Canada in 1981.[36]

The reasons for the small percentage of Chinese who are college-educated are not difficult to fathom. Intellectuals were a repeated target of political campaigns under Mao. Over 20,000, including many school teachers, were killed during the Anti-Rightist Campaign in 1957. More than 30,000 intellectuals were killed or committed suicide in the "Four Purification Campaign" of 1964. According to Communist Party figures, over 400,000 intellectuals perished during the Cultural Revolution, from abuse or suicide.[37]

More than that, during the Great Proletarian Cultural Revolution, all schools, colleges and universities were closed[38] so that young people could make a new revolution by declaring war on the "four olds" (ideas, culture, customs, and habits), and by travelling across the country to retrace the CCP's historic Long March of 1934–36. In 1969, Mao brought an end to the GPCR, blaming its chaos and destruction on precisely the youth whom he had summoned to revolution. In a meeting with leaders of the Red Guards, Mao tearfully accused them for having let him down. As punishment, millions of young people were "sent down" to the countryside to live in barren border regions or among the peasants. They would not begin to return to their city homes until after Mao's death in 1976. In the meantime, ten years were lost, along with the formal education of an entire generation.

After Mao's death, the Communist Party, as part of its reform, resolved to improve education by committing itself to yearly increases in educational funding. Since 1949, the PRC's educational expenditure had hovered around 4 to 7 percent of total government spending.[39] In 1978, when economic reform began, it was 5.9 percent. After 1978, the Chinese government began to apportion a larger share of its spending to education, reaching 11.6 percent in 1990 but dropping to 10.03 percent the following year. However, even the 1990 high figure of 11.6 percent compares unfavorably with other governments' spending on education. In 1988, for example, 22 percent of the United States' total government expenditure went to education. The respective figures for Japan, Mexico, South Korea, Thailand, and Malaysia were 17.9 percent, 25.3 percent, 28.2 percent, 18.5 percent, and 16.3 percent. Nor does the People's Republic compare well with its political rival, the Republic of China on Taiwan. The latter devoted 14.7 percent of its government spending in 1981 to education, increasing to 17.5 percent by 1990.[40]

China compares even less favorably with other countries when its educational spending is computed as a percentage of its GNP. Since the economic reforms began, that percentage remained essentially unchanged through the 1980s. It was 2.74 percent in 1981; 2.84 percent in 1983; 2.7 percent in 1985; 2.82 percent in 1986; and 2.51 percent in 1987.[41] In the 1990s, however, the percentage began to decline to 2.5 percent in 1992, then to 2 percent in 1993 and 1994.[42] The figures for other countries were 4.62 percent for Taiwan in 1983; and an average of 4.6 percent for Asian nations, 4 percent for developing nations, 6.1 percent for developed nations, and 5.7 percent for all the countries of the world.[43] In a study of thirty-eight countries, Beijing University professor Chen Liangkun found that those countries with an average per capita income of $400–500 generally devoted 3.52–3.69 percent of their GNP to education. China, however, accorded only 2.51 percent of its GNP to education in 1987 although its average per capita income had reached $420 by that time.[44]

Yet another way to assess the importance placed on education in China is to compare China's average per student educational spending with the figures for other countries. In 1978, developed and developing countries spent an average of $1,767 and $146, respectively, per student. In 1978, the PRC spent only $12 per student,[45] decreasing to $7 by 1984.[46]

In effect, despite increases in educational expenditure after 1978, every comparative indicator shows that the Chinese government's efforts are below the norm. It appears unlikely that the situation will improve in the future. In 1994, Beijing announced that badly needed public works projects requiring more than $500 billion in the next decade would necessitate deep cuts in funding for higher education.[47]

Nor does the future look promising for basic education. In 1985, Beijing passed a Resolution on Reform of the Educational System delegating the responsibility for basic education to the local-provincial authorities.[48] Given the phenomenon of regionalism and the increasing disposition of local officials to misuse public funds for private ends, there is little reason to expect that they will be assiduous in fulfilling their charge.

Still another problem of delegating basic education to local-provincial governments is that the quality of that education varies in accordance with local resources. A result is that, although the national dropout rate of China's elementary school children was 31.6 percent in 1985, the figure was substantially higher for nine western provinces and autonomous regions that are China's poorest areas. In 1984, 3.31 million children in Shanxi, Gansu, Ningxia, Qinghai, Xinjiang, Guangxi, Guizhou, Yunnan, and Tibet failed to complete all four years of elementary school—a drop-out rate of 51 percent.[49] By 1995, China had a total of 30 million children, from five to fourteen years old, who were not enrolled in schools. Those children, when they become adults, can only add to the PRC's present adult illiteracy rate of 15.9 percent.[50]

There are other problems still. Like the state-owned enterprises, China's schools and universities are also plagued with the problem of redundant labor. Seventy percent of the PRC's educational expenditure goes to salaries to support a bloated teaching corps. The average teacher-student ratio in Chinese elementary schools is 1:20; in secondary schools, 1:12; and in colleges and universities, the ratio is a generous 1:5.[51]

One consequence of a low investment in education is the small percentage of skilled labor in China. In 1989, only 3.4 out of every 10,000 people in the People's Republic were scientists and engineers. The comparable figures were 148 for the United States in 1982; 549 for the Soviet Union in 1987; and 595 for Japan in 1982.[52] Altogether, the number of skilled workers in China totalled 40 million in 1985, about 4 percent of the entire population. A majority (71 percent) of China's skilled labor had only a basic skills level; only a minuscule 3 percent (or 0.0012 percent of the PRC's population) could be considered highly skilled. Moreover, China's skilled labor is disproportionately concentrated in the cities. Only 4 out of every 10,000 rural residents (0.04 percent) were skilled—a situation that surely impedes the introduction and application of science and technology to improve agricultural production and crop yield.[53]

To compound the problem, whatever skilled labor there is is not being fully and properly utilized. An estimated 60 to 70 percent of China's skilled personnel are either unemployed or underemployed, because of an antiquated labor system.[54] Almost twenty years after economic reforms began, China still does not have a free labor market where worker mobility is governed by market signals of supply and demand. Instead, for much of the country's skilled workers, once they are employed in a state enterprise, they are assured of lifetime security. Nor are their skills necessarily matched to their positions. The problem is exacerbated by local-provincial protectionism over skilled workers, which further thwarts labor mobility and its rational allocation.[55]

To add to the problem, the Chinese government is not adequately investing in and nurturing its skilled talent. In 1994, only 0.56 percent of China's GNP went to research and development (R&D). The comparable figure for India, another overpopulated developing country, was 0.9 percent. The overall trend in China is not encouraging. R&D spending, as a proportion of GNP, declined from the relatively high points of 0.7 percent, 0.72 percent, and 0.71 percent attained in 1990–1992, to 0.62 percent in 1993 and 0.56 percent in 1994.[56]

Threats to Social Cooperation

While Deng's revival of material incentives clearly contributed to the success of his economic reforms, his injunction to "let some get rich first" also led to widening gaps in income and wealth between the coastal provinces and inland regions; between the cities and the villages; between entrepreneurs and those on fixed income; and between Han Chinese and the minority nationalities. After decades of Communist Party propaganda that understood socialism to mean economic equality, the new wealth and income differences can only foment envy and resentment among the less prosperous, which in turn could affect social cooperation.

Social cooperation is also undermined by the general moral decay and *anomie* of society. The individualism, materialism, hedonism, and nihilism that are increasingly evident in Chinese society are the inevitable result of the Communist Party's loss of its radical vision and ideals. At the same time, the economic reforms' employment and affirmation of capitalist tenets also contribute to the moral decay. As people's cynicism develops over time about the telos of communism, which is also the very raison d'être of the Communist Party-state, the collective and socialist values of the past inevitably become increasingly replaced by "a more individualistic, self-regarding approach."[57]

Threats to Order and Stability

Without order and stability, it would be difficult to attain the other preconditions of economic development. Today, there is increasing evidence that social order is in precipitous decline. Overall crime rates, including violent crimes, increase by the year despite the government's repeated efforts at combatting. Criminal activities are becoming organized. Passage by rail in China is vulnerable to attacks by roving bands of peasant bandits. Women and children are kidnapped and sold like slaves. Theft of public property is pandemic.

The rising incidence of crime will only worsen in the coming years as more and more of China's surplus males enter puberty. This, as was explained, is another unintended consequence of government policy. The one-child-per-couple policy indirectly spawned a gender birth-ratio imbalance that, by official estimates, will mean some 70 million young males by the year 2000 who will be without marital prospects and who can be expected to present a serious threat to law and order. As it is already, young men not only comprise the majority of China's mobile population,[58] they also make up the corps of organized crime in China. In some areas, they account for as much as 70 percent of criminal gang members.[59]

Added to the overall deterioration of law and order are unemployment pressures, a problem that expresses itself most vividly in a mobile population that may number as much as 120 million, almost half the population of the United States. Those 120 million, most of whom are poor illiterate peasants who abandoned farming to converge on already congested cities in search of employment, defy government's effective control. In a tacit admission that it could no longer control the movement of China's teeming masses, Beijing recently abolished the *hukou* (residential registration) system, instituted since 1958, whereby it used to maintain control over the populace.[60]

Wang Shan, in his bestseller *Looking at China Through the Third Eye*, highlighted the problem of the mobile population when he reminded his readers that every dynasty was brought down by roving hordes of peasants who eventually organized in a successful rebellion. The mobile population today "is like an explosive in society" that could be set off by the slightest conflict, disgruntlement, or extremist appeal. They represent the tip of the iceberg of the underlying problem of the peasantry who still comprise a majority of China's 1.215 billion population. It is that peasantry, including the mobile masses, who represent a "live volcano" that can erupt any moment to engulf China in yet another end-of-the-dynasty convulsion.[61]

The Problem of the State

In the last analysis, the responsibility for both the creation as well as the containment of the threats to economic development is with the state. Deng Xiaoping was right when he said that "If any problem arises in China, it will arise from inside the Communist Party."[62]

Societies that are late to modernization require the state to assume a strong role in planning, coordinating, executing, and managing economic development. If the state's plans are flawed, if the government is divided among itself, if officials are corrupt, and if the state's ability to implement its decisions is eroding—all this could negatively impact the country's chances for successful development.

The Flawed State Sector

To begin with, it is the government's inability to deal decisively with the inherited problem of the planned economy which drains the country of its capital, leaving China's growth and political stability increasingly dependent on foreign funding. About two-thirds of the PRC's national savings and most of its skilled human resources are presently wasted because the dysfunctional state-owned sector absorbs and distorts the allocation of well over 70 percent of the country's resources. All of which means that China must depend on foreign savings in the form of foreign direct investment—currently equal to 6 percent of China's GDP—and other foreign exchange inflows to keep the economy growing.[63] Foreign-invested enterprises in China have become a major player in the country's foreign trade, accounting for 39.1 percent of the PRC's total bilateral trade in 1995.[64]

Given all this, how much of China's spectacular economic growth has actually been fueled by domestic capital is genuinely questionable. Even the Chinese government admitted that foreign investment has been a "main" contributor to the country's "sustained" industrial growth.[65] In effect, as one economic analyst put it, "Foreign cash is the fuel in the tank of the Chinese economic miracle." Without this foreign capital, the result could be "wholesale social instability."[66]

Despite its dependence on foreign capital, the Chinese government seems bent on inflaming an increasingly strident nationalism because Beijing sees it as a panacea for mounting and interrelated domestic problems. But the appeal to nationalism could backfire when foreign traders and investors become alienated by the rising xenophobia.

The Problem of Regionalism

In addition to the moribund state economy, decentralization of power and authority has resulted in the phenomenon of regionalism, which has also hurt China's economic development. At the same time that Dietrich Rueschemeyer and Peter B. Evans recommended decentralization as a prerequisite feature of the successful developmental state, they cautioned that serious problems of corporate cohesion and coordination could result, especially when "strong and divergent forces" in society "are bent on capturing parts of the state apparatus and using them for their purposes." When that happens, the state is in danger of "dissipating" its critical role in economic development. Also endangered is the "general and inclusive vision" needed for social cooperation towards the accomplishment of the common task of industrialization.[67] The result is the "degeneration" of decentralization "into inefficiency and chaos."[68]

That seems precisely to be what decentralization of political power and authority has wrought in China. Regional protectionism hurts social cooperation by impeding the smooth operation of the national economy. Increasingly independent local and provincial officials undertake indiscriminate construction projects to pursue quick profits. Many of these projects not only consume precious arable land, they waste capital resources as well as contravene the development plans of the central government.

The Problem of Political Corruption

Regionalism aside, there are also the many deleterious economic effects of political corruption in China which more than outweigh whatever arguments there are that corruption can be functional for economic development. As an example, it is argued that bribery improves bureaucratic efficiency by acting as "speed money" to cut through bureaucratic red tape, enabling the entrepreneur (the briber) to avoid costly delays. In effect, bribes motivate government employees to work harder, particularly when the money is given out on a piece rate basis.[69] It is also argued that corruption is conducive to allocative efficiency in that the successful briber is probably also the most efficient entrepreneur because the "ability to offer massive bribes . . . could be correlated with entrepreneurial efficiency."[70]

Whatever the particular argument, the overall reasoning is that corruption can be beneficial if it helps to move the economy in a free-market direction—what David Osterfeld called "expansive corruption." Corruption in the form of bribery, it is argued, can be conducive to economic development by reducing the harm of government policy, increasing competition, and creating new jobs in businesses that otherwise would not exist due to government restrictions.[71]

But the counterarguments against this functional view of corruption are more numerous and compelling. As Syed Hussein Alatas put it, "almost everything happening under the sun can be said to be positive in some way." It is only when graft is considered "in the total context that we get a different picture of the function of extortive corruption."[72]

To begin with, the speeding of bureaucracy by bribes may actually induce corruption[73] in that the bribes become incentives for officials not to reform the system. Neither does corruption promote entrepreneurship, allocative efficiency, or the public good. Corruption causes decisions to be weighed in terms of money, not in terms of human need.[74] Success in bribery is not necessarily correlated with business efficiency. Not only is graft often directed to avoid rules and procedures that were instituted to ensure quality control,[75] inefficient firms tend to be the more dishonest, so that their bribery would actually harm rather than enhance economic competitiveness.[76]

The reality is that pandemic political corruption in the People's Republic hurts economic development in every possible way, beginning with its effects on capital accumulation. Corruption discourages work because bribery and expropriation undermine the incentive to produce by severing the connection between work and wealth. Corruption diverts investment in time, effort, and money away from activities that expand the production of wealth into those that merely transfer wealth from the briber to the bribee.[77]

Rural capital accumulation is hurt by the extortionary fees and taxes that local officials extract from peasants, which rob them of hard-earned income and savings. Bribes to officials by native and foreign businessmen not only must be subtracted from operating expenses and investment capital, but are a kind of illegal taxation, the cost of which is inevitably passed on to the consumer.[78]

Not only does political corruption hurt capital accumulation, it also negatively affects capital investment. Bribery of officials for tax evasion purpose means a net loss for the state treasury. The lavishing of public funds on entertainment such as the "imperial dinners" is a gross misuse of surplus capital. In both cases, revenue that otherwise could be used by the state for economic development is either wasted on conspicuous consumption or is diverted to private pockets.

Since corruption, by its very nature, is a secretive enterprise, little is known about the use to which corrupt officials put their ill-gotten gains. But if the money "winds up in Swiss banks" instead of as investment capital in business ventures, it becomes a net loss for the developing country.[79] In the case of China, it was reported that although the country has enjoyed an inflow of foreign capital, it has also experienced significant capital flight[80]—which suggests that the proceeds from corruption are being exported.

The most compelling study on the negative impact of corruption on capital investment is that undertaken by Paolo Mauro. In the first systematic cross-country empirical study of the economic impact of political corruption, Mauro concluded that corruption dampens economic growth because it lowers the private marginal product of capital by acting as a tax on the proceeds of investment. This was true even for countries burdened with cumbersome bureaucratic regulations. Using a sample of seventy countries over a fifteen-year period (1960–1985), Mauro found a negative and significant association between corruption and the rate of private investment. Thus, if corruption is reduced by one standard deviation, the investment rate increases by 2.9 percent of the GDP.[81]

Mauro also discovered that corrupt governments tend to spend less on education because education offers "less abundant" opportunities for officials' private gain.[82] In effect, in addition to its impact on capital accumulation and investment, political corruption also hurts innovation because of reduced investment in education. There is more still.

Political corruption takes away from innovation by the incalculable amount of time, energy, and talent that it wastes. As Colin Leys put it,

"If the top political elite of a country consumes its time and energy in trying to get rich by corrupt means, it is not likely that the development plans will be fulfilled."[83] There is also the loss in productive effort because of the need of bribers to cultivate *guanxi* with officials, a loss that "defies estimation."[84] All of this is confirmed by a study that found that countries where talented people pursue "rent-seeking activities" tend to grow more slowly.[85] Finally, through the practice of nepotism, corruption further hurts innovation. By its very nature, nepotism—"the appointment of relatives, friends, or political associates to public offices regardless of their merits and the consequences on the public weal"[86]—works against the norms of merit and achievement that are essential to economic development.

Then there is corruption's negative impact on social cooperation. Already existing perceptions of inequality can be exacerbated if some citizens are believed to have illegitimate access of goods via corruption.[87] Social cooperation could also deteriorate because of society's general moral decline, as citizens emulate the example set by corrupt officialdom. Increasingly, as one writer put it, "the man-in-the-street will see little reason why he too should not gather what he can for himself and his loved ones."[88] Society comes to resemble "one of every man for himself," ultimately leading to "the impatient refusal of each sector of the population to accept the disciplines of planned development."[89] Regional economic protectionism and the increasing willfulness of local-provincial authorities in defiance of central policies are only some of the indicators of the breakdown of social cooperation in the People's Republic.

That breakdown must eventually affect the overall order and stability of society. Among the findings of Paolo Mauro is a strong association between bureaucratic efficiency and political stability, bureaucratic efficiency being the simple average of the judiciary system, red tape, and corruption indices. The correlation coefficient with political stability was 0.67, significant at the 1 percent level.[90] In other words, the more corrupt the government, the more unstable the polity.

Corruption's negative association with political stability is exercised through its corrosion of political legitimacy, a country's "most important asset."[91] A survey in 1995 of over 6000 youth in ten provinces of China found that 89.32 percent regarded political corruption as a serious problem, for which they felt both rage and frustration.[92] By destroying the legitimacy of the Communist Party government in the eyes of the people, political corruption is contributing to China's growing instability and even its likely disintegration.

If that were to happen, it would not be the first time that corruption brought down a government. There are countless historical precedents. Corruption, in combination with other causes, had always played a role in the *denouement* and overthrow of dynasties in ancient China. More recently, corruption, and the public reaction to it, was a primary factor in the collapse of communist power in the Soviet Union and Eastern Europe, as well as the 1989 democracy movement in China that ended in the violence at Tiananmen Square.[93] Today, in the unstable climate of rapid socioeconomic change and disruption, it is not far-fetched to imagine that pandemic political corruption could, once again as in China's millennial past, wreak disastrous consequences.

The Decline in State Capacity

Rising regionalism and pandemic corruption could account for the steady erosion in the Chinese government's extractive capacity, which would inevitably affect the overall capacity of the state. And as state capacity diminishes, so too its ability to plan, coordinate, manage, and execute the nation's economic development.

The statistics that are available are not encouraging. Although the Chinese economy grew by an average of 9 percent a year since 1978, total government revenue[94] as a percentage of GDP has steadily declined from 31.2 percent in 1978 to 14.2 percent in 1992 and to an expected 13.3 percent in 1995. If that trend continues, total state revenue will decrease to 11.3 percent of the GNP by the year 2000.[95]

For those statistics to be meaningful, they need to be placed in a comparative perspective. In a comparison of the People's Republic with twelve other countries[96] from 1979 to 1989, aside from China, only three countries experienced a decrease in government revenue as a percentage of GDP. They are Indonesia (20.44 percent to 17.06 percent); Egypt (37 percent to 34.94 percent); and Yugoslavia (32.46 percent to 22.21 percent). The decline in China, however, was more precipitous, from 31.2 percent in 1978 to 14.2 percent by 1992.[97]

More troubling still is a comparison of the PRC's central government revenue as a percentage of GDP with the same twelve countries from 1980 to 1989/1990. Aside from China, four other countries experienced a decline. They are the United States (a marginal decline from

20.85 percent to 20.24 percent); Indonesia (21.4 percent to 16.62 percent); Egypt (47.07 percent in 1981 to 34.94 percent in 1989); and Yugoslavia (8.12 percent to 4.27 percent). In the case of China, central government revenue fell from 14.57 to 8.85 percent of GDP.[98]

Not only is China's 1990 figure of 8.85 percent uncomfortably close to Yugoslavia's 8.12 percent in 1980, if China's percentage declines even more, the consequences may be calamitous if past experience is any indication. The PRC's present circumstances are approaching those of two dangerous historical precedents. In 1934, the Kuomintang central government's revenue was only 4.8 percent of GNP; fifteen years later, the Nationalist regime fell to the Chinese Communists. The comparable figure for Yugoslavia was 4.27 percent in 1989; a year later, Yugoslavia completely disintegrated.[99]

Conclusion

Almost twenty years after economic reforms began, China finds itself in uneasy transit between tradition and modernity; between ideology and pragmatism; and between the collectivist ethic of the past and a new self-regarding individualism. Amidst this time of immense flux, the People's Republic is suspended between the known past and an uncertain future. If it manages to transform economic growth into development, China will become the world's new superpower. But it may also explode under the cumulative weight of its problems.

If the PRC continues on its course of economic growth and, at the same time, manages to peaceably absorb Hong Kong and Taiwan, unified China will be an economic colossus. Already in 1996, the combined foreign exchange reserves (excluding gold) of mainland China, Taiwan, and Hong Kong totalled $223.7 billion—a figure that is close to the $278.9 billion in foreign reserves of the United States and Japan. The 1996 combined purchasing-power parity GDP of Hong Kong, Taiwan, and the PRC was $3,591 billion, a little more than half that of the United States.[100] The total imports of China, Hong Kong, and Taiwan are two-thirds those of Japan. If the three Chinese entities were to unite, the Asian Development Bank expects it will displace Japan as the dominant economic power in Asia in the future.[101] And if United China were to maintain an annual growth rate of 7 percent, by 2020, its combined GNP will be $9,000 billion, roughly equivalent to the GNP of the United States in 2002.[102]

More than that, should the People's Republic maintain a course of positive nationalism and continue to attract the investment capital, talent, and skills of the overseas Chinese, the future United China would maximally profit from the contributions of the Chinese "global tribe."[103] Ethnic Chinese number 2.36 million in Singapore; 6.16 million in Malaysia; 6.58 million in Thailand; 5.05 million in Indonesia; 760,000 in the Philippines; 2.46 million in Vietnam, Laos, and Cambodia; 170,000 in Japan and South Korea; 120,000 in India and Pakistan; 2.32 million in North America; 800,000 in Latin America; 620,000 in Europe; 490,000 in Australia and New Zealand; and 100,000 in other places.[104] Altogether, overseas Chinese living outside of mainland China (including those in Hong Kong and Taiwan) number 55.79 million. Together with mainland China's 1.215 billion, this super United China would comprise 1.27 billion people and has the potential to be an economic behemoth.

As it is now, overseas Chinese dominate the Southeast Asian economies, excepting Brunei. To illustrate, in Indonesia, ethnic Chinese constitute only 3.5 percent of the population but control 73 percent of the country's private capital. The respective figures for the Philippines are 2 percent of the population and 50 percent of the country's private capital; for Thailand, 10 percent of the population, 81 percent of private capital; and for Malaysia, 29 percent of the population and 61 percent of all private capital.[105] Ethnic Chinese own twenty of Indonesia's twenty-five largest enterprises; account for 35 percent of the Philippines' domestic retail sales; control more than half of Thailand's banking capital as well as 90 percent of Thailand's industrial and commercial capital.[106]

According to the *Australian*, Chinese in Asia (excluding those in the People's Republic) commanded a cumulative GNP of 670 billion Australian dollars in 1992, more than Australia's GNP of 420 billion Australian dollars. Not counting stock shares, the liquid capital of overseas Chinese in the world may be as much as $2 trillion.[107] It is that wealth that had enabled the PRC's impressive economic growth since 1978.

Overseas Chinese investments in the People's Republic account for as much as 70 to 80 percent of the country's total foreign direct investment.[108] Hong Kong and Taiwan together account for two-thirds of FDI flows to the mainland, with the Southeast Asian Chinese responsible for another 10 to 15 percent.[109] One may legitimately wonder whether the People's Republic would have its much vaunted economic boom were it not for the overseas Chinese.

The Chinese expression for "crisis" is comprised of two ideograms: *wei* (danger) and *ji* (opportunity). At the same time that China holds a real potential of becoming a superpower, there are also mounting problems that could jeopardize that future. And the responsibility for most, if not all, of the problems ultimately rest within the Chinese Communist Party-state.

Rueschemeyer and Evans had specified that the successful developmental state needs certain requisite attributes. They are the relative autonomy of the state from the dominant class; an extensive, internally coherent bureaucratic machinery; decentralization of authority that is not dysfunctional; and a limited state enterprise sector.[110] By all these criteria, the Chinese developmental state is a failure.

To begin with, nothing can be further than Rueschemeyer and Evans' prescription of a limited state enterprise sector than China's state enterprises that squander two-thirds of national savings. The rising regionalism thwarts the creation of that "extensive, internally coherent" bureaucracy that is needed. At the same time, the chaos wrought by regionalism is evidence of the degeneration of decentralization. Most grievously, perhaps, is the rampant corruption—testimony to the Chinese state's failure at achieving autonomy from its dominant class of cadres and officials. Corruption by China's ruling apparatchik pillages private and public capital; distorts development plans; thwarts productive investment; discourages achievement and innovation; and, by setting a poor example, is a cancer that infects the entire society.

Through its inadequate investment in education, research and development, the PRC government is not following J. J. Spengler's advice to provide needed public services and "growth-supporting arrangements".[111] More than that, China's bloated political bureaucracy makes a mockery of Spengler's prescription that the developmental state must judiciously utilize its personnel.[112]

All of these are traceable to the inherent flaws and disabilities of the ruling CCP. In the last analysis, it is the single party-state in China that is the chief impediment and endangerment to economic development, a task at which the Chinese had been endeavoring for a century and a half. As a consequence, it may be that, like Sisyphus of Greek mythology, China is doomed, once again, to fail at its historic project.

Even if the People's Republic were to overcome all odds and become a superpower, without systemic political reform, it would be a superpower that could threaten the world. Today, China remains a society without the rule of law, a political system without checks and balances where power is still monopolized by a party without an ideological *raison d'être*. Instead of a China mired in underdevelopment, the problem is as likely to be a different one. That problem, in the words of the *Christian Science Monitor*, is "the arrival on the world stage of a giant economic power that is also an arbitrary, often a xenophobic, despotism." While this is surely grim for the Chinese, it "would be fearful for everyone else." [113]

More than thirty years ago, Geoffrey Hudson observed that inherent in the communist system of China are both strength and weakness. There is cohesion of leadership, along with an unwillingness to abdicate political leadership to an alternative ready to accept responsibility "when the passion of the Party in power has been spent."[114] Hudson's observation remains relevant today, more than ever.

Notes

1. Alvin Rabushka, *The New China: Comparative Economic Development in Mainland China, Taiwan, and Hong Kong* (Boulder, CO: Westview, 1987), 206, 217. The year 1957 was chosen as the benchmark because there was no appropriate exchange rate for the PRC before 1957.
2. Jan S. Prybyla, "China's New Economic Strategy: Defining the U.S. Role," *Backgrounder* (Washington, DC: The Heritage Foundation, 1985), 3.
3. *Newsweek*, 1 April 1996, p. 26.
4. Kenneth Auchincloss, "Friend or Foe?", ibid., 32–33; "China on the Edge . . . of What?" *New York Times Magazine*, 18 February 1996, p. 25.
5. Geoffrey Hudson, "Conclusion: The Chinese Model and the Developing Countries," in *The Chinese Model: A Political, Economic and Social Survey*, ed. Werner Klatt (Hong Kong: Hong Kong University, 1965), 218, 217.
6. See Sun Yat-sen's disagreement with the Marxist notion of class struggle in "The Principle of Livelihood," *San Min Chu I* (Shanghai: Commercial Press, 1929): 391, 440–441.
7. Jonathan D. Spence, *The Search for Modern China* (New York: W. W. Norton & Co., 1991), 583.
8. Editorial, "Market Knows Best," *Far Eastern Economic Review* (hereafter, FEER), 13 June 1996, p. 5.
9. Hudson, "The Chinese Model," 218.
10. Ibid., 218.
11. Communist systems' disposition to use idealized, sometimes fictitious, role models to inspire the masses began during the Soviet Union's drive to industrialization in the 1930s, when Stalin elevated a factory worker named Aleksei Stakhanov for national emulation. Under Mao, a soldier named Lei Feng and the Dazhai Commune were among those held as role models for the masses.

12. During the Cultural Revolution, peasants in China's Guangxi Autonomous Region committed cannibalism in the name of "class struggle." See Liu Binyan's "An Unnatural Disaster" in the *New York Review* of 8 April 1993, pp. 3–5. Liu's essay was a review of two autobiographical accounts by Zheng Yi. They are *Lishi de yibufen* (A Part of History) (Tianyuan Publishers) and *Hongse jinianbei* (Red Memorial), an unpublished manuscript.

13. According to a PRC bestseller, during the Cultural Revolution, the peasants in the countryside massacred whole families, including women and infants. The result was that "in the two years from 1967 to the end of 1968, Chinese villages resembled slaughter houses." Wang Shan, *Disanzhi yanjing kan zhongguo* (Looking at China Through the Third Eye) (Taipei: Zhouzhi wenhua, 1994), 60, 57.

14. As quoted in "The Price of Deng's Pragmatism," *Christian Science Monitor*, 26 August 1994, p. 19.

15. See the CCP's Central Committee's "Guiding Principles for Inner-Party Political Life," in *Foreign Broadcast Information Service*, 17 March 1980, p. L3.

16. For much of its history, the CCP violated its own rules on the management of internal conflicts and disputes. See Maria Hsia Chang, "Factions," in *Human Rights in the People's Republic of China*, ed. Yuan-li Wu et al. (Boulder, CO: Westview, 1988), 233–249.

17. Deng Xiaoping, "On the Reform of the System of Party and State Leadership," in *Selected Works (1975–1982)* (Beijing: Foreign Languages, 1984), 319.

18. Mary Matossian, "Ideologies of Delayed Industrialization," in *Political Development and Social Change*, eds. Jason L. Finkle and Richard W. Gable (New York: John Wiley and Sons, 1971), 122, 120.

19. S. N. Eisenstadt, "The Protestant Ethic Thesis in an Analytical and Comparative Framework," in *The Protestant Ethic and Modernization*, ed. Eisenstadt (New York: Basic Books, 1968), 10.

20. E. Troeltsch, *Protestantism and Progress* (Boston: Beacon, 1958), 90–91.

21. W. W. Rostow, *The Process of Economic Growth* (New York: W. W. Norton, 1962), chs. 1–3.

22. "The Price of Deng's Pragmatism."

23. *Xinwen ziyou daobao* (*Press Freedom Guardian*), 17 February 1995.

24. *Shijie ribao* (*World Journal*, hereafter *WJ*), 31 October 1996, p. A12.

25. Chen Chaozhe, "Zhongguo dalu di xiaofei chao (The Rising Tide of Consumerism in Mainland China)," *Zhongguo dalu yanjiu* (*Mainland China Studies*, hereafter *MCS*) (Taipei) 37 (September 1994): 59–60.

26. In 1989, price subsidies consumed nearly 13 percent of state income.

27. *WJ*, 12 November 1996, p. A19.

28. Matt Forney, "Trials by Fire," *FEER*, 12 September 1996, pp. 62, 63.

29. David Roche, "Faltering Investment Haunts China's Leaders," *Wall Street Journal*, 12 February 1996, p. A14.

30. Matt Forney, "Back to the Future," *FEER*, 29 August 1996, p. 40.

31. The estimated figure of 305 million tons of foodgrains is 105 million tons more than the current annual world grain export total of 200 million tons. *WJ*, 23 August 1994, p. A2.

32. Roche, "Faltering Investment."

33. Dong Ruiqi, "Dalu zhuanbian jingji zengchang fangshi zhi yanxi (An Analysis of Changes in Mainland China's Pattern of Economic Growth)," *MCS* 39 (June 1996): 14.

34. James O'Connor, "Best and Brightest Leaving China," *San Francisco Chronicle*, 24 May 1995, p. A1.

35. Dong Ruiqi, "Mainland China's Pattern," 17.
36. Lin Wenxian, "Zhonggong jianli shehui zhuyi rencai shichang tanxi (An Analysis of the Establishment of a Socialist Talent Market in Communist China)," *Gongdang wenti yanjiu* (*Studies in Communism*) (Taipei) 21 (June 1995): 68.
37. *1990 Zhonggong nianbao* (*1990 China Yearbook*) (Taipei: Zhonggong yanjiu zazhishe, 1990) section 3, p. 43.
38. Occupational and trade schools remained closed for another seven more years, until 1976. Wang Xuewen, "Zhonggong zhiye jishu jiaoyu zhi yanxi (An Analysis of Communist China's Occupational Skills Education)," *MCS* 28 (April 1986): 39.
39. Liu Shengji, "Zhongguo dalu geji xuexiao xueli caizheng wenti (Problems about the Reliability of Diplomas Issued by Schools in Mainland China)," *MCS* 37 (August 1994): 74.
40. Liu Shengji, "Zhonggong jing shinian lai jiaoyu jingfei zhi fenxi (An Analysis of Communist China's Educational Funding over the Past Decade)," *MCS* 38 (January 1995): 9, 15.
41. Ibid., 7.
42. Yan Hua, "Dalu jiaoyu xianzhuang yu minzu weiji (Mainland China's Educational Situation and National Crisis)," *Zhongguo dalu* (*Mainland China Monthly*) (Taipei) no. 332 (April 1995): 38.
43. Liu Shengji, "Diplomas," 75.
44. Liu Shengji, "Educational Funding," 15–16.
45. Liu Shengji, "Diplomas," 75.
46. Wang Xuewen, "Occupational Skills," 44.
47. James Hertling, "China's Colleges Feel the Pinch," *San Francisco Chronicle*, 23 November 1994, p. A12.
48. Wang Xuewen, "Occupational Skills," 38, 44.
49. Liu Shengji, "Diplomas," 77.
50. Yan Hua, "Educational Situation," 40.
51. Liu Shengji, "Educational Funding," 16.
52. Lin Wenxian, "Socialist Talent Market," 68.
53. Wang Xuewen, "Occupational Skills," 38.
54. Wang Xiaorong, "Dalu jishu shichang fazhan di xiankuang yu wenti (The Development and Problems of Mainland China's Technology Market)," *MCS* 36 (April 1993): 61.
55. For a discussion of China's skilled labor market, see Lin Wenxian, "Socialist Talent Market," 60–69.
56. Dong Ruiqi, "Mainland China's Pattern," 16.
57. Leslie Holmes, *The End of Communist Power: Anti-Corruption Campaigns and Legitimation Crisis* (New York: Oxford University, 1993), 271.
58. Men comprise 80 percent of migrant laborers in Anhui province. Males, forty-nine years old and younger, constitute 82.4 percent of Shanghai's mobile populace, 41.6 percent of whom are from twenty to twenty-nine years of age. Xu Qi, "Wuoguo renkou yidong ruogan wenti tantao (Analysis of Certain Problems concerning Our Nation's Population Mobility)," in *Xueshu jie* (*Academy*), published by Anhui province's Social Science Association, no. 6 (1995): 89.
59. Article in the PRC's *Zhongguo qingnian bao* (*China Youth Daily*), reprinted as "Zhuanjia tantao heishehui (Experts Explore the Criminal Underworld)," in *Press Freedom Guardian*, 17 February 1995.
60. See *WJ*, 13 June 1996, A13.
61. Wang Shan, *Third Eye*, 72, 78, 35.

62. Deng Xiaoping, "Excerpts from Talks Given in Wuchang, Shenzhen, Zhuhai and Shanghai," 18 January-21 February 1992, in *Selected Works of Deng Xiaoping (1982–1992)* III (Beijing: Foreign Languages, 1994): 368.

63. Roche, "Faltering Investment."

64. WJ, 13 January 1996, p. A1.

65. China Daily, 11 August 1994, p. 1.

66. Roche, "Faltering Investment." Roche is a global strategist for the London-based Independent Strategy Ltd.

67. Dietrich Rueschemeyer and Peter B. Evans, "The State and Economic Transformation: Toward an Analysis of the Conditions Underlying Effective Intervention," in *Bringing the State Back In*, eds. Peter Evans, Dietrich Rueschemeyer, and Theda Skocpol (London: Cambridge University, 1985), 55–56.

68. Robert Klitgaard, *Adjusting to Reality: Beyond "State versus Market" in Economic Development* (San Francisco, CA: ICS, 1991), 244.

69. Paolo Mauro, "Corruption and Growth," *Quarterly Journal of Economics* 110 (August 1995): 681.

70. David Bayley, "The Effects of Corruption in a Developing Nation," *Western Political Quarterly* 19 (December 1966): 727.

71. David Osterfeld, *Prosperity Versus Planning: How Government Stifles Economic Growth* (New York: Oxford University, 1992), 209, 214.

72. Syed Hussein Alatas, *The Problem of Corruption* (Singapore: Times Books International, 1986), 17.

73. M. Shahid Alam, "Anatomy of Corruption: An Approach to the Political Economy of Underdevelopment," *American Journal of Economics and Sociology* 48 (October 1989): 448.

74. Bayley, "Effects of Corruption," 726.

75. Alatas, *The Problem of Corruption*, 33.

76. Michael Beenstock, "Corruption and Development," *World Development* 7 (1979): 24.

77. Osterfeld, *Prosperity*, 211.

78. Alatas, *The Problem of Corruption*, 17–18.

79. J. S. Nye, "Corruption and Political Development: A Cost-Benefit Analysis," *American Political Science Review* LXI:2 (June 1967): 421.

80. "China," *Asia 1994* (Hong Kong: *Far Eastern Economic Review*, 1994), 118–119.

81. Mauro, "Corruption and Growth," 683, 700, 695.

82. Ibid., 706.

83. Colin Leys, "What is the Problem About Corruption?" *Journal of Modern African Studies* 3, no. 2 (1965): 229.

84. Bayley, "Effects of Corruption," 726.

85. See Kevin M. Murphy, Andrei Shleifer, and Robert W. Vishny, "The Allocation of Talent: Implications for Growth," *Quarterly Journal of Economics* CVI (1991): 503–530.

86. Alatas, *The Problem of Corruption*, 9.

87. Holmes, *End of Communist Power*, 213.

88. Bayley, "Effects of Corruption," 725.

89. Selig Harrison, "Troubled India and Her Neighbors," *Foreign Affairs* (January 1965), 314.

90. Mauro, "Corruption and Growth," 687, 688.

91. Nye, "Political Development," 423.

92. *Press Freedom Guardian*, 3 February 1995, p. 1.

93. Holmes, *End of Communist Power*, 214.
94. Total government revenue includes the revenue of both the central and the local-provincial governments.
95. Wang Shaoguang and Hu Angang, "Zhongguo zhengfu qiqu nengli di xiajiang jiqi houguo (The Decline and Implications of the Chinese Government's Extractive Capacity)," *Ershiyi shiji (21st Century Bimonthly)* (Hong Kong), no. 21 (February 1994): 8.
96. They are the United States, Canada, France, Germany, Great Britain, India, Indonesia, Malaysia, Thailand, Egypt, Brazil, Mexico, and Yugoslavia.
97. Wang and Hu, "Chinese Government's Extractive Power," 9.
98. Ibid., 9.
99. Ibid., 11.
100. In June 1996, the U.S. foreign reserves were $73.2 billion and its GDP (PPP) was $6,738 billion. Japan's foreign exchange reserves, the largest in the world, were $205.7 billion, its GDP (PPP) was $2,668 billion. See "The Bottom Line," *AsiaWeek*, 14 June 1996, p. 63.
101. WJ, 13 July 1994, p. A2; and 23 October 1993, p. A1.
102. Cheng Chu-yuan, "Dalu jingji shili xin pinggu (A New Assessment of Mainland China's Economic Power)," *WJ*, 27 May 1993, p. A12.
103. A concept of Joel Kotkin in *Tribes: How Race, Religion, and Identity Determine Success in the New Global Economy* (New York: Random House, 1993).
104. Cheng Chu-yuan, "Haiwai huaren yu zhongguo jingji jiangshe (Overseas Chinese and the Economic Construction of China)," *WJ*, 29 May 1994, p. A5; and Ming Zongguang, "Huaren jiang zuoyou jingnian yatai jingji fazhan (The Chinese Will Determine This Year's Asian-Pacific Economic Development)," *WJ*, 21 January 1994, p. A4.
105. WJ, 15 March 1994, p. A15.
106. Cheng, "Overseas Chinese."
107. *WJ*, 15 March 1994, p. A15.
108. Sheila Tefft, "The Rootless Chinese: Repatriates Transform Economy, Yet Endure Persistent Resentment," *Christian Science Monitor*, 30 March 1994, p. 11.
109. "The Overseas Chinese: A Driving Force," *Economist*, 18 July 1992, p. 21.
110. Rueschemeyer and Evans, *Bringing the State Back In*, 49, 50–51, 55, 57–58.
111. J. J. Spengler, "Economic Development: Political Preconditions and Political Consequences," in Finkle and Gable, *Political Development*, 172–173.
112. Ibid., 171–172.
113. "The Price of Deng's Pragmatism."
114. Hudson, "The Chinese Model," 217.

Index